The Homilies of St. John Chrysostom

The Homilies of St. John Chrysostom

The Homilies of St. John Chrysostom

© Lighthouse Publishing 2025

Written by: St. Chrysostom (347-407 AD)
Translated by: REV. W. R. W. STEPHENS, M.A., (1839-1902)
Updated into Modern U.S English: A.M. Overett (b.1960)

All rights reserved. Without limiting the rights under copyright reserved above, no part of this publication may be reproduced, stored in a retrieval system, or transmitted, in any form or by any means (electronic, mechanical, photocopying, recording or otherwise), without the prior written permission of the copyright owner of this book.

Published by
Lighthouse Publishing
SAN 257-4330
228 Freedom Parkway
Hoschton, GA 30548
United States of America

www.lighthousechristianpublishing.com

St. John Chrysostom

HOMILIES ON S. IGNATIUS AND S. BABYLAS

INTRODUCTION TO THE HOMILIES ON S. IGNATIUS AND S. BABYLAS.

The following have been selected out of a large number delivered by Chrysostom on the festivals of saints and martyrs, not only because they are good samples of his discourses on such occasions, but also on account of the celebrity of the two saints in whose honor they were spoken. There is really very little known about Ignatius beyond the fact that he was Bishop of Antioch, and suffered martyrdom at Rome in the reign of Trajan about the year 110 a.d.: being torn to death by wild beasts in the colossal amphitheater erected for the display of such inhuman sports by the emperors of the Flavian dynasty. The tradition that he was a disciple of St. John does not rest on any trustworthy evidence, but on the other hand there is nothing inherently impossible or even improbable in the supposition.

According to a tradition which cannot be traced back earlier than the latter part of the fourth century the reliques were translated from Rome to Antioch and deposited in the Christian cemetery outside the gates called the Daphnitic gate, because it led from the city to the famous suburb of Daphne, on which we shall have more to say presently. It is clear from the following eulogy that Chrysostom accepted this tradition, and his repeated invitation to his hearers to "come hither" to enjoy the beneficent influence of the saint seems to imply that his discourse was delivered in the "martyr," that is

1

the chapel erected to contain the martyr's remains, not in the "Great Church" of Antioch where he commonly preached. In the next generation the reliques of the saint were again translated by the Emperor, the younger Theodosius, to the building which had been the temple of the "Fortune of Antioch," and then the illustrious Christian martyr was substituted for the mythical goddess on the tutelary genius of the city.

The fame of S. Babylas rivalled and for a time almost threatened to overshadow that of S. Ignatius. He had been Bishop of Antioch about 237 to 250. The heroic courage with which he had once repulsed the Emperor Philip from the church until he should have submitted to penance for some offence committed, and his martyrdom in the persecution under Decius were his original claims to popular veneration. But some later events shed a fresh luster on his name. In the year 351 the Cæsar Gallus, brother of Julian, being resident in Antioch, transferred the reliques of Babylas from their resting place within the city to the beautiful suburb the garden or grove of Daphne. "In the history of this spot we have a singular instance of the way in which Grecian legend was transplanted into foreign soil. Daphne the daughter of the river-god Ladon were according to the Syrian version of the myth, overtaken by her lover Apollo near Antioch. Here it was, on the banks not of the Peneus but of the Oronete, that the maiden prayed to her mother earth to open her arms and shelter her from the pursuit of the amorous god, and that the laurel plant sprang out of the spot where she vanished from the eyes of her disappointed lover. The house of Seleucus Nicator, founder of the Syrian monarchy was said to have struck his hoof upon one of the arrows dropped by Apollo in the hurry of his pursuit; in consequence of which the king dedicated the place to the god. A temple was erected in his honor, ample in its proportions, sumptuous in its adornments; the internal walls were resplendent with polished marbles, the lofty ceiling was of cypress wood. The colossal image of the god, enriched with gold and gems, nearly reached the top of the roof. * * * With one hand the deity lightly touched the lyre which hung from his shoulders and in the other he held a golden dish, as if about to pour a libation on the earth "and supplicate the venerable mother to give to his arms the cold and beauteous Daphne." The whole grove became consecrated to pleasure under the guise of festivity in honor of the god. * * * It contained everything which could gratify and charm the senses; the deep impenetrable shade of cypress trees, the delicious noise and coolness of falling waters, the fragrance of aromatic shrubs; there were also baths, and grottos, porticoes, and colonnades. Such materials for voluptuous enjoyment told with fatal effect upon the morals of a people addicted at all times to an immoderate indulgence in luxurious pleasure. Daphne became one of those places where gross and shameless vice was practiced under the sanction of religion. The intention of Cæsar Gallus in translating the reliques of Babylas to Daphne was as Chrysostom expresses it to "bring a physician to the sick;" to introduce a pure and Christian association into a spot hitherto consecrated to Pagan and licentious rites. The bones of the saint were laid near the shrine of Apollo, and the Christian church standing hard by the heathen temple was a visible warning to any Christian who might visit the place to abstain from deeds abhorrent to the faith for which the bishop had died. But the remains of the martyr were not permitted to rest in peace. When the Emperor Julian visited Antioch, he consulted the oracle of Apollo at Daphne respecting the issue of the expedition which he was about to make into Persia. But the oracle was dumb. At length the god yielded to the importunity of prayers and sacrifices so far as to explain the cause of his silence. He was offended by the proximity of dead men. "Break open the sepulchers, take up the bones, and carry them hence." No name was mentioned, but the demand was interpreted as referring to the remains of Babylas, and the wishes of the affronted deity were complied with. The Christians were commanded by Julian to remove the bones of their saint from the neighborhood of Apollo's sanctuary. They obeyed, but what was intended to be a humiliation was converted into a triumph. The reliques were conveyed to their resting place within the city as in a kind of festive procession, accompanied by crowds along the whole way, four or five miles, chanting the words of the Psalm, "Confounded be all they that worship carved images and delight in vain gods." In vain were some of the Christians seized and tortured. The popularity of the saint grew in proportion as Julian tried to put it down; and the insults done to him were speedily avenged. A fire, mysterious in its origin, broke out soon after the removal of the martyr's reliques in the shrine of Apollo, consuming the roof of the building, and the statue of the god. At the time when Chrysostom preached, about twenty years later, the columns and walls were still standing, the melancholy wreck serving as a memorial and witness of the judgment which had fallen upon the place.

The remains of Babylas were not brought back to Daphne but removed from the city to a magnificent church built to receive them on the other side of Orontes.

Near the close of his discourse Chrysostom refers to the erection of this church and to the zeal of the Bishop Meletius in promoting it, who actually took part in the work with his own hands, as we are told that Hugh did in the building of the Minster at Lincoln. But although the body of the martyr rested elsewhere, his spirit and influence were supposed to inhabit in a special manner the spot where he had put the heathen deity to silence and shame, and to confer blessings on the pilgrims who resorted in crowds to his martyr in Daphne. The ruined and deserted temple indeed, and the well preserved Christian church thronged with worshippers, standing as they did side by side, formed a striking emblem of the two religions to which they were devoted—the one destined to crumble and vanish away, the other to endure and conquer.

HOMILIES ON S. IGNATIUS AND S. BABYLAS.

Eulogy.

On the holy martyr Saint Ignatius, the god-bearer, archbishop of Antioch the great, who was carried off to Rome, and there suffered martyrdom, and thence was conveyed back again to Antioch.

1. Sumptuous and splendid entertainers give frequent and constant entertainments, alike to display their own wealth, and to show goodwill to their acquaintance. So also the grace of the Spirit, affording us a proof of his own power, and displaying much good-will towards the friends of God, sets before us successively and constantly the tables of the martyrs. Lately, for instance, a maiden quite young, and unmarried, the blessed martyr Pelagia, entertained us, with much joy. Today again, this blessed and noble martyr Ignatius has succeeded to her feast. The persons are different: The table is one. The wrestling are varied: The crown is one. The contests are manifold: The prize is the same. For in the case of the heathen contests, since the tasks are bodily, men alone are, with reason, admitted. But here, since the contest is wholly concerning the soul, the lists are open to each sex, for each kind the theatre is arranged. Neither do men alone disrobe, in order that the women may not take refuge in the weakness of their nature, and seem to have a plausible excuse, nor have women only quitted themselves like men, lest the race of men be put to shame; but on this side and on that many are proclaimed

conquerors, and are crowned, in order that thou may learn by means of the exploits themselves that in Christ Jesus neither male nor female, neither sex, nor weakness of body, nor age, nor any such thing could be a hindrance to those who run in the course of religion; if there be a noble readiness, and an eager mind, and a fear of God, fervent and kindling, be established in our souls. On this account both maidens and women, and men, both young and old, and slaves, and freemen, and every rank, and every age, and each sex, disrobe for those contests, and in no respect suffer harm, since they have brought a noble purpose to these wrestling. The season then already calls us to discourse of the mighty works of this saint. But our reckoning is disturbed and confused, not knowing what to say first, what second, what third, so great a multitude of things calling for eulogy surrounds us, on every side; and we experience the same thing as if anyone went into a meadow, and seeing many a rosebush and many a violet, and an abundance of lilies, and other spring flowers manifold and varied, should be in doubt what he should look at first, what second, since each of those he saw invites him to bestow his glances on itself. For we too, coming to this spiritual meadow of the mighty works of Ignatius, and beholding not the flowers of spring, but the manifold and varied fruit of the spirit in the soul of this man, are confused and in perplexity, not knowing to which we are first to give our consideration, as each of the things we see draws us away from its neighbors, and entices the eye of the soul to the sight of its own beauty. For see, he presided over the Church among us nobly, and with such carefulness as Christ desires. For that which Christ declared to be the highest standard and rule of the Episcopal office, did this man display by his deeds. For having heard Christ saying, the good shepherd lays down his life for the sheep with all courage he did lay it down for the sheep.

He held true converse with the apostles and drank of spiritual fountains. What kind of person then is it likely that he was who had been reared, and who had everywhere held converse with them, and had shared with them truths both lawful and unlawful to utter, and who seemed to them worthy of so great a dignity? The time again came on, which demanded courage; and a soul which despised all things present, glowed with Divine love, and valued things unseen before the things which are seen; and he lay aside the flesh with as much ease as one would put off a garment. What then shall we speak of first? The teaching of the apostles which he gave proof of throughout, or his indifference to this present life, or the strictness of his virtue, with which he administered his rule over the Church; which shall we first call to mind? The martyr or the bishop or the apostle. For the grace of the spirit having woven a threefold crown, thus bound it on his holy head, yea rather a manifold crown. For if anyone will consider them carefully, he will find each of the crowns, blossoming with other crowns for us.

2. And if you will, let us come first to the praise of his episcopate. Does this seem to be one crown alone? Come, then, let us unfold it in speech, and you will see both two, and three, and more produced from it. For I do not wonder at the man alone that he seemed to be worthy of so great an office, but that he obtained this office from those saints, and that the hands of the blessed apostles touched his sacred head. For not even is this a slight thing to be said in his praise, nor because he won greater grace from above, nor only because they caused more abundant

energy of the Spirit to come upon him, but because they bore witness that every virtue possessed by man was in him. Now how this is, I tell you. Paul writing to Titus once on a time—and when I say Paul, I do not speak of him alone, but also of Peter and James and John, and the whole band of them; for as in one lyre, the strings are different strings, but the harmony is one, so also in the band of the apostles the persons are different, but the teaching is one, since the artificer is one, I mean the Holy Spirit, who moves their souls, and Paul showing this said, "Whether therefore they, or I, so we preach." This man, then, writing to Titus, and showing what kind of man the bishop ought to be, says, "For the bishop must be blameless as God's steward; not self-willed, not soon angry, no brawler, no striker, not greedy of filthy lucre; but given to hospitality, a lover of good, sober-minded, just, holy, temperate, holding to the faithful word, which is according to the teaching, that he may be able both to exhort in the sound doctrine, and to convict the gainsayers;" and to Timothy again, when writing upon this subject, he says somewhat like this: "If a man seeks the office of a bishop, he desires a good work. The bishop, therefore, must be without reproach, the husband of one wife, temperate, sober-minded, orderly, given to hospitality, apt to teach, no brawler, no striker, but gentle, not contentious, no lover of money. Do you see what strictness of virtue he demands from the bishop? For as some most excellent painter from life, having mixed many colors, if he be about to furnish an original likeness of the royal form, works with all accuracy, so that all who are copying it, and painting from it, may have a likeness accurately drawn, so accordingly the blessed Paul, as though painting some royal likeness, and furnishing an original sketch of it, having mixed the different colors of virtue, has painted in the features of the office of bishop complete, in order that each of those who mount to that dignity, looking thereupon, may administer their own affairs with just such strictness.

Boldly, therefore, would I say that Ignatius took an accurate impression of the whole of this, in his own soul; and was blameless and without reproach, and neither self-willed, nor soon angry, nor given to wine, nor a striker, but gentle, not contentious, no lover of money, just, holy, temperate, holding to the faithful word which is according to the teaching, sober, sober-minded, orderly, and all the rest which Paul demanded. "And what is the proof of this?" says one. They who said these things ordained him, and they who suggest to others with so great strictness to make proof of those who are about to mount to the throne of this office, would not themselves have done this negligently. But had they not seen all this virtue planted in the soul of this martyr would not have entrusted him with this office. For they knew accurately how great danger besets those who bring about such ordinations, carelessly and haphazard. And Paul again, when showing this very thing to the same Timothy wrote and says, "Lay hands suddenly on no man, neither be partaker of other men's sins." What dost thou say? Has another sinned, and do I share his blame and his punishment? Yes, says he, the man who authorizes evil; and just as in the case of any one entrusting into the hands of a raging and insane person a sharply pointed sword, with which the madman commits murder, that man who gave the sword incurs the blame; so anyone who gives the authority which arises from this office to a man living in evil, draws down on his own head all the fire of that man's sins and audacity. For he who provides the root, this man is the cause of all that springs from it on every side. Do you see how in the meanwhile a double crown of the episcopate has appeared, and how the dignity of those who ordained him has made the office more illustrious, bearing witness to every exhibition of virtue in him?

3. Do you wish that I should also reveal to you another crown springing from this very matter? Let us consider the time at which he obtained this dignity. For it is not the same thing to administer the Church now as then, just as it is not the same thing to travel along a road well-trodden, and prepared, after many wayfarers; and along one about to be cut for the first time, and containing ruts, and stones, and full of wild beasts, and which has never yet, received any traveler. For now, by the grace of God, there is no danger for bishops, but deep peace on all sides, and we all enjoy a calm, since the Word of piety has been extended to the ends of the world, and our rulers keep the faith with strictness. But then there was nothing of this, but wherever anyone might look, precipices and pitfalls, and wars, and fighting, and dangers; both rulers, and kings, and people and cities and nations, and men at home and abroad, laid snares for the faithful. And this was not the only serious thing, but also the fact that many of the believers themselves, inasmuch as they tasted for the first time strange doctrines, stood in need of great indulgence, and were still in a somewhat feeble condition and were often upset. And this was a thing which used to grieve the teachers, no less than the fighting without, nay rather much more. For the fighting without, and the plotting, afforded much pleasure to them on account of the hope of the rewards awaiting them. On this account the apostles returned from the presence of the Sanhedrin

rejoicing because they had been beaten; and Paul cries out, saying: "I rejoice in my sufferings," and he glories in his afflictions everywhere. But the wounds of those at home, and the falls of the brethren, do not suffer them to breathe again, but always, like some most heavy yoke, continually oppress and afflict the neck of their soul. Hear at least how Paul, thus rejoicing in suffering, is bitterly pained about these. "For who, says he, is weak, and I am not weak? who is offended, and I burn not?" and again, "I fear lest when I come I shall find you not such as I would, and I be found of you such as ye would not," and a little afterwards, "Lest when I come again to you, God humble me, and I shall mourn many of those who have sinned before, and have not repented of their uncleanness, and wantonness, and fornication which they have committed." And throughout thou sees that he is in tears and lamentations on account of members of the household and evermore fearing and trembling for the believers. Just as then we admire the pilot, not when he is able to bring those who are on board safe to shore when the sea is calm, and the ship is borne along by favorable winds, but when the deep is raging and the waves contending, and the passengers themselves within in revolt, and a great storm within and without besets those who are on board, and he is able to steer the ship with all security; so we ought to wonder at, and admire those who then had the Church committed to their hands, much more than those who now have the management of it; when there was a great war without and within, when the plant of the faith was more tender, and needed much care, when, as a newly-born babe, the multitude in the church required much forethought, and the greatest wisdom in any soul destined to nurse it; and in order that ye may more clearly learn, how great crowns they were worthy of, who then had the Church entrusted to them, and how great work and danger there was in undertaking the matter on the threshold and at the beginning, and in being the first to enter upon it, I bring forward for you the testimony of Christ, who pronounces a verdict on these things, and confirms the opinion which has been expressed by me. For when he saw many coming to him and was wishing to show the apostles that the prophets toiled more than they, he says: "Others have labored, and ye have entered into their labor." And yet the apostles toiled much more than the prophets. But since they first sowed the word of piety and won over the untaught souls of men to the truth, the greater part of the work is credited to them. For it is by no means the same thing for one to come and teach after many teachers, and himself to be the first to sow seeds. For that which has been already practiced, and has become customary with many, would be easily accepted; but that which is now for the first time heard, agitates the mind of the hearers, and gives the teacher a great deal to do. This at least it was which disturbed the audience at Athens, and on this account, they turned away from Paul, reproaching him with, "You bring certain strange things to our ears." For if the oversight of the Church now furnishes much weariness and work to those who govern it, consider how double and treble and manifold was the work then, when there were dangers and fighting and snares, and fear continually. It is not possible to set forth in words the difficulty which those saints then encountered, but he alone will know it who comes to it by experience.

    4. And I will speak of a fourth crown, arising for us out of this episcopate. What then is this? The fact that

he was entrusted with our own native city. For it is a laborious thing indeed to have the oversight of a hundred men, and of fifty alone. But to have on one's hands so great a city, and a population extending to two hundred thousand, of how great virtue and wisdom dost thou think there is a proof? For as in the care of armies, the wiser of the generals have on their hands the more leading and more numerous regiments, so, accordingly, in the care of cities. The more able of the rulers are entrusted with the larger and more populous. And at any rate this city was of much account to God, as indeed He manifested by the very deeds which He did. At all events the master of the whole world, Peter, to whose hands He committed the keys of heaven, whom He commanded to do and to bear all, He bade tarry here for a long period. Thus in His sight our city was equivalent to the whole world. But since I have mentioned Peter, I have perceived a fifth crown woven from him, and this is that this man succeeded to the office after him. For just as anyone taking a great stone from a foundation hastens by all means to introduce an equivalent to it, lest he should shake the whole building, and make it more unsound, so, accordingly, when Peter was about to depart from here, the grace of the Spirit introduced another teacher equivalent to Peter, so that the building already completed should not be made more unsound by the insignificance of the successor. We have reckoned up then five crowns, from the importance of the office, from the dignity of those who ordained to it, from the difficulty of the time, from the size of the city, from the virtue of him who transmitted the episcopate to him. Having woven all these, it was lawful to speak of a sixth, and seventh, and more than these; but in order that we may not, by spending the whole time on the consideration of the episcopate, miss the details about the martyr, come from this point, let us pass to that conflict. At one time a grievous warfare was rekindled against the Church, and as though a most grievous tyranny overspread the earth, all were carried off from the midst of the marketplace. Not indeed charged with anything monstrous, but because being freed from error, they hastened to piety; because they abstained from the service of demons, because they recognized the true God, and worshipped his only begotten Son, and for things for which they ought to have been crowned, and admired and honored, for these they were punished and encountered countless tortures, all who embraced the faith, and much more they who had the oversight of the churches. For the devil, being crafty, and apt to contrive plots of this kind, expected that if he took away the shepherds, he would easily be able to scatter the flocks. But He who takes the wise in their craftiness, wishing to show him that men do not govern His church, but that it is He himself who everywhere tends those who believe on Him, agreed that this should be, that he might see, when they were taken away, that the cause of piety was not defeated, nor the word of preaching quenched, but rather increased; that by these very works he might learn both himself, and all those who minister to him, that our affairs are not of men, but that the subject of our teaching has its root on high, from the heavens; and that it is God who everywhere leads the Church, and that it is not possible for him who fights against God, ever to win the day. But the Devil did not only work this evil, but another also not less than this. For not only in the cities over which they presided, did he suffer the Bishops to be slaughtered; but he took them into foreign territory and slew them; and he did this, in anxiety at once to take them when destitute of friends, and hoping to render them weaker with the toil of their journey, which accordingly he did with this saint. For he called him away from our city to Rome, making the course twice as long, expecting to depress his mind both by the length of the way and the number of the days, and not knowing that having Jesus with him, as a fellow traveler, and fellow exile on so long a journey, he rather became the stronger, and afforded more proof of the power that was with him, and to a greater degree knit the Churches together. For the cities which were on the road running together from all sides, encouraged the athlete, and sped him on his way with many supplies, sharing in his conflict by their prayers, and intercessions. And they derived no little comfort when they saw the martyr hastening to death with so much readiness, as is consistent in one called to the realms which are in the heaven, and by means of the works themselves, by the readiness and by the joyousness of that noble man, that it was not death to which he was hastening, but a kind of long journey and migration from this world, and ascension to heaven; and he departed teaching these things in every city, both by his words, and by his deeds, and as happened in the case of the Jews, when they bound Paul, and sent him to Rome, and thought that they were sending him to death, they were sending a teacher to the Jews who dwelt there. This indeed happened in the case of Ignatius in larger measure. For not to those alone who dwell in Rome, but to all the cities lying in the intervening space, he went forth as a wonderful teacher, persuading them to despise the present life, and to think naught of the things which are seen, and to love those which are to come, to look towards heaven, and to pay no regard to any of the terrors of this present life. For on this and on more than this, by means of his works, he went on his way instructing them, as a sun rising from the east, and hastening to the west. But rather more brilliant than this, for this is wont to run on high, bringing material light, but Ignatius shone below, imparting to men's souls the intellectual light of doctrine. And that light on departing into the regions of the west, is hidden and straightway causes the night to come on. But this on departing to the regions of the west, shone there more brilliantly, conferring the greatest benefits to all along the road. And when he arrived at the city, even *that* he instructed in Christian wisdom. For on this account God permitted him there to end his life, so that this man's death might be instructive to all who dwell in Rome. For *we* by the grace of God need henceforward no evidence, being rooted in the faith. But they who dwelt in Rome, inasmuch as there was great impiety there, required more help. On this account both Peter and Paul, and this man after them, were all slain there, partly, indeed, in order that they might purify with their own blood, the city which had been defiled with blood of idols, and partly in order that they might by their works afford a proof of the resurrection of the crucified Christ, persuading those who dwell in Rome, that they would not with so much pleasure disdain this present life, did they not firmly persuade themselves that they were about to ascend to the crucified Jesus, and to see him in the heavens. For in reality it is the greatest proof of the resurrection that the slain Christ should show forth so great power after death, as to persuade living men to despise both country and home and friends, and acquaintance and life itself, for the sake of confessing him, and to choose in place of present pleasures, both stripes and dangers and death. For these are not the achievements of any dead man, nor of one remaining in the tomb but of one risen and living. Since how could you account, when he was alive, for all the Apostles who companied with him becoming weaker through fear to betray their teachers and to flee and depart; but when he died, for not only Peter and Paul, but even Ignatius, who had not even seen him, nor enjoyed his companionship, showing such earnestness as to lay down life itself for his sake?

5. In order then that all who dwell in Rome might learn that these things are a reality, God allowed that there the saint should be perfected, and that this was the reason I will guarantee from the very manner of his death. For not outside the walls, in a dungeon, nor even in a court of justice, nor in some corner, did he receive the sentence which condemned him, but in the midst of the theatre, while the whole city was seated above him, he underwent this form of martyrdom, wild beasts being let loose upon him, in order that he might plant his trophy against the Devil, beneath the eyes of all, and make all spectators emulous of his own conflicts. Not dying thus nobly only, but dying even with pleasure. For not as though about to be severed from life, but as called to a better and more spiritual life, so he beheld the wild beasts gladly. Whence is this manifest? From the words which he uttered when about to die, for when he heard that this manner of punishment awaited him, "may I have joy," said he, "of these wild beasts." For such are the loving. For they receive with pleasure whatever they may suffer for the sake of those who are beloved, and they seem to have their desire satisfied when what happens to them is more than usually grievous. Which happened, therefore, in this man's case. For not by his death alone, but also by his

readiness he studied to emulate the apostles, and hearing that they, after they had been scourged retired with joy, himself too wished to imitate his teachers, not only by his death, but by his joy. On this account he said, "May I have joy of thy wild beasts," and much milder than the tongue of the tyrant did he consider the mouths of these; and very reasonably. For while that invited him to Gehenna, their mouths escorted him to a kingdom. When, therefore, he made an end of life there, yea rather, when he ascended to heaven, he departed henceforward crowned. For this also happened through the dispensation of God, that he restored him again to us, and distributed the martyr to the cities. For that city received his blood as it dropped, but ye were honored with his remains, ye enjoyed his episcopate, they enjoyed his martyrdom. They saw him in conflict, and victorious, and crowned, but ye have him continually. For a little time God removed him from you, and with greater glory granted him again to you. And as those who borrow money, return with interest what they receive, so also God, using this valued treasure of yours, for a little while, and having shown it to that city, with greater brilliancy gave it back to you. Ye sent forth a Bishop and received a martyr; ye sent him forth with prayers, and ye received him with crowns; and not only ye, but all the cities which intervene. For how do ye think that they behaved when they saw his remains being brought back? What pleasure was produced! How they rejoiced! With what applause on all sides they beset the crowned one! For as with a noble athlete, who has wrestled down all his antagonists, and who comes forth with radiant glory from the arena, the spectators receive him, and do not suffer him to tread the earth, bringing him home on their shoulders, and besetting him with countless praises: so also the cities in order receiving this saint then from Rome, and bearing him upon their shoulders as far as this city, escorted the crowned one with praises, celebrating the champion, in song; laughing the Devil to scorn, because his artifice was turned against him, and what he thought to do against the martyr, this turned out for his behoove. Then, indeed, he profited, and encouraged all the cities; and from that time to this day he enriches this city, and as some perpetual treasure, drawn upon every day, yet not failing, makes all who partake of it more prosperous, so also this blessed Ignatius fills those who come to him with blessings, with boldness, nobleness of spirit, and much courage, and so sent them home.

Not only today, therefore, but every day let us go forth to him, plucking spiritual fruits from him. For it is, it is possible for him who comes with faith to gather the fruit of many good things. For not the bodies only, but the very sepulchers of the saints have been filled with spiritual grace. For if in the case of Elisha this happened, and a corpse when it touched the sepulcher, burst the bands of death and returned to life again, much rather now, when grace is more abundant, when the energy of the spirit is greater, is it possible that one touching a sepulcher, with faith, should win great power; thence on this account God allowed us the remains of the saints, wishing to lead by them us to the same emulation, and to afford us a kind of haven, and a secure consolation for the evils which are ever overtaking us. Wherefore I beseech you all, if any is in despondency, if in disease, if under insult, if in any other circumstance of this life, if in the depth of sins, let him come hither with faith, and he will lay aside all those things, and will return with much joy, having procured a lighter conscience from the sight alone.

But more, it is not only necessary that those who are in affliction should come hither, but if anyone be in cheerfulness, in glory, in power, in much assurance towards God, let not this man despise the benefit. For coming hither and beholding this saint, he will keep these noble possessions unmoved, persuading his own soul to be moderate by the recollection of this man's mighty deeds, and not suffering his conscience by the mighty deeds to be lifted up to any self-conceit. And it is no slight thing for those in prosperity not to be puffed up at their good fortune, but to know how to bear their prosperity with moderation, so that the treasure is serviceable to all, the resting place is suitable, for the fallen, in order that they may escape from their temptations, for the fortunate, that their success may remain secure, for those in weakness indeed, that they may return to health, and for the healthy, that they may not fall into weakness. Considering all which things, let us prefer this way of spending our time, to all delight, all pleasure, in order that rejoicing at once, and profiting, we may be able to become partakers with these saints, both of their dwelling and of their home, through the prayers of the saints themselves, through the grace and lovingkindness of our Lord Jesus Christ, with whom be glory to the Father with the Holy Spirit, now and always forever and ever amen.

On the Holy Martyr, s. Babylas.

1. I was anxious today to pay the debt which I promised you when I was lately here. But what am I to do? In the meanwhile, the blessed Babylas has appeared, and has called me to himself, uttering no voice, but attracting our attention by the brightness of his countenance. Be ye not, therefore, displeased at the delay in my payment; at all events, the longer the time is, the more the interest will increase. For we will deposit this money with interest. Since thus did the master command who entrusted it to us. Being confident, therefore, about what is lent, that both the principal and the profit await you, let us not pass by the gain which falls in our way today, but revel in the noble actions of the blessed Babylas.

How, indeed, he presided over the Church which is among us, and saved that sacred ship, in storm, and in wave, and billow; and what a bold front he showed to the emperor, and how he lay down his life for the sheep and underwent that blessed slaughter; these things and such as these, we will leave to the elder among our teachers, and to our common father, to speak of. For the more remote matters, the aged can relate to you but as many things as happened lately, and within our lifetime, these, I a young man will relate to you, I mean those after death, those after the burial of the martyr, those which happened while he remained in the suburbs of the city. And I know indeed that the Greeks will laugh at my promise, if I promise to speak of the noble deeds after death and burial of one who was buried, and had crumbled to dust. We shall not assuredly on this account keep silence, but on this very account shall especially speak, in order that by showing this marvel truly, we may turn their laughter upon their own head. For of an ordinary man there would be no noble deeds after death. But of a martyr, many and great deeds, not in order that he might become more illustrious (for he has no need of glory from the multitude), but that thou, the unbeliever mayest learn that the death of the martyrs is not death, but the beginning of a better life, and the prelude of a more spiritual conversation, and a change from the worse to the better. Do not then look at the fact, that the mere body of the martyr lies destitute of energy of soul; but observe this, that a greater power takes its place by the side of it, different from the soul itself—I mean the grace of the Holy Spirit, which pleads to all on behalf of the resurrection, by means of the wonders which it works. For if God has granted greater power to bodies dead and crumbled to dust, than to all living, much more will he grant to them a better life than the former, and a longer, at the time of the bestowal of his crowns; what then are this saint's noble deeds? But be not disturbed, if we take our discourse a little further back. For they who wish to display their portraits to advantage, do not uncover them until they have placed the spectators a little way off from the picture, making the view clearer by the distance. Do you then also have patience with me while I direct my discourse into the past.

    For when Julian who surpassed all in impiety, ascended the imperial throne, and grasped the despotic scepter, straightway he lifted up his hands against the God who created him, and ignored his benefactor, and looking from the earth beneath to the heavens, howled after the manner of mad dogs, who alike bay at those who do not feed them and those who do feed them. But he rather was mad with a more savage madness than theirs. For they indeed turn from, and hate their friends and strangers alike. But this man used to fawn upon demons, strangers to his salvation, and used to worship them with every mode of worship. But his benefactor, and Savior, and him who spared not the only Begotten, for his sake, he turned from and used to hate, and made havoc of the cross, the very thing which uplifted the whole world when it was lying prostrate, and drove away the darkness on all sides, and brought in light more brilliant than the sunbeams; nor yet even then did he desist from his frenzy, but promised that he would tear the nation of the Galileans, out of the midst of the world; for thus he was wont to call us; and yet if he thought the names of the Christians an abomination, and Christianity itself to be full of much shame, for what reason did he not desire to put us to shame by that means, but with a strange name? Yea because he knew clearly, that to be called by what belongs to Christ, is a great ornament not only to men, but to angels, and to the powers above. On this account he set everything in motion, so as to strip us of this ornament, and put a stop to the preaching of it. But this was impossible, O wretched and miserable man! as it was impossible to destroy the heaven and to quench the sun, and to shake and cast down the foundations of the earth, and those things Christ foretold, thus saying: "Heaven and earth shall pass away, but my words shall not pass away."

    Well, thou dost not submit to Christ's words; accept therefore the utterance which thus his deeds give. For I indeed having been privileged to know what the declaration of God is, how strong, how invincible a thing, have believed that is more trustworthy than the order of nature, and than experience in all matters. But do thou still creeping on the ground, and agitated with the investigations of human reasoning, receive the witness of the deeds. I gainsay nothing. I strive not.

2. What then do the deeds say? Christ said that it was easier for heaven and earth to be destroyed, than for any of his words to fail. The emperor contradicted these words and threatened to destroy his decrees. Where then is the emperor who threatened these things? He perished and is corrupted, and is now in Hades, awaiting the inevitable punishment. But where is Christ who uttered these decrees? In Heaven, on the right hand of the Father, occupying the highest throne of glory; where are the blasphemous words of the Emperor, and his unchastened tongue? They are become ashes, and dust and the food of worms. Where is the sentence of Christ? It shines forth by the very truth of the deed, receiving its luster from the issue of the events, as from a golden column. And yet the emperor left nothing undone, when about to raise war against us, but used to call prophets together, and summon sorcerers, and everything was full of demons and evil spirits.

What then was the return for this worship? The overturning of cities, the bitterest famine of all famines. For you know doubtless, and remember, how empty indeed the marketplace was of wares, and the workshops full of confusion, when everyone strove to snatch up what came first and to depart. And why do I speak of famine, when the very fountains of waters were failing, fountains which by the abundance of their stream, used to eclipse the rivers. But since I have mentioned the fountains, come, forthwith, let us go up to Daphne, and conduct our discourse to the noble deeds of the martyr. Although you desire me still to parade the indecencies of the Greeks, although I too desire this, let us abstain; for wherever the commemoration of a martyr is, there certainly also is the shame of the Greeks. This emperor then, going up to

Daphne used to weary Apollo, praying, supplicating, entreating, so that the events of the future might be foretold to him. What then did the prophet, the great God of the Greeks? "The dead prevent me from uttering," saith he, "but break open the graves, dig up the bones, move the dead." What could be more impious than these commands? The Demon of grave-robbing introduces strange laws and devises new methods of expelling strangers. Who ever heard of the dead being driven forth? who ever saw lifeless bodies ordered to be moved as he commanded, overturning from their foundations the common laws of nature. For the laws of nature are common to all men, that he who departs this life should be hidden in the earth, and delivered over for burial, and be covered up in the bosom of the earth the mother of all; and these laws, neither Greek, barbarian, Scythian, nor if there be any more savage than they, ever changed, but all reverence them, and keep them, and thus they are sacred and venerated by all. But the Demon raises his mask, and with bare head, resists the common laws of nature. For the dead, he says, are a pollution. The dead are not a pollution, a most wicked demon, but a wicked intention is an abomination. But if one must say something startling, the bodies of the living full of evil are more polluting than those of the dead. For the one minister to the behests of the mind, but the other lie unmoved. Now that which is unmoved and destitute of all perception would be free from all accusation. Not that I even would say that the bodies of the living are by nature polluting; but that everywhere a wicked and perverted intention is open to accusations from all.

    The dead body then is not a pollution O Apollo, but to persecute a maiden who wishes to be modest, and to outrage the dignity of a virgin, and to lament at the failure of the shameless deed, this is worthy of accusation, and punishment. There were at all events, many wonderful and great prophets among ourselves, who spoke also many things concerning the future, and they in no case used to bid those who asked them to dig up the bones of the departed. Yea Ezekiel standing near the bones themselves was not only not hindered by them, but added flesh, and nerves and skin to them, and brought them back to life again. But the great Moses did not stand near the bones of the dead, but bearing off the whole dead body of Joseph, thus foretold things to come. And very reasonably, for their words were the grace of the Holy Spirit. But the words of these, a deceit, and a lie which is no wise able to be concealed. For that these things were an excuse, and pretense and that he feared the blessed Babylas, is manifest from what the emperor did. For leaving all the other dead, he only moved that martyr. And yet if he did these things, in disgust at him, and not in fear, it were necessary that he should order the coffin to be broken, thrown into the sea, carried to the desert, be made to disappear by some other method of destruction; for this is the part of one who is disgusted. Thus God did when he spoke to the Hebrews about the abominations of the Gentiles. He bade their statues to be broken, not to bring their abominations from the suburbs to the city.

3. The martyr then was moved, but the demon not even then enjoyed freedom from fear, but straightway learned that it is possible to move the bones of a martyr, but not to escape his hands. For as soon as the coffin was drawn into the city, a thunderbolt came from above upon the head of his image, and burnt it all up. And yet, if not before, then at least there was likelihood that the impious

emperor would be angry, and that he would send forth his anger against the testimony of the martyr. But not even then did he dare, so great fear possessed him. But although he saw that the burning was intolerable, and knew the cause accurately; he kept quiet. And this is not only wonderful that he did not destroy the testimony, but that he not even dared to put the roof on to the temple again. For he knew, he knew, that the stroke was divinely sent, and he feared lest by forming any further plan, he should call down that fire upon his own head. On this account he endured to see the shrine of Apollo brought to so great desolation; For there was no other cause, on account of which he did not rectify that which had happened, but fear alone. For which reason he unwillingly kept quiet, and knowing this left as much reproach to the demon, as distinction to the martyr. For the walls are now standing, instead of trophies, uttering a voice clearer than a trumpet. To those in Daphne, to those in the city, to those who arrive from far off, to those who are with us, to those men which shall be hereafter, they declare everything by their appearance, the wrestling, the struggle, the victory of the martyr. For it is likely that he who dwells far off from the suburb, when he sees the chapel of the saint deprived of a shrine, and the temple of Apollo deprived of its roof would ask the reason of each of these things; and then after learning the whole history would depart hence. Such are the noble deeds of the martyr after death, wherefore I count your city blessed, that ye have shown much zeal about this holy man. For then, when he returned from Daphne, all our city poured forth into the road, and the marketplaces were empty of men, and the houses were empty of women, and the bedchambers were destitute of maidens. Thus also every age and each sex passed forth from the city, as if to receive a father long absent who was returning from sojourn far away. And you indeed gave him back to the band of fellow enthusiasts. But the grace of God did not suffer him to remain there for good, but again removed him beyond the river, so that many parts of the country were filled with the sweet savor of the martyr. Neither even when he came hither was he destined to be alone, but he quickly received, a neighbor, and a fellow lodger, and one of similar life. For he shared with him the same dignity, and for the sake of religion showed forth equal boldness. Wherefore he obtained the same abode as he, this wonderful man being no vain imitator, as it seems, of the martyr. For so long a time he labored there, sending letters continually to the emperor, wearying the authorities, and bringing the ministry of the body to bear upon the martyr. For ye know, doubtless, and remember that when the midday summer sun possessed the heaven, he together with his acquaintances, used to walk thither every day, not as spectator only, but also, as intending to be a sharer in what was going on. For he often handled stone, and dragged a rope, and listened, in advance of the workmen themselves, to one who wanted to erect any building. For he knew, he knew what rewards lie in store for him for these things. And on this account, he continued doing service to the martyrs, not only by splendid buildings nor even by continual feasts, but by a better method than these. And what is this? He imitates their life, emulates their courage, throughout according to his ability he keeps the image of the martyrs alive, in himself. For see, they gave their bodies to the slaughter, he has mortified the members of his flesh which are upon the earth. They stopped the flame of fire; he quenched the flame of lust. They fought against the teeth of beasts, but this man bore off the most dangerous of our passions, anger. For all these things let us give thanks to God, because he hath thus granted us noble martyrs, and pastors worthy of martyrs, for the perfecting of the saints, for the edifying of the body of Christ with whom be glory, honor, and might to the Father, with the Holy and lifegiving Spirit, now and always, for ever and ever. Amen.

CONCERNING LOWLINESS OF MIND.

HOMILY.

Against those who improperly use the apostolic declaration which says, "Whether in pretense, or in sincerity, Christ is preached:" (Phil. i. 18), *and about humbleness of mind.*

Introduction.

There is an allusion at the beginning of this Homily to some remarks recently made on the parable of the Pharisee and the Publican. These occur in Chrysostom's fifth Homily against the Anomoeans, one of a set of Homilies which, from internal evidence, may be assigned to the close of the year 386, or beginning of 387. The following homily therefore was delivered at Antioch, probably just before Christmas 386. There were some persons who explained the words of St. Paul cited in the title as signifying that provided Christ was preached it mattered not whether the actual doctrines taught were true or heretical. The main object of the homily is to vindicate the language of the Apostle from this erroneous and mischievous interpretation.

1. When lately we made mention of the Pharisee and the publican, and hypothetically yoked two chariots out of virtue and vice; we pointed out each truth, how great is the gain of humbleness of mind, and how great the damage of pride. For this, even when conjoined with righteousness and fasting and tithes, fell behind; while that, even when yoked with sin, outstripped the Pharisee's

pair, even though the charioteer it had was a poor one. For what was worse than the publican? But all the same since he made his soul contrite, and called himself a sinner; which indeed he was; he surpassed the Pharisee, who had both fasting to tell of and tithes; and was removed from any vice. On account of what, and through what? Because even if he was removed from greed of gain and robbery, he had rooted over his soul the mother of all evils—vainglory and pride. On this account Paul also exhorts and says, "Let each one prove his own work; and then he will have his ground of boasting for himself, and not for the other." Whereas he publicly came forward as an accuser of the whole world; and said that he himself was better than all living men. And yet even if he had set himself before ten only, or if five, or if two, or if one, not even was this endurable; but as it was, he not only set himself before the whole world, but also accused all men. On this account he fell behind in the running. And just as a ship, after having run through innumerable surges, and having escaped many storms, then in the very mouth of the harbor having been dashed against some rock, loses the whole treasure which is stowed away in her—so truly did this Pharisee, after having undergone the labors of the fasting, and of all the rest of his virtue, since he did not master his tongue, in the very harbor underwent shipwreck of his cargo. For the going home from prayer, whence he ought to have derived gain, having rather been so greatly damaged, is nothing else than undergoing shipwreck in harbor.

  2. Knowing therefore these things, beloved even if we should have mounted to the very pinnacle of virtue, let us consider ourselves last of all; having learned that pride is able to cast down even from the heavens themselves

him who takes not heed, and humbleness of mind to bear up on high from the very abyss of sins him who knows how to be sober. For this it was that placed the publican before the Pharisee; whereas that, pride I mean and an overweening spirit, surpassed even an incorporeal power, that of the devil; while humbleness of mind and the acknowledgment of his own sins committed brought the robber into Paradise before the Apostles. Now if the confidence which they who confess their own sins effect for themselves is so great, they who are conscious to themselves of many good qualities, yet humble their own souls, how great crowns will they not win. For when sinfulness be put together with humbleness of mind it runs with such ease as to pass and out-strip righteousness combined with pride. If therefore thou have put it to with righteousness, whither will it not reach? through how many heavens will it not pass? By the throne of God itself surely it will stay its course; in the midst of the angels, with much confidence. On the other hand if pride, having been yoked with righteousness, by the excess and weight of its own wickedness had strength enough to drag down *its* confidence; if it be put together with sinfulness, into how deep a hell will it not be able to precipitate him who has it? These things I say, not in order that we should be careless of righteousness, but that we should avoid pride; not that we should sin, but that we should be soberminded. For humbleness of mind is the foundation of the love of wisdom which pertains to us. Even if thou shouldest have built a superstructure of things innumerable; even if almsgiving, even if prayers, even if fasting, even if all virtue; unless this have first been laid as a foundation, all will be built upon it to no purpose and in vain; and it will fall down easily, like that building which had been placed on the sand. For there is no one, no one of our good deeds, which does not need this; there is no one which separate from this will be able to stand. But even if thou shouldest mention temperance, even if virginity, even if despising of money, even if anything whatever, all are unclean and accursed and loathsome, humbleness of mind being absent. Everywhere therefore let us take her with us, in words, in deeds, in thoughts, and with this let us build these (graces).

3. But the things belonging to humbleness of mind have been sufficiently spoken of; not for the value of the virtue; for no one will be able to celebrate it in accordance with its value; but for the intelligence of your love. For well do I know that even from the few things that have been said you will embrace it with much zeal. But since it is also necessary to make clear and manifest the apostolic saying which has been to-day read; seeming as it does to many to afford a pretext for indolence; so that some may not, providing for themselves hence a certain frigid defense, neglect their own salvation—to this let us direct our discourse. What then is this saying? "Whether in pretense," it says, "or in sincerity, Christ is preached." This many wrest absolutely and just as happens, without reading what precedes and what comes after it; but having cut it off from the sequence of the remaining members, to the destruction of their own soul they put it forward to the more indolent. For attempting to seduce them from the sound faith; then seeing them afraid and trembling; on the ground of its not being without danger to do this, and desiring to relieve their fears, they bring forward this apostolic declaration, saying, Paul conceded this, by saying, "Whether in pretense or in sincerity, let Christ be proclaimed." But these things are not (true), they are not.

For in the first place he did not say "let him be proclaimed," but "he is proclaimed," and the difference between this and that is wide. For the saying "let him be proclaimed" belongs to a lawgiver; but the saying "he is proclaimed" to one announcing the event. For that Paul does not ordain a law that there should be heresies, but draws away all who attended to him, hear what he says, "If any one preaches to you a gospel besides what ye have received, let him be anathema, were it even I, were it even an angel from the heavens." Now he would not have anathematized both himself and an angel, if he had known the act to be without danger. And again— "I am jealous of you with a jealousy of God," he says; "for I have betrothed you to one husband a chaste virgin: and fear lest at some time, as the serpent beguiled Eve by his wiliness, so your thoughts should be corrupted from the singleness that is towards Christ." See, he both set down singleness, and granted no allowance. For if there were allowance, there was no danger: and if there was no danger Paul would not have feared: and Christ would not also have commanded that the tares should be burned up, if it were a thing indifferent to attend to this one or that or another: or to all indiscriminately.

4. Whatever then is what is meant? I wish to narrate to you the whole history from a point a little earlier; for it is needful to know in what circumstances Paul was when he was writing these things by letter. In what circumstances therefore was he? In prison and chains and intolerable perils. Whence is this manifest? From the epistle itself. For earlier than this he says, "Now I wish you to know, brethren, that the circumstances in which I am have come rather to the furtherance of the Gospel; so that my bonds have become manifest in Christ

in the whole Court, and to all the others; and a good many of the brethren, trusting to my bonds, the more exceedingly dare fearlessly to speak the word." Now Nero had then cast him into prison. For just as some robber having set foot in the house, while all are sleeping, when stealing everything, if he see anyone having lit a lamp, both extinguishes the light and slays him who holds the lamp, in order that he may be allowed in security to steal and rob the property of others; so truly also the Cæsar Nero then, just as any robber and burglar while all were sleeping a deep and unconscious slumber; robbing the property of all, breaking into marriage chambers, subverting houses, displaying every form of wickedness; when he saw Paul having lighted a lamp throughout the world; (the word of his teaching;) and reproving his wickedness, exerted himself both to extinguish what was preached, and to put the teachers out of the way; in order that he might be allowed with authority to do anything he pleased; and after binding that holy man, cast him into prison. It was at that time then that the blessed Paul wrote these things. Who would not have been astounded? who would not have marveled? or rather who could adequately have been astounded at and admired that noble and heaven-reaching soul; in that, while bound in Rome and imprisoned, at so great a distance as that, he wrote a letter to the Philippians? For you know how great is the distance between Macedonia and Rome. But neither did the length of the way, nor the amount of time (required), nor the press of business, nor the peril and the dangers coming one upon another, nor anything else, drive out his love for and remembrance of the disciples; but he retained them all in his mind; and not so strongly were his hands bound with the chains as his soul was bound together and rivetted by his longing for the disciples: which very thing itself indeed also declaring, in the preface of the Epistle he said, "On account of my having you in my heart, both in my bonds, and in the defense and confirmation of the Gospel." And just as a King, having ascended upon his throne at morning-tide and taken his seat in the royal courts, immediately receives from all quarters innumerable letters; so truly he also, just as in royal courts, seated in the dungeon, both received and sent his letters in far greater number; the nations from all quarters referring to his wisdom everything about what had taken place among themselves; and he administered more business than the reigning monarch in proportion to his having had a larger dominion entrusted to him. For in truth God had brought and put into his hands not those who inhabited the country of the Romans only, but also all the barbarians, both land and sea. And by way of showing this he said to the Romans, "Now I would not that ye should be ignorant, brethren, that ofttimes I have purposed to come to you, and have been hindered until the present; in order that I might have some fruit also among you, as among the rest of the Gentiles too. Both to Greeks and barbarians, both to wise and those without understanding I am a debtor." Every day therefore he was in anxious thought at one moment for Corinthians, at another for Macedonians; how Philippians, how Cappadocians, how Galatians, how Athenians, how they who inhabited Pontus, how all together were. But all the same, having had the whole world put into his hands, he continually cared not for entire nations only, but also for each single man; and now indeed he dispatched a letter on behalf of Onesimus, and now on behalf of him who among the Corinthians had committed fornication. For neither used he to regard this—that it was the individual who had sinned and needed advocacy; but that it was a human being; a human being, the living thing most precious to God; and for whose sake the Father had not spared even the Only-begotten.

5. For do not tell me that this or that man is a runaway slave, or a robber or thief, or laden with countless faults, or that he is a mendicant and abject, or of low value and worthy of no account; but consider that for his sake the Christ died; and this sufficed thee for a ground for all solicitude. Consider what sort of person *he* must be, whom Christ valued at so high a price as not to have spared even his own blood. For neither, if a king had chosen to sacrifice himself on any one's behalf, should we have sought out another demonstration of his being some one great and of deep interest to the King—I fancy not—for his death would suffice to show the love of him who had died towards him. But as it is not man, not angel, not archangel; but the Lord of the heavens himself, the only begotten Son of God himself having clothed himself with flesh, freely gave himself on our behalf. Shall we not do everything, and take every trouble, so that the men who have been thus valued may enjoy every solicitude at our hands? And what kind of defense shall we have? what allowance? This at least is the very thing by way of declaring which Paul also said, "Do not by thy meat destroy him for whose sake Christ died." For desiring to shame, and to bring to solicitude, and to persuade to care for their neighbors, those who despise their brethren, and look down upon them as being weak, instead of all else he set down the Master's death. Sitting then in the prison he wrote the letter to the Philippians from that so great distance. For such as this is the love that is according to

God: it is interrupted by no one of human things, since it has its roots from above in the heavens and its recompense. And what does he say? "Now I desire that ye should know, brethren." Seest thou solicitude for his scholars? sees thou a teacher's carefulness? Hear too of loving affection of scholars towards their teacher, that thou mayest know that this was what made them strong and unconquerable— the being bound together with one another. For if "Brother helped by brother is as a strong city;" far more so many bound together by the bonds of love would have entirely repulsed the plotting of the wicked demon. That indeed then Paul was bound up with the disciples, requires not even any demonstration further nor argument for us, since in truth even when in bonds he anxiously cared for them, and each day, he was also dying for them, burning with his longing.

6. And that the disciples too were bound up with Paul with all perfectness; and that not men only, but women also, hear what he says about Phoebe. "Now I commend to you Phoebe the sister, being a deaconess of the Church which is in Cenchreæ; that ye may receive her in the Lord worthily of the saints, and stand by her, in whatever matter she may require you, since she has proved a helper of many; and of me myself." But in this instance he bore witness to her of her zeal so far as help went (only:) but Priscilla and Aquilla went as far even as death for Paul's sake; and about them he thus writes, saying, "Aquila and Priscilla salute you, who for my life's sake laid down their own neck;" for death clearly. And about another again writing to these very persons he says, "Because he went as far as death; having counselled ill for his life, in order that he might supply your deficiency in your service towards me." Seest thou how they loved their

teacher? How they regarded his rest before their own life? On this account no one surpassed them then. Now this I say, not that we may hear only, but that we may also imitate; and not to the ruled only, but also to those who rule is what we say addressed; in order that both scholars may display much solicitude about their teachers, and the teachers may have the same loving affection as Paul about those placed under them; not those present only, but also those who are far off. For also Paul, dwelling in the whole world just as in one house, thus continually took thought for the salvation of all; and having dismissed everything of his own; bonds and troubles and stripes and straits, watched over and inquired into each day, in what state the affairs of the disciples were; and often for this very purpose alone sent, now Timothy, and now Tychicus; and about him he says, "That he may know your circumstances, and encourage your hearts:" and about Timothy; "I have sent him, being no longer able to contain myself; lest in some way the tempter have tempted you." And Titus again elsewhere, and another to another place. For since he himself, by the compulsion of his bonds being often detained in one place, was unable to meet those who were his vitals, he met them through the disciples.

7. And then therefore being in bonds he writes to the Philippians, saying, "Now I desire that ye should know, brethren," calling the disciples brethren. For such a thing as this is love; it casts out all inequality, and knows not superiority and dignity; but even if one be higher than all, he descends to the lowlier position of all; just what Paul also used to do. But let us hear what it is that he desires they should know. "That the things which happened unto me," he says, "have fallen out rather to the

furtherance of the gospel." Tell me, how and in what way? Hast thou then been released from thy bonds? hast thou then put off thy chain? and dost thou with free permission preach in the city? hast thou then, having gone into an assembly, drawn out many long discourses about the faith, and departed after gaining many disciples? hast thou then raised the dead and been made an object of wonder? hast thou then cleansed lepers, and all were astounded? hast thou driven away demons, and been exalted? No one of these things, he says. How then did the furtherance of the gospel take place? tell me. "So that my bonds," he says, "have become openly known in the whole Court, and to all the rest." What sayest thou? this then, this was the furtherance, this the advance, this the increase of the proclamation—that all knew that thou was bound. Yes, he says: Hear at least what comes next, that thou mayest learn that the bonds not only proved no hindrance, but also a ground of greater freedom of speech. "So that several of the brethren in the Lord, in reliance on my bonds, more abundantly dare fearlessly to speak the word." What sayest thou, O Paul? have thy bonds inspired not anxiety but confidence? not fear but earnest longing? The things mentioned have no consistency. I too know it. For neither did these things take place according to the consistency of human affairs, he means, but what came about was above nature, and the successes were of divine grace. On this account what used to cause anxiety to all others, that to him afforded confidence. For also if anyone having taken the leader of an army and confined him, have made this publicly known, he throws the whole camp into flight; and if anyone have carried a shepherd away from the flock, the security with which he drives off the sheep is great. But not in Paul's case was it thus, but the contrary entirely. For the leader of the army was bound, and the soldiers became more forward in the spirit; and the confidence with which they sprung upon their adversaries was greater: the shepherd was in confinement, and the sheep were not consumed, nor even scattered.

8. Who ever saw, whoever heard of, the scholars taking greater encouragement in the dangers of their teachers? How was it that they feared not? how was it that they were not terrified? how was it that they did not say to Paul, "Physician, heal thyself," deliver thyself from thy manifold perils, and then thou will be able to procure for us those countless good things? How was it they did not say these things? How! It was because they had been schooled, from the grace of the Spirit, that these things took place not out of weakness, but out of the permission of the Christ; in order that the truth might shine abroad more largely; through bonds and imprisonments and tribulations and straits increasing and rising, to a greater volume. Thus is the power of Christ in weakness perfected. For indeed if his bonds had crippled Paul and made him cowardly; either himself or those belonging to him; one could not but feel difficulty; but if rather they prepared him into greater renown, one must be astounded and marvel, how through a thing involving dishonor glory was procured for the disciple—through a thing inspiring cowardice confidence and encouragement resulted to them all. For who was not astounded at him then, seeing him encircled with a chain? Then demons took to flight all the more, when they saw him spending his time in a prison. For not so splendid does the diadem make a royal head, as the chain his hands; not owing to their proper nature, but owing to the grace that darted brightness on them. On this account it was that great encouragement

resulted to the disciples. For also they saw his body indeed bound, but his tongue not bound, his hands indeed tightly manacled, but his voice unshackled, and transversing the whole world more swiftly than the solar ray. And this became to them an encouragement; learning as they did from the facts that no one of present things is to be dreaded. For when the soul has been genuinely imbued by divine longing and love, it pays regard to no one of things present; but just as those who are mad venture themselves against fire and sword and wild beasts and sea and all else, so these too, maddened with a most noble and most spiritual frenzy, a frenzy arising from sanity, used to laugh at all things that are seen. On this account, seeing their teachers bound, they the more exulted, the more prided themselves; by facts giving to their adversaries a demonstration that on all sides they were impregnable and indomitable.

9. Then therefore, when matters were in this state, some of the enemies of Paul, desiring to fan up the war to greater vehemence, and to make the hatred of the tyrant, which was felt towards him greater, pretended that they themselves also preached; (and they did preach the right and sound faith,) for the sake of the doctrine advancing more rapidly: and this they did, not with the desire to disseminate the faith; but in order that Nero, having learnt that the preaching was increasing and the doctrine advancing, might the sooner have Paul led away to execution. There were therefore two schools; that of Paul's scholars and that of Paul's enemies; the one preaching out of sincerity, and the others out of love of contention and the hatred they felt towards Paul. And by way of declaring this he said, "Some indeed through envy and strife are preaching Christ," (pointing out those his

enemies) "but some also through good pleasure;" saying this about his own scholars. Then next about those; "Some indeed out of contentiousness," (his enemies,) not purely, not soundly, but, "thinking that they are thereby bringing pressure upon my bonds; but the others out of love;" (this again about his own brethren;) "knowing that I am set for the defense of the gospel." For what? Nevertheless, in any way; whether in pretense or in sincerity, Christ is being announced." So that vainly and to no purpose is this saying taken in reference to heresies. For those who then were preaching were not preaching corrupt doctrine; but sound and right belief. For if they were preaching corrupt doctrine, and were teaching other things contrary to Paul, what they desired was certain not to succeed to them. Now what did they desire? That the faith having grown, and the disciples of Paul having become numerous, it should rouse Nero to greater hostility. And if they were preaching different doctrines, they would not have made the disciples of Paul numerous; and by not doing so, they would not have exasperated the tyrant. He does not therefore say this—that they were bringing in corrupt doctrines—but that the motive from which they were preaching, *this* was corrupt. For it is one thing to state the pretext of their preaching itself was not sound. For the preaching does not become sound when the doctrine is laden with deception; and the pretext does not become sound when the preaching indeed is sound, but they who preach do not preach for the sake of God, but either with a view of enmity, or with a view to the favor of others.

10. He therefore does not say this—that they were bringing in heresies; but that it was not from a right motive, nor through piety that they were preaching what

they did preach. For it was not they might increase the gospel that they were doing this; but that they might wage war against him, and throw him into greater danger—on this account he accuses them. And see how with exactitude he laid it. "Thinking," he says, "that they were putting pressure upon my bonds." He did not say, putting, but "thinking they were putting upon," that is supposing, by way of pointing out that even if they so supposed, still he himself was not in such a position; but that he even rejoiced on account of the advance of the preaching. He added therefore saying, "But in this I both rejoice and will rejoice:" whereas if he held their doctrines deception, and they were bringing in heresies, Paul could not possibly rejoice. But since the doctrine was sound and of genuine parentage, on this account he says, "I rejoice and will rejoice." For what if they are destroying themselves by doing this out of contentiousness? Still, even unwillingly, they are strengthening my cause. Seest thou how great is Paul's power? how he is caught by no one of the devil's machinations? And not only is he not caught; but also by these themselves he subdues him. For great indeed is both the devil's craftiness, and the wickedness of those who minister to him; for under pretense of being of the same mind, they desired to extinguish the proclamation. But "he who seizes the cunning in their craftiness" did not permit that this should take place then. By way of declaring this very thing at least Paul said, "But the continuing in the flesh is the more necessary for your sake; and this I confidently know, that I shall continue and remain in company with you all." For those men indeed set their mind on casting me out of the present life, and are ready to endure anything for this object: but God does not permit it on your account.

11. These things therefore, all of them, remember with exactness in order that you may be able with all wisdom to correct those who use the Scriptures without reference to circumstances and at hap-hazard, and for the destruction of their neighbors. And we shall be able both to remember what has been said, and to correct others, if we always betake ourselves to prayers as a refuge, and beseech the God who gives the word of wisdom to grant both intelligence in hearing, and a careful and unconquerable guardianship of this spiritual deposit in our hands. For things which often we have not strength to perform successfully from our own exertions, these we shall have power to accomplish easily through prayers which are persevering. For always and without intermission it is a duty to pray, both for him who is in affliction, and him who is in dangers, and him who is in prosperity—for him who is in relief and much prosperity, that these may remain unmoved and without vicissitude, and may never change; and for him who is in affliction and his many dangers, that he may see some favorable change brought about to him, and be transported into a calm of consolation. Art thou in a calm? Then beseech God that this calm may continue settled to thee. Have you seen a storm risen up against thee? Beseech God earnestly to cause the billow to pass, and to make a calm out of the storm. Hast thou been heard? Be heartily thankful for this; because thou hast been heard. Hast thou not been heard? Persevere, in order that thou mayest be heard. For even if God at any time delay the giving, it is not in hatred and aversion;468 but from the desire by the deferring of the giving perpetually to retain thee with himself; just in the way also that affectionate fathers do; for they also adroitly manage the perpetual and assiduous attendance of

children who are rather indolent by the delay of the giving. There is to thee no need of mediators in audience with God; nor of that much canvassing; nor of the fawning upon others; but even if thou be destitute, even if bereft of advocacy, alone, by thyself, having called on God for help, thou wilt in any case succeed. He is not so wont to assent when entreated by others on our behalf, as by ourselves who are in need; even if we be laden with ten thousand evil deeds. For if in the case of men, even if we have come into countless collisions with them, when both at dawn and at mid-day and in the evening we show ourselves to those who are aggrieved against us, by the unbroken continuance and the persistent meeting and interview we easily demolish their enmity—far more in the case of God would this be effected.

12. But thou art unworthy. Become worthy by thy assiduity. For that it both is possible that the unworthy should become worthy from his assiduity; and that God assents more when called on by ourselves than by others; and that he often delays the giving, not from the wish that we should be utterly perplexed, nor to send us out with empty hands; but in order that he may become the author of greater good things to us—these three points I will endeavor to make evident by the parable which has to-day been read to you. The woman of Chanaan had come to Christ praying on behalf of a daughter possessed by a demon, and crying out with much earnestness (it says, "Have pity on me, Lord, my daughter is badly possessed by a demon.") See, the woman of a strange nation, and a barbarian, and outside of the Jewish commonwealth. For indeed what else (was she) than a dog, and unworthy of the receiving her request? For "it is not," he says, "good to take the children's bread, and to give it to the dogs."

But, all the same, from her assiduity, she became worthy. For not only did he admit her into the nobility of children, dog as she was; but also he sent her off with that high encomium saying, "O woman great is thy faith; be it done to thee as thou wilt." Now when the Christ says, "great is thy faith," seek thou no other demonstration of the greatness of soul which was in the woman. Seest thou how, from her assiduity the woman, being unworthy, became worthy? Desires thou also to learn that we accomplish (our wish) by calling on him by ourselves more than by others? She cried out, and the disciples having come to him say, "Let her go away, for she is crying after us:" and to them he says, "I am not sent, unless to the lost sheep of the house of Israel." But when she had come to him by herself and continued crying, and saying, "Yes, Lord, for even the dogs eat from the table of their masters," then he granted the favor and says, "Be it done unto thee as thou wilt." Seest thou how, when they were entreating him, he repelled; but when she who needed the gift herself cried out, he assented? For to them he says, "I am not sent, unless to the lost sheep of the house of Israel;" but to her he said, "Great is thy faith; be it done unto thee as thou wilt." Again, at the beginning and in the prelude of her request he answered nothing; but when both once and twice and thrice she had come to him, then he granted the boon; by the issue making us believe that he had delayed the giving, not that he might repel her but that he might display to us all the woman's endurance. For if he had delayed in order that he might repel her, he would have not granted it even at the end; but since he was waiting to display to all her spiritual wisdom, on this account he was silent. For if he had granted it immediately and at the beginning, we should not have known the woman's virtue. "Let her go" it says, "because she is clamoring behind us." But what (says) the Christ? "Ye hear a voice, but I see the mind: I know what she is going to say. I choose not to permit the treasure hidden in her mind to escape notice; but I am waiting and keeping silence; in order that having discovered it I may lay it down in publicity, and make it manifest to all.

13. Having therefore learned all these things, even if we be in sins, and unworthy of receiving, let us not despair; knowing, that by assiduity of soul we shall be able to become worthy of the request. Even if we be unaided by advocate and destitute, let us not faint; knowing that it is a strong advocacy—the coming to God one's self by one's self with much eagerness. Even if he delay and defer with respect to the giving, let us not be dispirited; having learned that the putting it off and delay is a sure proof of caring and love for mankind. If we have thus persuaded ourselves; and with a soul deeply pained and fervent, and thoroughly roused purpose; and such as that with which the woman of Chanaan approached, we too come to him, even if we be dogs; even if we have done anything whatever dreadful; we shall both rebut our own crimes, and obtain so great liberty of speech as also to be advocates for others; in the way in which also this woman of Chanaan not only herself enjoyed liberty of speech and ten thousand encomiums but had power to snatch her dear daughter out of her intolerable sufferings. For nothing—nothing is more powerful than prayer when fervent and genuine. This both disperses present dangers, and rescues from the penalties which take place at that hour. That therefore we may both complete our passage through the present life with ease, and depart thither with confidence, with much zeal and eagerness let us perform

this perpetually. For thus shall we be able both to attain the good things which are laid up, and to enjoy those excellent hopes; which God grant that we may all attain; by the grace and loving kindness and compassion of our Lord Jesus Christ—with whom to the Father together with the Holy Spirit be glory, honor, dominion, to the ages of the ages. Amen.

St. John Chrysostom

INSTRUCTIONS TO CATECHUMENS.

First instruction.

To those about to be illuminated, and for what reason the laver is said to be of regeneration and not of remission of sins; and that it is a dangerous thing not only to forswear oneself, but also to take an oath, even though we swear truly.

1. How delightful and lovable is our band of young brethren! For brethren I call you, even now before you have been brought forth, and before your birth I welcome this relationship with you: For I know, I know clearly, to how great an honor you are about to be led, and to how great a dignity; and those who are about to receive dignity, all are wont to honor, even before the dignity is conferred, laying up for themselves beforehand by their attention good will for the future. And this also I myself now do. For ye are not about to be led to an empty dignity, but to an actual kingdom: and not simply to a kingdom, but to the kingdom of the Heavens itself. Wherefore I beseech and entreat you that you remember me when you come into that kingdom, and as Joseph said to the chief butler "Remember me when it shall be well with thee," this also I say now to you, do ye remember me when it is well with you. I do not ask this in return for interpreting your dreams, as he; for I have not come to interpret dreams for you, but to discourse of matters celestial, and to convey to you glad tidings of such good things as "eye hath not seen, and ear hath not heard and which have entered not into the heart of man, such are the things which God hath prepared for them that love him."

Now Joseph indeed said to that chief butler, "yet three days and Pharaoh will restore thee to thy chief butlership." But I do not say, yet three days and ye shall be set to pour out the wine of a tyrant, but yet thirty days, and not Pharaoh but the king of Heaven shall restore you to the country which is on high, Jerusalem, which is free—to the city which is in the heavens; and *he* said indeed, "Thou shalt give the cup into the hands of Pharaoh." But I say not that you shall give the cup into the hands of the king, but that the king shall give the cup into your hand—that dread cup, full of much power, and more precious than any created thing. The initiated know the virtue of this cup, and you yourselves shall know it a little while hence. Remember me, therefore, when you come into that kingdom, when you receive the royal robe, when you are girt with the purple dipped in the master's blood, when you will be crowned with the diadem, which has luster leaping forth from it on all sides, more brilliant than the rays of the sun. Such are the gifts of the Bridegroom, greater indeed than your worth, but worthy of his loving kindness.

Wherefore, I count you blessed already before those sacred nuptials, and I do not only count you blessed, but I praise your prudence in that you have not come to your illumination as the most slothful among men, at your last breath, but already, like prudent servants, prepared with much goodwill to obey your master, have brought the neck of your soul with much meekness and readiness beneath the bands of Christ, and have received His easy yoke, and have taken His light burden. For if the grace bestowed be the same both for you and for those who are initiated at their last hour, yet the matter of the intention is not the same, nor yet the matter of the preparation for the rite. For they indeed receive it on their bed, but you in the bosom of the Church, which is the common mother of us all; they indeed with lamentation and weeping, but you rejoicing, and exceeding glad: they sighing, you giving thanks; they indeed lethargic with much fever, you filled with much spiritual pleasure; wherefore in your case all things are in harmony with the gift, but in theirs all are adverse to it. For there is wailing and much lamentation on the part of the initiated, and children stand around crying, wife tearing her cheeks, and dejected friends and tearful servants; the whole aspect of the house resembles some wintry and gloomy day. And if thou shalt open the heart of him who is lying there, thou wilt find it more downcast than are these. For as winds meeting one another with many a contrary blast, break up the sea into many parts, so too the thought of the terrors preying upon him assail the soul of the sick man, and distract his mind with many anxieties. Whenever he sees his children, he thinks of their fatherless condition; whenever he looks from them to his wife, he considers her widowhood; when he sees the servants, he beholds the desolation of the whole house; when he comes back to himself, he calls to mind his own present life, and being about to be torn from it, experiences a great cloud of despondency. Of such a kind is the soul of him who is about to be initiated. Then in the midst of its tumult and confusion, the Priest enters, more formidable than the fever itself, and more distressing than death to the relatives of the sick man. For the entrance of the Presbyter is thought to be a greater reason for despair than the voice of the physician despairing of his life, and that which suggests eternal life seems to be a symbol of death. But I have not yet put the finishing stroke to these ills. For in the midst of relatives raising a tumult and making preparations, the soul has often taken its flight, leaving the body desolate; and in many cases, while it was present it was useless, for when it neither recognizes those who are present, nor hears their voice, nor is able to answer those words by which it will make that blessed covenant with the common master of us all, but is as a useless log, or a stone, and he who is about to be illuminated lies there differing nothing from a corpse, what is the profit of initiation in a case of such insensibility?

2. For he who is about to approach these holy and dread mysteries must be awake and alert, must be clean from all cares of this life, full of much self-restraint, much readiness; he must banish from his mind every thought foreign to the mysteries, and on all sides cleanse and prepare his home, as if about to receive the king himself. Such is the preparation of your mind: such are your thoughts; such the purpose of your soul. Await therefore a return worthy of this most excellent decision from God, who overpowers with His recompense those who show forth obedience to Him. But since it is necessary for his fellow servants to contribute of their own, then we will contribute of our own; yea rather not even are these things our own, but these too are our Master's. "For what hast thou," saith He, "that thou didst not receive? but if thou didst receive it, why dost thou glory, as if thou hadst not received it?" I wished to say this first of all, why in the world our fathers, passing by the whole year, settled that the children of the Church should be initiated at this season; and for what reason, after the instruction from us, removing your shoes and raiment, unclad and unshod, with but one garment on, they conduct you to hear the words of the exorcisers. For it is not thoughtlessly and

rashly that they have planned this dress and this season for us. But both these things have a certain mystic and secret reason. And I wish to say this to you. But I see that our discourse now constrains us to something more necessary to say what baptism is, and for what reason it enters into our life, and what good things it conveys to us.

But, if you will, let us discourse about the name which this mystic cleansing bears: for its name is not one, but very many and various. For this purification is called the laver of regeneration. "He saved us," he saith, "through the laver of regeneration, and renewing of the Holy Ghost." It is called also illumination, and this St. Paul again has called it, "For call to remembrance the former days in which after ye were illuminated ye endured a great conflict of sufferings;" and again, "For it is impossible for those who were once illuminated, and have tasted of the heavenly gift, and then fell away, to renew them again unto repentance." It is called also, baptism: "For as many of you as were baptized into Christ did put on Christ." It is called also burial: "For we were buried" saith he, "with him, through baptism, into death." It is called circumcision: "In whom ye were also circumcised, with a circumcision not made with hands, in the putting off of the body of the sins of the flesh." It is called a cross: "Our old man was crucified with him that the body of sin might be done away." It is also possible to speak of other names besides these, but in order that we should not spend our whole time over the names of this free gift, come, return to the first name, and let us finish our discourse by declaring its meaning; but in the meantime, let us extend our teaching a little further. There is that laver by means of the baths, common to all men, which is wont to wipe off bodily uncleanness; and there is the Jewish laver, more honorable than the other, but far inferior to that of grace; and it too wipes off bodily uncleanness but not simply uncleanness of body, since it even reaches to the weak conscience. For there are many matters, which by nature indeed are not unclean, but which become unclean from the weakness of the conscience. And as in the case of little children, masks, and other bugbears are not in themselves alarming, but seem to little children to be alarming, by reason of the weakness of their nature, so it is in the case of those things of which I was speaking; just as to touch dead bodies is not naturally unclean, but when this comes into contact with a weak conscience, it makes him who touches them unclean. For that the thing in question is not unclean naturally, Moses himself who ordained this law showed, when he bore off the entire corpse of Joseph, and yet remained clean. On this account Paul also, discoursing to us about this uncleanness which does not come naturally but by reason of the weakness of the conscience, speaks somewhat in this way, "Nothing is common of itself save to him who accounted anything to be common." Dost thou not see that uncleanness does not arise from the nature of the thing, but from the weakness of the reasoning about it? And again: "All things indeed are clean, howbeit it is evil to that man who eats with offense." Do you see that it is not to eat, but to eat with offense, that is the cause of uncleanness?

    3. Such is the defilement from which the laver of the Jews cleansed. But the laver of grace, not such, but the real uncleanness which has introduced defilement into the soul as well as into the body. For it does not make those who have touched dead bodies clean, but those who have set their hand to dead works: and if any man be

effeminate, or a fornicator, or an idolator, or a doer of whatever ill you please, or if he be full of all the wickedness there is among men: should he fall into this pool of waters, he comes up again from the divine fountain purer than the sun's rays. And in order that thou mayest not think that what is said is mere vain boasting, hear Paul speaking of the power of the laver, "Be not deceived: neither idolators, nor fornicators, nor adulterers, nor effeminate, nor abusers of themselves with men, nor covetous, not drunkards, not revilers, not extortioners shall inherit the kingdom of God." And what has this to do with what has been spoken? says one, "for prove the question whether the power of the laver thoroughly cleanses all these things." Hear therefore what follows: "And such were some of you, but ye were washed, but ye were sanctified, but ye were justified in the name of the Lord Jesus Christ, and in the spirit of our God." *We promise to show you that they who approach the laver become clean from all fornication: but the word has shown more, that they have become not only clean, but both holy and just, for it does not say only "ye were washed," but also "ye were sanctified and were justified." What could be stranger than this, when without toil, and exertion, and good works, righteousness is produced? For such is the lovingkindness of the Divine gift that it makes men just without this exertion. For if a letter of the Emperor, a few words being added, sets free those who are liable to countless accusations, and brings others to the highest honors; much rather will the Holy Spirit of God, who is able to do all things, free us from all evil and grant us much righteousness, and fill us with much assurance, and as a spark falling into the wide sea would straightway be quenched, or would become invisible, being overwhelmed by the multitude of the waters, so also all human wickedness, when it falls into the pool of the divine fountain, is more swiftly and easily overwhelmed, and made invisible, than that spark. And for what reason, says one, if the laver take away all our sins, is it called, not a laver of remission of sins, nor a laver of cleansing, but a laver of regeneration? Because it does not simply take away our sins, nor simply cleanse us from our faults, but so as if we were born again. For it creates and fashions us anew not forming us again out of earth, but creating us out of another element, namely, of the nature of water. For it does not simply wipe the vessel clean, but entirely remolds it again. For that which is wiped clean, even if it be cleaned with care, has traces of its former condition, and bears the remains of its defilement, but that which falls into the new mold, and is renewed by means of the flames, laying aside all uncleanness, comes forth from the furnace, and sends forth the same brilliancy with things newly formed. As therefore anyone who takes and recasts a golden statue which has been tarnished by time, smoke, dust, rust, restores it to us thoroughly cleansed and glistening: so too this nature of ours, rusted with the rust of sin, and having gathered much smoke from our faults, and having lost its beauty, which He had from the beginning bestowed upon it from himself, God has taken and cast anew, and throwing it into the waters as into a mold, and instead of fire sending forth the grace of the Spirit, then brings us forth with much brightness, renewed, and made afresh, to rival the beams of the sun, having crushed the old man, and having fashioned a new man, more brilliant than the former.

4. And speaking darkly of this crushing, and this mystic cleansing, the prophet of old said, "Thou shalt

dash them in pieces like a potter's vessel." For that the word is in reference to the faithful, what goes before sufficiently shows us, "For thou art my Son," he says, "to-day have I begotten thee, ask of me and I will give the heathen for three inheritance, the utmost parts of the earth for thy possession." Do you see how he has made mention of the church of the Gentiles, and has spoken of the kingdom of Christ extended on all sides? Then he says again, "Thou shalt rule them with a rod of iron;" not grievous, but strong: "thou shalt break them in pieces like a potter's vessel." Behold then, the laver is more mystically brought forward. For he does not say earthen vessels: but vessels of the potter. But, give heed: For earthen vessels when crushed would not admit of refashioning, on account of the hardness which was gained by them from the fire. But the fact is that the vessels of the potter are not earthen, but of clay; wherefore, also, when they have been distorted, they can easily, by the skill of the artificer, be brought again to a second shape. When, therefore, God speaks of an irremediable calamity, he does not say vessels of the potter, but an earthen vessel; when, for instance, he wished to teach the prophet and the Jews that he delivered up the city to an irremediable calamity, he bade him take an earthen wine-vessel, and crush it before all the people, and say, "Thus shall this city be destroyed, be broken in pieces." But when he wishes to hold out good hopes to them, he brings the prophet to a pottery, and does not show him an earthen vessel, but shows him a vessel of clay, which was in the hands of the potter, falling to the ground: and brings him to it saying, "If this potter has taken up and remodeled his vessel which has fallen, shall I not much rather be able to restore you when you have fallen?" It is possible therefore for God not only to restore those who are made of clay, through the laver of regeneration, but to bring back again to their original state, on their careful repentance, those who have received the power of the Spirit, and have lapsed. But this is not the time for you to hear words about repentance, rather may the time never come for you to fall into the need of these remedies, but may you always remain in preservation of the beauty and the brightness which ye are now about to receive, unsullied. In order, then, that ye may ever remain thus, come and let us discourse to you a little about your manner of life. For in the wrestling schools falls of the athletes are devoid of danger. For the wrestling is with friends, and they practice all their exercises on the persons of their teachers. But when the time of the contest has come, when the lists are open, when the spectators are seated above, when the president has arrived, it necessarily follows that the combatants, if they become careless, fall and retire in great disgrace, or if they are in earnest, win the crowns and the prizes. So then, in your case these thirty days are like some wrestling school, both for exercise and practice: let us learn from thence already to get the better of that evil demon. For it is to contend with him that we have to strip ourselves, with him after baptism are we to box and fight. Let us learn from thence already his grip, on what side he is aggressive, on what side he can easily threaten us, in order that, when the contest comes on, we may not feel strange, nor become confused, as seeing new forms of wrestling; but having already practiced them amongst ourselves, and having learnt all his methods, may engage in these forms of wrestling against him with courage. In all ways, therefore, is he accustomed to threaten us, but especially by means of the tongue, and the mouth. For there is no organ so convenient for him for our deception and our destruction as an unchastened tongue and an unchecked utterance. Hence come many slips on our part: hence many serious accusations against us. And the ease of these falls through the tongue a certain one showed, when he said, "Many fell by the sword, but not so many as by the tongue." Now the gravity of the fall the same person shows us again when he says: "To slip upon a pavement is better than to slip with the tongue." And what he speaks of is of this kind. Better it is, says he, that the body should fall and be crushed, than that such a word should go forth as destroys the soul; and he does not speak of falls merely; he also admonishes us that much forethought should be exercised, so that we should not be tripped up, thus saying "Make a door and bars for thy mouth," not that we should prepare doors and bars, but that with much security, we should shut the tongue off from outrageous words; and again in another place, after showing that we need influence from above, both as accompanying and preceding our own effort so as to keep this wild beast within: stretching forth his hands to God, the prophet said, "Let the lifting up of my hands be an evening sacrifice, set a watch, O Lord, before my mouth, keep the door of my lips;" and he who before admonished, himself too says again "Who shall set a watch before my mouth, and a seal of wisdom upon my lips?" Dost thou not see, each one fearing these falls and bewailing them, both giving advice, and praying that the tongue may have the benefit of much watchfulness? and for what reason, says one, if this organ brings us such ruin, did God originally place it within us? Because indeed, it is of great use, and if we are careful, it is of use only, and brings no ruin. Hear, for example, what he says who spoke the former words, "Death and life are in the power of the tongue." And Christ points to the same thing when he says, "By thy words thou shalt be condemned, and by thy words thou shalt be justified." For the tongue stands in the midst ready for use on either hand. Thou art its master. Thus indeed a sword lies in the midst, and if thou use it against thine enemies, this organ becomes a means of safety for thee. But if thou thrust its stroke against thyself, not the nature of the iron, but thine own transgression becomes the cause of thy slaughter. Let us then take this view of the tongue. It is a sword lying in the midst; sharpen it for the purpose of accusing thine own sins. Thrust not the stroke against thy brother. For this reason God surrounded it with a double fortification; with the fence of the teeth and the barrier of the lips, that it may not rashly and without circumspection utter words which are not convenient. Well, dost thou say it will not endure this? Bridle it therefore within. Restrain it by means of the teeth, as though giving over its body to these executioners and making them bite it. For it is better that when it sins now it should be bitten by the teeth, than one day when it seeks a drop of water and is parched with heat, to be unable to obtain this consolation. In many other ways indeed it is wont to sin, by raillery and blasphemy, by uttering foul words, by slander, swearing, and perjury.

5. But in order that we may not by saying everything at once to-day, confuse your minds, we put before you one custom, namely, about the avoidance of oaths, saying this much by way of preface, and speaking plainly—that if you do not avoid oaths, I say not perjury merely, but those too which happen in the cause of

justice, we shall not further discourse upon any other subject. For it is monstrous that teachers of letters should not give a second lesson to their children until they see the former one fixed well in their memory, but that we, without being able to express our first lessons clearly, should inculcate others before the first are completed. For this is nothing else than to pour into a perforated jar. Give great care, then, that ye silence not our mouth. For this error is grave, and it is exceedingly grave because it does not seem to be grave, and on this account I fear it, because no one fears it. On this account the disease is incurable, because it does not seem to be a disease; but just as simple speech is not a crime, so neither does this seem to be a crime, but with much boldness this transgression is committed: and if any one call it in question, straightway laughter follows, and much ridicule, not of those who are called in question for their oaths, but of those who wish to rectify the disease. On this account I largely extend my discourse about these matters. For I wish to pull up a deep root, and to wipe out a long-standing evil: I speak not of perjury alone, but even of oaths in good faith. But so and so, says one, a forbearing man, consecrated to the priesthood, living in much self-control and piety, takes an oath. Do not speak to me of this forbearing person, this self-controlled, pious man who is consecrated to the priesthood; but if thou wilt, add that this man is Peter, or Paul, or even an angel descended out of heaven. For not even in such a case do I regard the dignity of their persons. For the law which I read upon oaths, is not that of the servant, but of the King: and when the edicts of a king are read, let every claim of the servants be silent. But if thou art able to say that Christ bade us use oaths, or that Christ did not punish the doing of this, show me, and I am persuaded. But if he forbids it with so much care, and takes so much thought about the matter as to class him who takes an oath with the evil one (for whatsoever is more than these, namely, than yea and nay, saith he, is of the devil), why dost thou bring this person and that person forward? For not because of the carelessness of thy fellow servants, but from the injunctions of his own laws, will God record his vote against thee. I have commanded, he says, you ought to obey, not to shelter thyself behind such and such a person and concern thyself with other persons' evil. Since the great David sinned a grievous sin, is it then safe for us to sin? Tell me: on this account then we ought to make sure of this point, and only to emulate the good works of the saints; and if there is carelessness, and transgression of the law anywhere, we ought to flee from it with great care. For our reckoning is not with our fellow-servants, but with our Master, and to him we shall give account for all done in our life. Let us prepare ourselves therefore for this tribunal. For even if he who transgresses this law be beyond everything revered and great, he shall certainly pay the penalty attaching to the transgression. For God is no respecter of persons. How then and in what way is it possible to flee from this sin? For one ought to show not only that the crime is grievous, but to give counsel how we may escape from it. Hast thou a wife, hast thou a servant, children, friends, acquaintance, neighbors? To all these enjoin caution on these matters. Custom is a grievous thing, terrible to supplant, and hard to guard against, and it often attacks us unwilling and unknowing; therefore in so far as thou knowest the power of custom, to such an extent study to be freed from any evil custom, and transfer thyself to any other most useful one. For as that custom is often able to trip thee up, though thou art careful, and guards thyself, and takes thought, and consideration, so if thou transfer thyself to the good custom of abstaining from oaths, thou wilt not be able, either involuntarily or carelessly, to fall into the fault of oaths. For custom is really great and has the power of nature. In order then that we do not continually distress ourselves let us transfer ourselves to another custom, and ask thou each one of thy kindred and acquaintance this favor, that he advise thee and exhort thee to flee from oaths, and reprove thee, when detected in them. For the watch over thee which takes place on their part, is to them too counsel and a suggestion to what is right. For he who reproves another for oaths, will not himself easily fall into this pit. For much swearing is no ordinary pit, not only when it is about little matters but about the greatest. And we, whether buying vegetables, or quarrelling over two farthings, or in a rage with our servants and threatening them, always call upon God as our witness. But a freeman, possessed of some barren dignity, thou would not dare to call upon as witness in the market to such things; but even if thou attempted it, thou wilt pay the penalty of thine insolence. But the King of Heaven, the Lord of Angels, when disputing both about purchases and money, and what not, thou drags in for a testimony. And how can these things be borne? Whence then should we escape from this evil custom? After setting those guards of which I spoke round us, let us fix on a specified time to ourselves for amendment, and adding thereto condemnation if, when the time has passed, we have not amended this. How long will suffice for the purpose? I do not think that they who are very wary, and on the alert, and watchful about their own salvation, should need more than ten days, so as to be altogether free from the evil custom of oaths. But if after ten days we be detected swearing, let us add a penalty due to ourselves, and let us fix upon the greatest punishment and condemnation of the transgression; what then is this condemnation? This I do not fix upon, but will suffer you yourselves to determine the sentence. So we arrange matters in our own case, not only in respect of oaths but in respect of other defects, and fixing a time for ourselves, with most grievous punishments, if at any time we have fallen into them, shall come clean to our Master, and shall escape the fire of hell, and shall stand before the judgment seat of Christ with boldness, to which may we all attain, by the grace and lovingkindness of our Lord Jesus Christ, with whom be glory to the Father together with the Holy Spirit for ever and ever:

Amen.

Second instruction.

To those about to be illuminated and concerning women who adorn themselves with plaiting of hair, and gold, and concerning those who have used omens, and amulets, and incantations, all which are foreign to Christianity.

1. I have come to ask first of all for some fruit in return for the words lately said out of brotherly love to you. For we do not speak in order that ye should hear simply, but in order that ye should remember what has been said, and may afford us evidence of this, by your works. Yea, rather, not us, but, God, who knows the secrets of the heart. On this account indeed instruction is so called, in order that even when we are absent, our

discourse may instruct your hearts. And be not surprised if, after an interval of ten days only, we have come asking for fruit from the seed sown. For in one day it is possible at once to let the seed fall, and to accomplish the harvest. For strengthened not by our own power alone, but by the influence which comes from God, we are summoned to the conflict. Let as many therefore as have received what has been spoken, and have fulfilled it by their works, remain reaching forth to the things which are before. But let as many as have not yet arrived at this good achievement, arrive at it straightway, that they may dispel the condemnation which arises out of their sloth by their diligence for the future. For it is possible, it is indeed possible for him who has been very slothful, by using diligence for the future to recover the whole loss of the time that is past. Wherefore, He says, "To-day if ye will hear his voice, harden not your hearts, as in the day of provocation." And this, He says, exhorting and counselling us; that we should never despair, but so long as we are here, should have good hopes, and should lay hold on what is before us, and hasten towards the prize of our high calling of God. This then let us do, and let us inquire into the names of this great gift. For as ignorance of the greatness of this dignity makes those who are honored with it more slothful, so when it is known it renders them thankful, and makes them more earnest; and anyhow it would be disgraceful and ridiculous that they who enjoy such glory and honors from God, should not even know what the names of it are intended to show forth. And why do I speak about this gift, for if thou wilt consider the common name of our race, thou wilt receive the greatest instruction and incentive to virtue. For this name "Man," we do not define according as they who are without define it, but as the Divine Scripture has bidden us. For a man is not merely whosoever has hands and feet of a man, nor whosoever is rational only, but whosoever practices piety and virtue with boldness. Hear, at least, what he says concerning Job. For in saying that "there was a man in the land of Ausis," he does not describe him in those terms in which they who are without describe him, nor does he say this because he had two feet and broad nails, but he added the evidences of his piety and said, "just, true, fearing God, eschewing every evil deed," showing that this is a man; even as therefore another says, "Fear God, and keep his commandments, because this is the whole man." But if the name man affords such a great incentive to virtue, much rather the term faithful. For thou art called faithful on this account, because thou hast faith in God, and thyself art entrusted from Him with righteousness, sanctification, cleansing of soul, adoption, the kingdom of heaven. He entrusted thee with these, and handed them over to thee. Thou in turn hast entrusted, and handed over other things to him, almsgiving, prayers, self-control and every other virtue. And why do I say almsgiving? If thou gives him even a cup of cold water, thou shalt not indeed lose this, but even this he keeps with care against that day and will restore it with overflowing abundance. For this truly is wonderful, that he does not keep only that which has been entrusted to him, but in recompensing it increases it.

  This too he has bidden thee do according to thy power, with what has been entrusted to thee, to extend the holiness which thou hast received, and to make the righteousness which comes from the laver brighter, and the gift of grace more radiant; even as therefore Paul did, increasing all the good things which he received by his subsequent labors, and his zeal, and his diligence. And look at the carefulness of God; neither did he give the whole to thee then, nor withhold the whole, but gave part, and promised part. And for what reason did he not give the whole then? In order that thou might show thy faith about Him, believing, on his promise alone, in what was not yet given. And for what reason again did he not there dispense the whole, but did give the grace of the Spirit, and righteousness and sanctification? In order that he might lighten thy labors for thee, and by what has been already given may also put thee in good hope for that which is to come. On this account, too, thou art about to be called newly enlightened, because thy light is ever new, if thou wilt, and is never quenched. For this light of day, whether we will or no, the night succeeds, but darkness knows not that light's ray. "For the light shineth in the darkness, and the darkness apprehended it not." Not so bright at least is the world, when the sunbeams come forth, as the soul shines and becomes brighter when it has received grace from the Spirit and learns more exactly the nature of the case. For when night prevails, and there is darkness, often a man has seen a coil of rope and has thought it was a serpent, and has fled from an approaching friend as from an enemy, and being aware of some noise, has become very much alarmed; but when the day has come, nothing of this sort could happen, but all appears just as it really is; which thing also occurs in the case of our soul. For when grace has come, and driven away the darkness of the understanding, we learn the exact nature of things, and what was before dreadful to us becomes contemptible. For we no longer fear death, after learning exactly, from this sacred initiation, that death is not death, but a sleep and a seasonable slumber; nor poverty nor disease, nor any other such thing, knowing that we are on our way to a better life, undefiled and incorruptible, and free from all such vicissitudes.

2. Let us not therefore remain craving after the things of this life, neither after the luxury of the table, or costliness of raiment. For thou hast the most excellent of raiment, thou hast a spiritual table thou hast the glory from on high, and Christ is become to thee all things, thy table, thy raiment, thy home, thy head, thy stem. "For as many of you as were baptized into Christ, did put on Christ." See how he has become raiment for thee. Do you wish to learn how he becomes a table for thee? "He who eats me," says He, "as I live because of the Father, he also shall live because of me;" and that he becometh a home for thee, "he that eats my flesh abides in me, and I in him;" and that He is stem He says again, "I am the vine, ye the branches," and that he is brother, and friend, and bride-groom, "I no longer call you servants: for ye are my friends;" and Paul again, "I espoused you to one husband, that I might present you as a pure virgin to Christ;" and again, "That he might be the first-born among many brethren;" and we become not his brethren only, but also his children, "For behold," he says, "I and the children which God has given me" and not this only, but His members, and His body. For as if what has been said were not enough to show forth the love and the goodwill which He has shown forth towards us, He has added another thing greater and nearer still, calling himself besides, our head. Knowing all these matters, beloved, requite thy benefactor by the best conversation, and considering the greatness of the sacrifice, adorn the members of thy body; consider what thou receives in thine hand, and never suffer it to strike any one, nor shame what has been

honored with so great a gift by the sin of a blow. Consider what thou receives in thine hand, and keep it clean from all covetousness and extortion; think that thou dost not receive this in thy hand, but also puts it to thy mouth, and guard thy tongue in purity from base and insolent words, blasphemy, perjury, and all other such things. For it is disastrous that what is ministered to by such most dreadful mysteries, and has been dyed red with such blood, and has become a golden sword, should be perverted to purposes of raillery, and insult, and buffoonery. Reverence the honor with which God has honored it, and bring it not down to the vileness of sin, but having reflected again that after the hand and the tongue, the heart receives this dread mystery, do not ever weave a plot against thy neighbor, but keep thy thoughts pure from all evil. Thus thou shalt be able to keep thine eyes too, and thy hearing safe. For is it not monstrous, after this mystic voice is borne from heaven—I mean the voice of the Cherubim—to defile thy hearing with lewd songs, and dissolute melodies? and does it not deserve the utmost punishment if, with the same eyes with which thou looks upon the unspeakable and dread mysteries, thou looks upon harlots, and dost commit adultery in thy heart. Thou art called to a marriage, beloved: enter not in clad in sordid raiment, but take a robe suitable to the marriage. For if when men are called to a material marriage, though they be poorer than all others, they often possess themselves of or buy clean raiment, and so go to meet those who called them. Do thou too who hast been called to a spiritual marriage, and to a royal banquet, consider what kind of raiment it would be right for thee to buy, but rather there is not even need to purchase, yea he himself who calls thee gives it thee gratis, in order that thou mayest not be able to plead poverty in excuse. Keep, therefore, the raiment which thou receives. For if thou loses it, thou wilt not be able to use it henceforth, or to buy it. For this kind of raiment is nowhere sold. Have you heard how those who were initiated, in old times, groaned, and beat their breasts, their conscience thereupon exciting them? Beware then, beloved, that thou do not at any time suffer like this. But how wilt thou not suffer, if thou dost not cast off the wicked habit of evil men? For this reason I said before, and speak now and will not cease speaking, if any has not rectified the defects in his morals, nor furnished himself with easily acquired virtue, let him not be baptized. For the laver is able to remit former sins, but there is no little fear, and no ordinary danger lest we return to them, and our remedy become a wound. For by how much greater the grace is, by so much is the punishment more for those who sin after these things.

3. In order, therefore, that we return not to our former vomit, let us henceforward discipline ourselves. For that we must repent beforehand, and desist from our former evil, and so come forward for grace, hear what John says, and what the leader of the apostles says to those who are about to be baptized. For the one says, "Bring forth fruit worthy of repentance, and begin not to say within yourselves, we have Abraham to our Father;" and the other says again to those who question him, "Repent ye and be baptized every one of you in the name of the Lord Jesus Christ." Now he who repents, no longer touches the same matters of which he repented. On this account, also, we are bidden to say, "I renounce thee, Satan," in order that we may never more return to him. As therefore happens in the case of painters from life, so let it

happen in your case. For they, arranging their boards, and tracing white lines upon them, and sketching the royal likeness in outline, before they apply the actual colors, rub out some lines, and change some for others, rectifying mistakes, and altering what is amiss with all freedom. But when they put on the coloring for good, it is no longer in their power to rub out again, and to change one thing for another, since they injure the beauty of the portrait, and the result becomes an eyesore. Consider that thy soul is the portrait; before therefore the true coloring of the spirit comes, wipe out habits which have wrongly been implanted in thee, whether swearing, or falsehood, or insolence, or base talking, or jesting, or whatever else thou hast a habit of doing of things unlawful. Away with the habit, in order that thou mayest not return to it, after baptism. The laver causes the sins to disappear. Correct thy habits, so that when the colors are applied, and the royal likeness is brought out, thou mayest no more wipe them out in the future; and add damage and scars to the beauty which has been given thee by God. Restrain therefore anger, extinguish passion. Be not thou vexed, be sympathizing, be not exasperated, nor say, "I have been injured in regard to my soul." No one is injured in regard to the soul if we do not injure ourselves in regard to the soul; and how this is, I now say. Has anyone taken away thy substance? He has not injured thee in regard to thy soul, but thy money. But if thou cherish ill-will against him, thou hast injured thyself in regard to thy soul. For the money taken away has wrought thee no damage, nay has even been profitable, but thou by not dismissing thine anger wilt give account in the other world for this cherishing of ill-will. Has anyone reviled thee and insulted thee. He has in no way injured thy soul, and not even thy body. Have you reviled in return and insulted? Thou hast injured thyself in regard to thy soul, for the words which thou hast said thou art about to render account there; and this I wish you to know chiefly of all, that the Christian, and faithful man, no one is able to injure in regard to the soul, not even the devil himself; and not only is this wonderful, that God hath made us inaccessible to all his designs, but that he has constituted us fit for the practice of virtue, and there is no hinderance, if we will, even though we be poor, weak in body, outcast, nameless, bondservants. For neither poverty, nor infirmity, nor deformity of body, nor servitude, nor any other of such things could ever become a hinderance to virtue; and why do I say, poor, and a bondservant, and nameless? Even if thou art a prisoner, not even this would be ever any hinderance to thee as regards virtue. And how this is I proceed to say. Has any of thy household grieved thee and provoked thee? dismiss thy wrath against him. Have bonds, and poverty, and obscurity been any hinderance to thee in this respect? and why do I say hinderance? They have both helped and contributed to restrain pride. Have you seen another prospering? do not envy him. For not even in this case is poverty a bar. Again, whenever thou needs to pray, do so with a sober and watchful mind, and nothing shall be a bar even in that case. Show all meekness, forbearance, self-restraint, gravity. For these things need no external helps. And this especially is the chief point about virtue, that it has no necessity for wealth, power, glory, nor anything of that kind, but of a sanctified soul alone, and it seeks for nothing more. And behold, also, the same thing happening in respect of grace. For if anyone be lame, if he has had his eyes put out, if he be maimed in body, if he has fallen into the last extremity of weakness, grace is not hindered from coming by any of these things. For it only seeks a soul receiving it with readiness, and all these external things it passes over. For in the case of worldly soldiers, those who are about to enlist them for the army seek for stature of body and healthy condition, and it is not only necessary that he who is about to become a soldier should have these alone, but he must also be free. For if anybody be a slave, he is rejected. But the King of Heaven seeks for nothing of this kind, but receives slaves into his army, and aged people, and the languid in limb, and is not ashamed. What is more merciful than this? What could be more kind? For he seeks for what is in our own power, but they seek for what is not in our power. For to be a slave or free is not our doing. To be tall, again, or short is not in our own power, or to be aged, or well grown, and such like. But to be forbearing and kind, and so forth, are matters of our own choice; and God demands of us only those things of which we have control. And quite reasonably. For He does not call us to grace because of his own need, but because of doing us kindness; but kings, because of services required by them; and they carry men off to an outward and material warfare, but He to a spiritual combat; and it is not only in the case of heathen wars, but in the case of the games also that one may see the same analogy. For they who are about to be brought into the theatre, do not descend to the contest until the herald himself takes them beneath the gaze of all, and leads them round, shouting out and saying, "Has anyone a charge against this person?" although in that case the struggle is not concerned with the soul, but with the body. Wherefore then dost thou demand proofs of nobleness? But in this case there is nothing of the kind, but all is different, our contest not consisting of hand locked in hand, but in philosophy of soul, and excellence of mind. The president of our conflicts does the opposite. For he does not take us, and lead us round and say, "Has anyone a charge against this man?" but cries out, "Though all men, though demons, stand up with the devil and accuse him of extreme and unspeakable crimes, I reject him not, nor abhor him, but removing him from his accusers, and freeing him from his wickedness, thus I bring him to the contest. And this is very reasonable. For there indeed the president contributes nothing towards the victory, in the case of the combatants, but stands still in the midst. But here, the President of the contests for holiness becomes a fellow-combatant, and helper, sharing with them the conflict against the devil.

4. And not only is this the wonderful thing that he remits our sins, but that he not even reveals them nor makes them manifest and patent, nor compels us to come forward into the midst, and to tell out our errors, but bids us make our defense to him alone, and to confess ourselves to him. And yet among secular judges, if any tell any of the robbers or grave-riflers, when they are arrested, to tell their errors and be quit of their punishment, they would accede to this with all readiness, despising the shame through desire of safety. But in this case there is nothing of this kind, but he both remits the sins, nor compels us to marshal them in array before any spectators. But one thing alone he seeks, that he who enjoys this remission should learn the greatness of the gift. How is it not, therefore, absurd that in case where he does us service, he should be content with our testimony only, but in those where we serve him we seek for others as witnesses, and do a thing for ostentation's sake? While

we wonder then at his kindliness, let us show forth our doings, and before all others let us curb the vehemence of our tongue, and not always be giving utterance. "For in the multitude of words there wanted not transgression." If indeed then thou hast anything useful to say, open thy lips. But if there be nothing necessary for thee to say, be silent, for it is better. Art thou a handicraftsman? As thou sits at work, sing psalms. Do you not wish to sing with thy mouth? do this in thine heart; a psalm is a great companion. In this case thou shalt undergo nothing serious, but shalt be able to sit in thy workshop as in a monastery. For not suitableness of place, but strictness of morals will afford us quiet. Paul, at least, pursuing his trade in a workshop, suffered no injury to his own virtue. Do not thou therefore say, How can I, being a handicraftsman and a poor man, be a philosopher? This is indeed the very reason why thou mayest be a philosopher. For poverty is far more conducive to piety for us than wealth, and work than idleness; since wealth is even a hinderance to those who do not take heed. For when it is needful to dismiss anger, to extinguish envy, to curb passion, to offer prayer, to exhibit forbearance and meekness, kindliness and charity, when would poverty be a bar? For it is not possible by spending money to accomplish these things, but by exhibiting a right disposition; almsgiving especially needs money, but even it shines forth in greater degree through poverty. For she who spent the two mites was poorer than all men, and yet surpassed all. Let us not then consider wealth to be anything great, nor gold to be better than clay. For the value of material things is not owing to their nature, but to our estimate of them. For if anyone would inquire carefully, iron is much more necessary than gold. For the one contributes to no need of our life, but the other has furnished us with the greater part of our needs, ministering to countless arts; and why do I speak of a comparison between gold and iron? For these stones are more necessary than precious stones. For of those nothing serviceable could be made, but out of these, houses and walls and cities are erected. But do thou show me what gain could be derived from these pearls, rather what harm would not happen? For in order that thou mayest wear one pearl drop, countless poor people are pinched with hunger. What excuse wilt thou hit upon? what pardon?

Do you wish to adorn thy face? Do so not with pearls, but with modesty, and dignity. So thy countenance will be more full of grace in the eyes of thy husband. For the other kind of adorning is wont to plunge him into a suspicion of jealousy, and into enmity, quarrelsomeness and strife, for nothing is more annoying than a face which is suspected. But the ornament of compassion and modesty casts out all evil suspicion, and will draw thy partner to thee more strongly than any bond. For natural beauty does not impart such comeliness to the face as does the disposition of him who beholds it, and nothing is so wont to produce that disposition as modesty and dignity; so that if any woman be comely, and her husband be ill affected towards her, she appears to him the most worthless of all women; and if she do not happen to be fair of face, but her husband be well affected towards her, she appears more comely than all. For sentence is given not according to the nature of what is beheld, but according to the disposition of the beholders. Adorn thy face then with modesty, dignity, pity, lovingkindness, charity, affection for thy husband, forbearance, meekness, endurance of ill. These are the tints of virtue. By means of these thou wilt attract angels not human beings to be thy lovers. By means of these thou hast God to commend thee, and when God receives thee, he will certainly win over thy husband for thee. For if the wisdom of a man illuminates his countenance, much more does the virtue of a woman illuminate her face; and if thou considers this to be a great ornament, tell me what will be the advantage of the pearls in that day? But why is it necessary to speak of that day, since it is possible to show all this from what happens now. When, then, they who thought fit to revile the emperor were dragged to the judgment hall, and were in danger of extreme measures being taken, then the mothers, and the wives, laying aside their necklaces, and their golden ornaments, and pearls, and all adornment, and golden raiment, wearing a simple and mean dress, and besprinkled with ashes, prostrated themselves before the doors of the judgment hall and thus won over the judges; and if in the case of these earthly courts of justice, the golden ornaments, and the pearls, and the variegated dress would have been a snare and a betrayal, but forbearance, and meekness, and ashes, and tears, and mean garments persuaded the judge, much more would this take place in the case of that impartial and dread tribunal. For what reason wilt thou be able to state, what defense, when the Master lays these pearls to thy charge, and brings the poor who have perished with hunger into the midst? On this account Paul said, "not with braided hair, or gold, or pearls, or costly raiment." For therein would be a snare. And if we were to enjoy them continually, yet we shall lay them aside with death. But arising out of virtue there is all security, and no vicissitude and changeableness, but here it makes us more secure, and also accompanies us there. Do you wish to possess pearls, and never to lay aside this wealth? Take off all ornament and place it in the hands of Christ through the poor. He will keep all thy wealth for thee, when He shall raise up thy body with much radiancy. Then He shall invest thee with better wealth and greater ornament, since this present is mean and absurd. Consider then whom thou wishes to please, and for whose sake thou puts on this ornament, not in order that the ropemaker and the coppersmith and the huckster may admire. Then art thou not ashamed, nor blushes thou when thou shows thyself to them? doing all on their account whom thou dost not consider worthy of accosting.

How then wilt thou laugh this fancy to scorn? If thou wilt remember that word, which thou sent forth when thou wert initiated, I renounce thee, Satan, and thy pomp, and thy service. For the frenzy about pearls is a pomp of Satan. For thou didst receive gold not in order that thou might bind it on to thy body, but in order that thou might release and nourish the poor. Say therefore constantly, I renounce thee, Satan. Nothing is safer than this word if we shall prove it by our deeds.

5. This I think it right that you who are about to be initiated should learn. For this word is a covenant with the Master. And just as we, when we buy slaves, first ask those who are being sold if they are willing to be our servants: So also does Christ. When He is about to receive thee into service, He first asks if thou wishes to leave that cruel and relentless tyrant, and He receives covenants from thee. For his service is not forced upon thee. And see the lovingkindness of God. For we, before we put down the price, ask those who are being sold, and when we have learned that they are willing, then we put down

the price. But Christ not so, but He even put down the price for us all, his precious blood. For, He says, ye were bought with a price. Notwithstanding, not even then does He compel those who are unwilling, to serve him; but except thou hast grace, He says, and of thine own accord and will determine to enroll thyself under my rule, I do not compel, nor force thee. And *we* should not have chosen to buy wicked slaves. But if we should at any time have so chosen, we buy them with a perverted choice, and put down a corresponding price for them. But Christ, buying ungrateful and lawless slaves, put down the price of a servant of first quality, nay rather much more, and so much greater that neither speech nor thought can set forth its greatness. For neither giving heaven, nor earth, nor sea, but giving up that which is more valuable than all these, his own blood, thus He bought us. And after all these things, he does not require of us witnesses, or registration, but is content with the single word, if thou sayest it from thy heart. "I renounce thee, Satan, and thy pomp," has included all. Let us then say this, "I renounce thee, Satan," as men who are about in that world at that day to have that word demanded of them, and let us keep it in order that we may then return this deposit safe. But Satan's pomps are theatres, and the circus, and all sin, and observance of days, and incantations and omens.

"And what are omens?" says one. Often when going forth from his own house he has seen a one-eyed or lame man, and has shunned him as an omen. This is a pomp of Satan. For meeting the man does not make the day turn out ill, but to live in sin. When thou goes forth, then, beware of one thing—that sin does not meet thee. For this it is which trips us up. And without this the devil will be able to do us no harm. What say you? Thou sees a man, and shunned him as an omen, and dost not see the snare of the devil, how he sets thee at war with him who has done thee no wrong, how he makes thee the enemy of thy brother on no just pretext; but God has bidden us love our enemies; but thou art turned away from him who did thee no wrong, having nothing to charge him with, and dost thou not consider how great is the absurdity, how great the shame, rather how great is the danger? Can I speak of anything more absurd? I am ashamed, indeed, and I blush: But for your salvation's sake, I am, I am compelled to speak of it. If a virgin meet him, he says the day becomes unsuccessful; but if a harlot meet him, it is propitious, and profitable, and full of much business; are you ashamed? and do you smite your foreheads, and bend to the ground? But do not this on account of the words which I have spoken, but of the deeds which have been done. See then, in this case, how the devil hid his snare, in order that we might turn away from the modest, but salute and be friendly to the unchaste. For since he has heard Christ saying that "He who looked on a woman to desire her, has already committed adultery with her," and has seen many get the better of unchastity, wishing by another wrong to cast them again into sin, by this superstitious observance he gladly persuades them to pay attention to whorish women.

And what is one to say about them who use charms and amulets, and encircle their heads and feet with golden coins of Alexander of Macedon. Are these our hopes, tell me, that after the cross and death of our Master, we should place our hopes of salvation on an image of a Greek king? Dost thou not know what great result the cross has achieved? It has abolished death, has extinguished sin, has made Hades useless, has undone the power of the devil, and is it not worth trusting for the health of the body? It has raised up the whole world, and dost thou not take courage in it? And what would you be worthy to suffer, tell me? Thou dost not only have amulets always with thee, but incantations bringing drunken and half-witted old women into thine house, and art thou not ashamed, and dost thou not blush, after so great philosophy, to be terrified at such things? and there is a graver thing than this error. For when we deliver these exhortations, and lead them away, thinking that they defend themselves, they say, that the woman is a Christian who makes these incantations, and utters nothing else than the name of God. On this account I especially hate and turn away from her, because she makes use of the name of God, with a view to ribaldry. For even the demons uttered the name of God, but still they were demons, and thus they used to say to Christ, "We know thee who thou art, the Holy One of God," and notwithstanding, he rebuked them, and drove them away. On this account, then, I beseech you to cleanse yourselves from this error, and to keep hold of this word as a staff; and just as without sandals, and cloak, no one of you would choose to go down to the market-place, so without this word never enter the market-place, but when thou art about to pass over the threshold of the gateway, say this word first: I leave thy ranks, Satan, and thy pomp, and thy service, and I join the ranks of Christ. And never go forth without this word. This shall be a staff to thee, this thine armor, this an impregnable fortress, and accompany this word with the sign of the cross on thy forehead. For thus not only a man who meets you, but even the devil himself, will be unable to hurt you at all, when he sees thee everywhere appearing with these weapons; and discipline thyself by these means henceforth, in order that when thou receives the seal thou mayest be a well-equipped soldier, and planting thy trophy against the devil, may receive the crown of righteousness, which may it be the lot of us all to obtain, through the grace and lovingkindness of our Lord Jesus Christ, with whom be glory to the Father and to the Holy Spirit for ever and ever—Amen.

HOMILY I

AGAINST THOSE WHO SAY THAT DEMONS GOVERN HUMAN AFFAIRS.

HOMILIES II AND III

ON THE POWER OF MAN TO RESIST THE DEVIL.

TRANSLATED BY

T. P. BRANDRAM, M.A.,

RECTOR OF RUMBOLDSWHYKE, CHICHESTER.

THREE HOMILIES CONCERNING THE POWER OF DEMONS.

Introduction by rev. w. r. w. Stephens.

The three following Homilies are closely connected in subject, and the opening sentence of the third clearly proves that it was delivered two days after the second; but it is impossible to say whether that which is placed first was really delivered before the other two. It must however have been spoken at Antioch, since Chrysostom refers at the beginning of it to his sermons "on the obscurity of prophecies" in which passages occur which clearly imply that he was not then a Bishop. The second of the three homilies here translated was delivered in the presence of a Bishop, as is clearly indicated by the commencement, and as the third was as already mentioned delivered two days after the second we may safely affirm that they were all spoken at Antioch when Chrysostom was a presbyter there under the Episcopate of Flavian.

They deal with errors against which Chrysostom throughout his life most strenuously contended. In an age of great depravity there seem to have been many who tried to excuse the weak resistance which they made to evil, both in themselves, and in others, by maintaining that the world was abandoned to the dominion of devils, or to the irresistible course of fate. To counteract the disastrous effects of such philosophy, which surrendered man to the current of his passions, it was necessary to insist very boldly and resolutely on the essential freedom of the will, on moral responsibility, and the duty of vigorous exertion in resisting temptation. And

Chrysostom did this to an extent which some thought carried him perilously near the errors of the Pelagian heresy. No one however has described in more forcible language the powerful hold of sin upon human nature, and the insufficiency of man to shake it off without the assistance of divine grace. What he does most earnestly combat, both in the following homilies and very many others, is the doctrine that evil was an original integral part of our nature: he maintains that it is not a substantial inherent force (δύναμις ἐνυπόστατος). If evil was a part of our nature in this sense it would be no more reprehensible than natural appetites and affections. We do not try to alter that which is by nature (φύσει): sin therefore is not by nature, because by means of education, laws, and punishments we do seek to alter that. Sin comes through defect in the moral purpose (προαίρεσις). Our first parents fell through indolence of moral purpose (ῥ‹θυμία) and this is the principal cause of sin now. They marked out a path which has been trodden ever since: the force of will has been weakened in all their posterity: so that though evil is not an inherent part of man's nature yet he is readily inclined to it (ὀξυρρεπὴς πρὸς κακι€ν); and this tendency must be perpetually counteracted by vigorous exertion, and a bracing up of the moral purpose, with the aid of divine grace. Profoundly convinced therefore on the one hand of a strong and universal tendency to sin, but on the other of an essential freedom of the will, Chrysostom sounds alternately the note of warning and encouragement,—warning against that weakness, indolence, languor of moral purpose which occasions a fall,—encouragement to use to the full all the powers with which man is gifted, in reliance on God's forbearance and love, and on His willingness to help those who do not despair of themselves. Despair is the devil's most potent instrument for effecting the ruin of man; for it is that which prevents him from rising again after he has fallen. St. Paul repented, and, not despairing, became equal to angels: Judas repenting, but despairing, rushed into perdition.

Homily I.

Against those who say that demons govern human affairs, and who are displeased at the chastisement of God, and are offended at the prosperity of the wicked and the hardships of the just.

I indeed was hoping, that from the continuance of my discourse, you would have had a surfeit of my words: but I see that the contrary is happening: that no surfeit is taking place from this continuance, but that your desire is increased, that an addition is made not to your satiety but to your pleasure, that the same thing is happening which the winebibbers at heathen drinking-bouts experience; for they, the more they pour down unmixed wine, so much the rather they kindle their thirst, and in your case the more teaching we inculcate, so much the rather do we kindle your desire, we make your longing greater, your love for it the stronger. On this account, although I am conscious of extreme poverty, I do not cease to imitate the ostentatious among entertainers, both setting before you my table continuously, and placing on it the cup of my teaching, filled full: for I see that after having drunk it all, you retire again thirsting. And this indeed has become evident during the whole time, but especially since the last Lord's Day: For that ye partake of the divine oracles insatiably, that day particularly shewed: whereon I discoursed about the unlawfulness of speaking ill one of another, when I furnished you with a sure subject for self-accusation, suggesting that you should speak ill of your own sins, but should not busy yourselves about those of other people: when I brought forward the Saints as accusing themselves indeed, but sparing others: Paul saying I am the chief of sinners, and that God had compassion on him who was a blasphemer, and a persecutor, and injurious, and calling himself one born out of due time, and not even thinking himself worthy of the title of Apostle: Peter saying "Depart from me because I am a sinful man:" Matthew styling himself a publican even in the days of his Apostleship: David crying out and saying "My iniquities have gone over my head, and as a heavy burden have been burdensome to me:" and Isaiah lamenting and bewailing "I am unclean, and have unclean lips:" The three children in the furnace of fire, confessing and saying that they have sinned and transgressed, and have not kept the commandments of God. Daniel again makes the same lamentation. When after the enumeration of these Saints, I called their accusers flies, and introduced the right reason for the comparison, saying, that just as they fasten themselves upon the wounds of others, so also the accusers bite at other people's sins, collecting disease therefrom for their acquaintance, and those who do the opposite, I designated bees, not gathering together diseases, but building honeycombs with the greatest devotion, and so flying to the meadow of the virtue of the Saint: Then accordingly— then ye shewed your insatiable longing. For when my discourse was extended to some length, yea to an interminable length, such as never was, many indeed expected that your eagerness would be quenched by the abundance of what was said. But the contrary happened. For your heart was the rather warmed, your desire was the rather kindled: and whence was this evident? The acclamations at least which took place at the end were greater, and the shouts more clear, and the same thing took place as at the forge. For as there at the beginning indeed the light of the fire is not very clear, but when the flame has caught the whole of the wood that is laid upon it, it is raised to a great height; so also accordingly this happened on the occasion of that day. At the beginning indeed, this assembly was not vehemently stirred by me. But when the discourse was extended to some length, and gradually took hold of all the subjects and the teaching spread more widely, then accordingly, then the desire of listening was kindled in you, and the applause broke forth, more vehemently. On this account, although I had been prepared to say less than was spoken, I then exceeded the measure, nay rather *I* never exceeded the measure. For I want to measure the amount of the teaching not by the multitude of the words spoken, but by the disposition of the audience. For he who meets with a disgusted audience, even if he abridge his teaching, seems to be vexatious, but he who meets with eager, and wide-awake, and attentive hearers, though he extend his discourse to some length, not even thus fulfils their desire.

But since it happens that there are in so great a congregation, certain weak ones, unable to follow the length of the discourse, I wish to suggest this to them, that they should hear and receive, as much as they can, and having received enough should retire: There is no one who forbids, or compels them to remain beyond their natural strength. Let them not however necessitate the abridgement of the discourse before the time and the proper hours. Thou art replete, but thy brother still hungers. Thou art drunk with the multitude of the things spoken, but thy brother is still thirsty. Let him then not distress thy weakness, compelling thee to receive more than thine own power allows: nor do thou vex his zeal by preventing him from receiving all that he can take in.

2. This also happens at secular feasts. Some indeed are more quickly satisfied, some more tardily, and neither do these blame those, nor do they condemn these. But there indeed to withdraw more quickly is praiseworthy, but here to withdraw more quickly is not praiseworthy, but excusable. There to leave off more slowly, is culpable and faulty, here to withdraw more tardily, brings the greatest commendation, and good report. Pray why is this? Because there indeed the tardiness arises from greediness, but here the endurance, and patience are made up of spiritual desire and divine longing.

But enough of preamble. And we will proceed hereupon to that business which remained over to us from that day. What then was that which was then spoken? that all men had one speech, just as also they had one nature, and no one was different in speech, or in tongue. Whence then comes so great a distinction in speech? From the carelessness of those who received the gift—of both of which matters we then spoke, shewing both the lovingkindness of the Master through this unity of speech, and the senselessness of the servants through their distinction of speech. For he indeed foreseeing that we should waste the gift nevertheless gave it: and they to whom it was entrusted, waxed evil over their charge. This is then one way of explanation, not that God wrested the gift from us but that we wasted what had been given. Then next after that, that we received afterwards gifts greater than those lost. In place of temporal toil he honored us with eternal life. In place of thorns and thistles he prepared the fruit of the Spirit to grow in our souls. Nothing was more insignificant than man, and nothing became more honored than man. He was the last item of the reasonable creation. But the feet became the head, and by means of the first fruits, were raised to the royal throne. For just as some generous and opulent man who has seen some one escape from shipwreck and only able to save his bare body from the waves, cradles him in his hands, and casts about him a bright garment, and conducts him to the highest honors; so also God has done in the case of our nature. Man cast aside all that he had, his right to speak freely, his communion with God, his sojourn in Paradise, his unclouded life, and as from a shipwreck, went forth bare. But God received him and straightway clothed him, and taking him by the hand gradually conducted him to heaven. And yet the shipwreck was quite unpardonable. For this tempest was due entirely not to the force of the winds, but to the carelessness of the sailor.

      And yet God did not look at this, but had compassion for the magnitude of the calamity, and him who had suffered shipwreck in harbor, he received as lovingly as if he had undergone this in the midst of the open sea. For to fall in Paradise is to undergo shipwreck in harbor. Why so? Because when no sadness, or care, or labor, or toil, or countless waves of desire assaulted our nature, it was upset and it fell. And as the miscreants who sail the sea, often bore through the ship with a small iron tool, and let in the whole sea to the ship from below; so accordingly then, when the Devil saw the ship of Adam, that is his soul, full of many good things, he came and bored it through with his mere voice, as with some small iron tool, and emptied him of all his wealth and sank the ship itself. But God made the gain greater than the loss and brought our nature to the royal throne. Wherefore Paul cries out and says, "He raised us up with him, and made us to sit with him, on his right hand in the heavenly places, that in the ages to come he might shew the exceeding riches of his grace in kindness towards us." What dost thou say? the thing has already happened and has an end, and dost thou say, "in order that he might shew to the ages to come?" Has he not shown? He has already shewn, but not to all men, but to me who am faithful, but the unbelieving has not yet seen the wonder. But then, in that day the whole nature of man will come forward, and will wonder at that which has been done, but especially will it be more manifest to us. For we believe even now; but hearing and sight do not put a wonder before us in the same way, but just as in the case of kings when we hear of the purple robe, and the diadem, and the golden raiment, and the royal throne, we wonder indeed, but experience this in greater degree when the curtains are drawn aside and we see him seated on the lofty judgment seat. So also in the case of the Only Begotten, when we see the curtains of heaven drawn aside, and the King of angels descending thence, and with his bodyguard of the heavenly hosts, then we perceive the wonder to be greater from our sight of it. For consider with me what it is to see our nature borne upon the Cherubim, and the whole angelic force surrounding it.

3. But look, with me, too, at the wisdom of Paul, how many expressions he seeks for, so as to present to us the lovingkindness of God. For he did not speak merely the word grace, nor riches, but what did he say? "The exceeding riches of his grace in kindness." But notwithstanding even so, he is below the mark; and even as the slippery bodies when grasped by countless hands, escape our hold, and slip through easily; so also are we unable to get hold of the lovingkindness of God in

whatever expressions we may try to grasp it, but the exceeding magnitude of it baffles the feebleness of our utterances. And Paul therefore experiencing this, and seeing the force of words defeated by its magnitude, desists after saying one word: and what is this? "Thanks be to God for his unspeakable gift." For neither speech, nor any mind is able to set forth the tender care of God. On this account he then says that it is past finding out, and elsewhere "The peace of God which passes all understanding shall keep your hearts."

But, as I was saying, these two ways of explanation are found in the meantime: one indeed that God has not wrested the gift that we have lost; and next, that the good things which have been given to us are even greater than those which we have lost. And I wish also to mention a third too. What then is the third? That even if he had not given the things after these, which were greater than those we had lost, but had only taken away what had been given to us, as we furnished the reason why, (for let this be added); even this is enough of itself to shew his tender care towards us. For not only to give, but also to take away what was given, is a mark of the greatest lovingkindness, and, if you will, let us lay bare the matter, in the case of Paradise. He gave Paradise. This of his own tender care. We were seen to be unworthy of the gift. This of our own senselessness. He took away the gift from those who became unworthy of it. This came of his own goodness. And what kind of goodness is it, says one, to take away the gift? Wait, and thou shalt fully hear. For think, what Cain would have been, dwelling in Paradise after his blood guiltiness. For if, when he was expelled from that abode, if when condemned to toil and labor, and beholding the threat of death hanging over his head, if seeing the calamity of his father before his eyes, and holding the traces of the wrath of God still in his hands, and encompassed with so great horrors, he lashed out into such great wickedness, as to ignore nature, and to forget one born from the same birth pangs, and to slay him who had done him no wrong, to lay hold on his brother's person, and to dye his right hand with blood, and when God wanted him to be still, to refuse submission and to affront his maker, to dishonor his parents; if this man had continued to dwell in Paradise—look, into how great evil he would have rushed. For if when so many restraints were laid upon him, he leapt with fatal leaps; and if these walls were set at nought, whither would he not have precipitated himself?

Would you learn too from the mother of this man, what a good result the expulsion from the life of Paradise had, compare what Eve was before this, and what she became afterwards. Before this indeed, she considered that deceiving Devil, that wicked Demon to be more worth believing than the commandments of God, and at the mere sight of the tree, she trampled underfoot the law which had been laid down by Him. But when the expulsion from Paradise came, consider how much better and wiser she grew. For when she bare a son, she says "I have gotten a man through the Lord." She straightway flew to the master, who before this had despised the master, and she neither ascribes the matter to nature, nor puts the birth down to the laws of marriage, but she recognizes the Lord of Nature, and acknowledges thanks to Him for the birth of the little child. And she who before this deceived her husband, afterwards even trained the little child, and gave him a name which of itself was able to bring the gift of God to her remembrance: and again when she bare another, she says "God hath raised up seed to me in place of Abel whom Cain slew." The woman remembers her calamity, and does not become impatient but she gives thanks to God, and calls the little child after his gift, furnishing it with constant material for instruction. Thus even in his very deprivation God conferred greater benefit. The woman suffered expulsion from Paradise, but by means of her ejection she was led to a knowledge of God, so that she found a greater thing than she lost. And if it were profitable, says one, to suffer expulsion from Paradise, for what cause did God give Paradise at the beginning? This turned out profitably to man, on account of our carelessness, since, if at least, they had taken heed to themselves, and had acknowledged their master, and had known how to be self-restrained, and to keep within bounds, they would have remained in honor. But when they treated the gifts which had been given them with insolence, then it became profitable, that they should be ejected. For what cause then did God give at first? In order that he might shew forth his own lovingkindness, and because He himself was prepared to bring us even to greater honor. But we were the cause of chastisement and punishment on all sides, ejecting ourselves through our indifference to goods which were given to us. Just as therefore an affectionate father, at first indeed, suffers his own son to dwell in his home, and to enjoy all his father's goods, but when he sees that he has become worthless of the honor, he leads him away from his table, and puts him far from his own sight, and often casts him forth from his paternal home, in order that he, suffering expulsion, and becoming better by this slight and this dishonor, may again shew himself worthy of restoration, and may succeed to his father's inheritance:

So has God done. He gave Paradise to man. He cast him out when he appeared unworthy, in order that by his dwelling outside, and through his dishonor, he might become better, and more self-restrained, and might appear worthy again of restoration. Since after those things he did become better, he brings him back again and says "Today shalt thou be with me in Paradise." Do you see that not the gift of Paradise but even the ejection from Paradise was a token of the greatest tender care? For had he not suffered expulsion from Paradise, he would not again have appeared worthy of Paradise.

4. This argument therefore let us maintain throughout and let us apply it to the case of the subject lying before us. God gave a speech common to all. This is part of his loving kindness to men. They did not use the gift rightly, but they lapsed to utter folly. He took away again that which had been given. For if when they had one speech, they fell into so great folly, as to wish to build a tower to heaven: had they not immediately been chastised would they not have desired to lay hold on the height of heaven itself? For why? If indeed that were impossible for them, yet notwithstanding their impious thoughts are made out from their plan. All which things God foresaw, and since they did not use their oneness of speech rightly, he rightly divided them by difference of speech. And see with me, his lovingkindness. "Behold," saith he "they all have one speech, and this they have begun to do."

For what reason did he not at once proceed to the division of tongues, but first of all defend himself, as if about to be judged in a law court? And yet at least no one can say to him why hast thou thus done? yea he is at liberty to do all things as he wills. But still as one about to give account, he thus sets up a defense, teaching us to be gentle and loving. For if the master defends himself to his servants, even when they have done him this wrong; much more ought we to defend ourselves to one another, even if we are wronged to the highest degree. See at least how he defends himself. "Behold they have all one mouth and one speech" saith he, "and this they have begun to do," as if he said let no one accuse me of this when he sees the division of tongues. Let no one consider that this difference of speech was made over to men from the beginning. "Behold they all have one mouth, and one speech." But they did not use the gift aright. And in order that thou mayest understand that he does not chastise for what has taken place so much as he provides for improvement in the future, hear the sequel "and now none of all the things will fail them, which they set on foot to do." Now what he says, is of such a kind as this. If they do not pay the penalty now, and be restrained from the very root of their sins, they will never cease from wickedness. For this is what "none of the things will fail them which they set on foot to do" means, as if he said, and they will add other deeds yet more monstrous. For such a thing is wickedness; if when it has taken a start it be not hindered, as fire catching wood, so it rises to an unspeakable height. Do you see that the deprivation of oneness of speech was a work of much lovingkindness? He inflicted difference of speech upon them, in order that they might not fall into greater wickedness. Hold fast this argument then with me and let it ever be fixed and immoveable in your minds, that not only when he confers benefits but even when he chastises God is good and loving. For even his chastisements and his punishments are the greatest part of his beneficence, the greatest form of his providence. Whenever therefore thou sees that famines have taken place, and pestilences, and drought and immoderate rains, and irregularities in the atmosphere, or any other of the things which chasten human nature, be not distressed, nor be despondent, but worship Him who caused them, marvel at Him for His tender care. For He who does these things is such that He even chastens the body that the soul may become sound. Then does God these things saith one? God does these things, and even if the whole city, nay even if the whole universe were here, I will not shrink from saying this. Would that my voice were clearer than a trumpet, and that it were possible to stand in a lofty place, and to cry aloud to all men, and to testify that God does these things. I do not say these things in arrogance but I have the prophet standing at my side, crying and saying, "There is no evil in the city which the Lord hath not done"—now evil is an ambiguous term; and I wish that you shall learn the exact meaning of each expression, in order that on account of ambiguity you may not confound the nature of the things, and fall into blasphemy.

5. There is then evil, which is really evil; fornication, adultery, covetousness, and the countless dreadful things, which are worthy of the utmost reproach and punishment. Again there is evil, which rather is not evil, but is called so, famine, pestilence, death, disease, and others of a like kind. For these would not be evils. On this account I said they are called so only. Why then? Because, were they evils, they would not have become the sources of good to us, chastening our pride, goading our sloth, and leading us on to zeal, making us more attentive. "For when," saith one, "he slew them, then they sought him, and they returned, and came early to God." He *calls*

this evil therefore which chastens them, which makes them purer, which renders them more zealous, which leads them on to love of wisdom; not that which comes under suspicion and is worthy of reproach; for that is not a work of God, but an invention of our own will, but this is for the destruction of the other. He calls then by the name of evil the affliction, which arises from our punishment; thus naming it not in regard to its own nature, but according to that view which men take of it. For since we are accustomed to call by the name of evil, not only thefts and adulteries, but also calamities; so he has called the matter, according to the estimate of mankind. This then is that which the prophet saith "There is no evil in the city which the Lord hath not done." This too by means of Isaiah God has made clear saying "I am God who makes peace and creates evil," again naming calamities evils. This evil also Christ hints at, thus saying to the disciples, "sufficient for the day is the evil thereof," that is to say the affliction, the misery. It is manifest then on all sides, that he here calls punishment evil; and himself brings these upon us, affording us the greatest view of his providence. For the physician is not only to be commended when he leads forth the patient into gardens and meadows, nor even into baths and pools of water, nor yet when he sets before him a well-furnished table, but when he orders him to remain without food, when he oppresses him with hunger and lays him low with thirst, confines him to his bed, both making his house a prison, and depriving him of the very light, and shadowing his room on all sides with curtains, and when he cuts, and when he cauterizes, and when he brings his bitter medicines, he is equally a physician. How is it not then preposterous to call him a physician who does so many evil things, but to blaspheme God, if at any time He doeth one of these things, if He bring on either famine or death, and to reject his providence over all? And yet He is the only true physician both of souls and bodies. On this account He often seizes this nature of ours wantoning in prosperity, and travailing with a fever of sins, and by want, and hunger, and death and other calamities and the rest of the medicines of which He knows, frees us from diseases. But the poor alone feel hunger, says one. But He does not chasten with hunger alone, but with countless other things. Him who is in poverty He has often corrected with hunger, but the rich and him who enjoys prosperity, with dangers, diseases, untimely deaths. For He is full of resources, and the medicines which He has for our salvation are manifold.

Thus too the judges do. They do not honor, or crown those only who dwell in cities, nor do they provide gifts alone, but they also often correct. On this account both the sword is sharpened by them, and tortures are prepared; both the wheel and the stocks, and the executioners, and countless other forms of chastisement. That which the executioner is to the judges, famine is to God—as an executioner correcting us and leading us away from vice. This too, it is possible to see in the case of the husbandmen: They do not then, only protect the root of the vine, nor hedge it round but prune it, and lop off many of the branches; on this account not only have they a hoe, but a sickle too, suitable for cutting: yet notwithstanding we do not find fault with them, but then above all we admire them, when we see them cutting off much that is unserviceable, so as through the rejection of what is superfluous to afford great security to that which remains. How is it not then preposterous, that we should thus approve of a father indeed and a physician and a judge, and a husbandman, and should neither blame nor censure him who casts his son out of his house nor the physician who puts his patient to torture nor the judge who corrects, nor the husbandman who prunes: but that we should blame and smite with countless accusations God, if he would at any time raise us up, when we are as it were, besotted through the great drunkenness which comes of wickedness? How great madness would it not be, not even to allow God a share of the same self-justification, of which we allow our fellow servants a share?

6. Fearing these things for them who reproach God, I speak now, in order that they may not kick against the pricks, and cover their own feet with blood, that they may not throw stones to heaven, and receive wounds on their own head. But I have somewhat else far beyond this to say. For omitting to ask (I say this by way of concession) if God took from us to our profit, I only say this; that if He took what had been given, not even thus, could anyone be able to reproach Him. For He was Lord of his own. Among men indeed, when they entrust us with money, and lend us silver, we give them our thanks for the time during which they lent it, we are not indignant at the time at which they take back their own. And shall we reproach God who wishes to take back his own? Indeed now is this not the extreme of folly? yea the great and noble Job did not act thus. For not only when he received, but even when he was deprived, he gives the greatest thanks to God saying, "The Lord gave, the Lord hath taken away; may the name of the Lord be blessed forever." But if it is right to give thanks for both these even separately, and deprivation is not the less serviceable

than bestowal; what excusableness should we have, tell me, in recompensing in a contrary spirit, and being impatient with Him when we ought to worship, who is so gentle, and loving and careful, who is wiser than every Physician, and more full of affection than any father, juster than any judge, and more anxious than any husbandman, in healing these souls of ours? What then could be more insane and senseless than they who in the midst of so great good order, say that we are deprived of the providence of God? For just as if someone were to contend that the soul was murky and cold, he would produce an example of extreme insanity, by his opinion; so if anyone doubts about the providence of God, much rather is he liable to charges of madness.

Not so manifest is the Sun, as the providence of God is clear. But nevertheless some dare to say that Demons administer our affairs. What can I do? Thou hast a loving Master. He chooses rather to be blasphemed by thee through these words, than to commit thine affairs to the Demons and persuade thee by the reality how Demons administer. For then thou would know their wickedness well by the experience of it. But rather indeed now it is possible to set it before you as it were by a certain small example. Certain men possessed of Demons coming forth out of the tombs met Christ, and the Demons kept beseeching him to suffer them to enter the herd of swine. And he suffered them, and they went away, and straightway precipitated them all headlong. Thus do Demons govern; and yet to them the swine were of no particular account, but with thee there is ever a warfare without a truce, and an implacable fight, and undying hatred. And if in the case of those with whom they had nothing in common they did not even endure that they should be allowed a brief breathing space of time: if they had gotten unto their power us their enemies who are perpetually stinging them what would they not have done? and what incurable mischief would they not have accomplished? For this reason God let them fall upon the herd of swine, in order that in the case of the bodies of irrational animals thou mayest learn their wickedness, and that they would have done to the possessed the things which they did to the swine, had not the demoniacs in their very madness experienced the providence of God, is evident to all: and now therefore when thou sees a man excited by a Demon, worship the Master. Learn the wickedness of the Demons. For it is possible to see both things in the case of these Demons, the lovingkindness of God, and the evil of the Demons. The evil of the Demons when they harass and disturb the soul of the demented: and the lovingkindness of God whenever he restrains and hinders so savage a Demon, who has taken up his abode within, and desires to hurl the man headlong, and does not allow him to use his own power to the full, but suffers him to exhibit just so much strength, as both to bring the man to his senses, and make his own wickedness apparent. Do you wish to form another example to see once more how a Demon arranges matters when God allows him to use his own power? Consider the herds, the flocks of Job, how in one instant of time he annihilated all, consider the pitiable death of the children, the blow that was dealt to his body: and thou shalt see the savage and inhuman and unsparing character of the wickedness of the Demons, and from these things thou shalt know clearly that if God had entrusted the whole of this world to their authority, they would have confused and disturbed everything, and would have assigned to us their treatment of the swine, and of those herds, since not even for a little breathing space of time could they have endured to spare us our salvation. If Demons were to arrange affairs, we should be in no better condition than possessed men, yea rather we should be worse than they. For God did not give them over entirely to the tyranny of the Demons, otherwise they would suffer far worse things than these which they now suffer. And I would ask this of those who say these things, what kind of disorder they behold in the present, that they set down all our affairs to the arrangement of Demons? And yet we behold the sun for so many years proceeding day by day in regular order, a manifold band of stars keeping their own order, the courses of the moon unimpeded, an invariable succession of night and day, all things, both above and below, as it were in a certain fitting harmony, yea rather even far more, and more accurately each keeping his own place, and not departing from the order which God who made them ordained from the beginning.

7. And what is the use of all this, says one, when the heaven indeed, and sun, and moon, and the band of stars, and all the rest keep much good order, but our affairs are full of confusion and disorder. What kind of confusion, O man, and disorder? A certain one says he, is rich, and overbearing, He is rapacious and covetous, he drains the substance of the poor day by day and suffers no terrible affliction. Another lives in forbearance, self-restraint, and uprightness, and is adorned with all other good qualities, and is chastened with poverty and disease, and extremely terrible afflictions. Are these then the matters which offend thee? Yes, these, says he. If then thou sees both of the rapacious, many chastened, and of those living virtuously, yea some even enjoying countless

goods, why dost thou not abandon thine opinion, and be content with the Almighty? Because it is this very thing which offends me more. For why when there are two evil men, is one chastened, and another gets off, and escapes; and when there are two good men, one is honored, and the other continues under punishment? And this very thing is a very great work of God's providence. For if he were to chasten all the evil men, here; and were to honor here all the good men, a day of judgment were superfluous. Again if he were to chasten no wicked man, nor were to honor any of the good, then the base would become baser and worse, as being more careless than the excellent, and they who were minded to blaspheme would accuse God all the more, and say that our affairs were altogether deprived of his providence. For if when certain evil men are chastened, and certain good men punished, they likewise say that human affairs are subject to no providence; if even this did not happen, what would they not say? and what words would they not send forth? On this account some of the wicked he chastens, and some he does not chasten and some of the good he honors and some he does not honor. He does not chasten all, in order that he may persuade thee, that there is a Resurrection. But he chastens some in order that he may make the more careless, through fear by means of the punishment of the others, more in earnest. Again he honors certain of the good, in order that he may lead on others by his honors to emulate their virtue. But he does not honor all, in order that thou mayest learn that there is another season for rendering to all their recompense. For if indeed all were to receive their deserts here, they would disbelieve the account of the Resurrection. But if no one were to receive his desert here, the majority would become more careless.

On this account some he chastens, and others he does not chasten, profiting both those who are chastened, and those who are not chastened. For he separates their wickedness from those, and he makes the others by their punishment, more self-restrained. And this is manifest from what Christ himself said. For when they announced to him that a tower had been brought to the ground, and had buried certain men, he saith to them "What think ye? that these men were sinners only? I say to you nay, but if ye do not repent ye also shall suffer the same thing."

Do you see how those perished on account of their sin, and the rest did not escape on account of their righteousness, but in order that they might become better by the punishment of the others? Were not then the chastened unjustly dealt with says one? For they could without being chastened themselves become better by the punishment of others. But if He had known that they would become better from penitence God would not have chastened them. For if when he foresaw that many would profit nothing from his longsuffering, he nevertheless bears with them, with much tolerance, fulfilling his own part, and affording them an opportunity of coming out of their own senselessness to their sober senses one day; how could he deprive those who were about to become better from the punishment of others, of the benefit of repentance? So that they are in no way unjustly treated, both their evil being cut off by their punishment, and their chastening is to be lighter there, because they suffered here beforehand. Again, they who were not chastened are in no way unjustly treated; for it was possible for them, had they wished, to have used the longsuffering of God, to accomplish a most excellent change, and wondering at his tolerance, to have become ashamed at his exceeding forbearance, and one day to have gone over to virtue, and to have gained their own salvation by the punishment of others. But if they remain in wickedness, God is not to blame, who on this account was longsuffering, that he might recover them, but they are unworthy of pardon, who did not rightly use the longsuffering of God: and it is not only possible to use this argument as a reason why all the wicked are not chastened here, but another also not less than this. Of what kind then is this? That if God brought upon all, the chastening which their sins deserved, our race would have been carried off, and would have failed to come down to posterity. And in order that thou mayest learn that this is true, hear the prophet saying, "If Thou observes iniquity O Lord, who shall stand?" And if it seems good to thee to investigate this saying, leaving the accurate enquiry into the life of each, alone: (For it is not possible even to know all that has been accomplished by each man) let us bring forward those sins which all, without contradiction, commit: and from these it will be plain and manifest to us, that if we were chastened for each of our sins, we should long ago have perished. He who has called his brother fool, "is liable to the hell of fire" saith He. Is there then any one of us who has never sinned this sin? What then? ought he to be straightway carried off? Therefore we should have been all carried off and would have disappeared, long ago, indeed very long ago. Again he who swears, saith he, even if he fulfil his oath, doeth the works of the wicked one. Who is there then, who has not sworn? Yea rather who is there who has never sworn falsely? He who looked on a woman, saith he, with unchaste eyes, is wholly an adulterer, and of this sin anyone would find many guilty. When then these acknowledged sins are such and so insufferable, and each of these of itself brings upon us inevitable chastisement, if we were to reckon up the secret sins committed by us, then we shall see especially that the providence of God does not bring upon us punishment for each sin. So that when thou sees anyone rapacious, covetous, and not chastened, then do thou unfold thine own conscience; reckon up thine own life, go over the sins which have been committed and thou shalt learn rightly that in thine own case first, it is not expedient to be chastened for each of thy sins: for on this account the majority make reckless utterances, since they do not look on their own case before that of others, but we all leaving our own alone, examine that of the rest. But let us no longer do this, but the reverse, and if thou sees any righteous man chastened, remember Job: for if anyone be righteous, he will not be more righteous than that man, nor within a small distance of approaching him. And if he suffer countless ills, he has not yet suffered so much, as that man.

8. Taking this then into thy mind, cease charging the master; learning that it is not by way of deserting him does God let such a one suffer ill, but through desire to crown him, and make him more distinguished. And if thou sees a sinner punished, remember the paralytic who passed thirty-eight years on his bed. For that that man was delivered over then to that disease through sin, hear Christ saying, "Behold thou art made whole; sin no more lest a worse thing happen to thee." For either when we are chastened, we pay the penalty of our sins, or else we receive the occasion of crowning if, when we live in rectitude, we suffer ill. So that whether we live in righteousness, or in sins, chastening is a useful thing for us, sometimes making us more distinguished, sometimes

rendering us more self-controlled, and lightening our punishment to come for us. For that it is possible that one chastened here, and bearing it thankfully should experience milder punishment there hear St. Paul saying "For this reason many are weak and sickly, and some sleep. For if we judge ourselves, we should not be judged. But when we are judged we are corrected by the Lord, that we should not be condemned with the world." Knowing all these things therefore, Let us both moralize in this way on the providence of God, and stop the mouths of the gainsayers. And if any of the events which happen pass our understanding, let us not from this consider that our affairs are not governed by providence, but perceiving His providence in part, in things incomprehensible let us yield to the unsearchableness of His wisdom. For if it is not possible for one not conversant with it to understand a man's art, much rather is it impossible for the human understanding to comprehend the infinity of the providence of God. "For his judgments are unsearchable and his ways past finding out." But nevertheless from small portions we gain a clear and manifest faith about the whole, we give thanks to him for all that happens. For there is even another consideration that cannot be contradicted, for those who wish to moralize about the providence of God. For we would ask the gainsayers, is there then a God? and if they should say there is not, let us not answer them. For just as it is worthless to answer madmen, so too those who say there is no God. For if a ship having few sailors, and passengers, would not be conducted safely for one mile even, without the hand which guides it, much more, such a world as this, having so many persons in it, composed of different elements, would not have continued so long a time, were there not a certain providence presiding over it, both governing, and continually maintaining this whole fabric, and if in shame, through the common opinion of all men, and the experience of affairs, they confess that there is a God, let us say this to them. If there is a God, as indeed there is, it follows that He is just, for if He is not just neither is He God, and if He is just He recompenses to each according to their desert. But we do not see all here receiving according to their desert. Therefore it is necessary to hope for some other requital awaiting us, in order that by each one receiving according to his desert, the justice of God may be made manifest. For this consideration does not only contribute to our wisdom about providence alone, but about the Resurrection; and let us teach others, and let us do all diligence to shut the mouths of them who rave against the master, and let us ourselves glorify him in all things. For thus shall we win more of his care, and enjoy much of his influence, and thus shall we be able to escape from real evil, and obtain future good, through the grace and lovingkindness of our Lord Jesus Christ, By whom and with whom be glory to the Father, with the Holy Spirit, now and always, for ever and ever. Amen.

Homily II.

Against those who object because the devil has not been put out of the world: and to prove that his wickedness does no harm to us—if we take heed: and concerning repentance.

1. When Isaac, in old times, was desirous to eat a meal at the hands of his son, he sent his son forth from the house to the chase. But when this Isaac was desirous to accept a meal at my hands he did not send me forth from the house, but himself ran to our table. What could be more tenderly affectionate than he? What more humble? who thought fit to show his warm love thus, and deigned to descend so far. On this account surely, we also having spent the tones of our voice, and the strength of our feet over the morning discourse, when we saw his fatherly face, forgot our weakness, laid aside our fatigue, were uplifted with pleasure; we saw his illustrious hoary head, and our soul was filled with light. On this account too, we set out our table with readiness, in order that he should eat and bless us. There is no fraud and guile, here, as there was then, there. One indeed was commanded to bring the meal—but another brought it. But *I* was commanded to bring it, and brought it too. Bless me then, O my father, with spiritual blessing, which we all also pray ever to receive, and which is profitable not only to thee, but also to me, and to all these. Entreat the common master of us all, to prolong thy life to the old age of Isaac. For this is both for me, and for these, more valuable, and more needful than the dew of heaven, and the fatness of the earth.

But it is time to proceed to set out our table; what then is this? The remains of what was lately said with a view to our love of you. For still—still—we renew our discourse concerning the Devil, which we started two days ago, which we also addressed to the initiated, this morning when we discoursed to them about renunciation, and covenant. And we do this, not because our discourse about the Devil is sweet to us, but because the doctrine about him is full of security for you. For he is an enemy and a foe, and it is a great security to know clearly, the tactics of your enemies. We have said lately, that he does not overcome by force, nor by tyranny, nor through compulsion, nor through violence. Since were this so, he would have destroyed all men. And in testimony of this we brought forward the swine, against which the Demons were unable to venture anything, before the permission of the Master. The herds and flocks of Job. For not even did the Devil venture to destroy these, until he received power from above. We learned therefore this one thing first, that he does not overcome us by force, or by compulsion; next after that, we added that even when he overcomes by deceitfulness, not thus does he get the better of all men, Then again we brought that athlete Job, himself into the midst, against whom he set countless schemes going, and not even thus got the better of him, but withdrew defeated. One question still remains. What then is this matter? That if he does not overcome says one, by force, yet by deceitfulness. And on this account it were better that he should be destroyed. For if Job got the better of him, yet Adam was deceived and overthrown. Now if once for all he had been removed from the world, Adam would never have been overthrown. But now he remains, and is defeated indeed by one, but gets the better of many.

Ten overcame him, but he himself overcomes and wrestles down ten thousand and if God took him away from the world, these ten thousand would not have perished. What then shall we say to this? That first of all they who overcame are more valuable far than they who are defeated, even if the latter be more, and the former less. "For better is one," saith he "that doeth the will of God than ten thousand transgressors." And next, that if the antagonist were taken away he who overcomes is thereby injured. For if you let the adversary remain, the more slothful are injured, not on account of the more diligent, but by their own slothfulness; whereas if thou takes away the antagonist, the more diligent are betrayed on account of the slothful, and neither exhibit their own power, nor win crowns.

2. Perhaps ye have not yet understood what has been said. Therefore it is necessary that I should say it again more clearly. Let there be one antagonist. But let there be also two athletes about to wrestle against him, and of these two athletes let one be consumed with gluttony, unprepared, void of strength, nerveless; but the other diligent, of good habit, passing his time in the wrestling school, in many gymnastic exercises, and exhibiting all the practice which bears upon the contest. If then thou takes away the antagonist, which of these two hast thou injured? The slothful, pray, and unprepared, or the earnest one who has toiled so much? It is quite clear that it is the earnest one: For the one indeed is wronged by the slothful, after the antagonist has been taken away. But the slothful, while he remains, is no longer injured on account of the earnest. For he has fallen, owing to his own slothfulness.

I will state another solution of this question, in order that thou mayest learn, that the Devil does not injure, but their own slothfulness everywhere overthrows those who do not take heed. Let the Devil be allowed to be exceeding wicked, not by nature, but by choice and conviction. For that the Devil is not by nature wicked, learn from his very names. For the Devil, the slanderer that is, is called so from slandering; for he slandered man to God saying "Doth Job reverence thee for nought? but put out thine hand, and touch what he hath, see if he will not blaspheme thee to thy face." He slandered God again to man saying, "Fire fell from heaven and burnt up the sheep." For he was anxious to persuade him, that this warfare was stirred up from above, out of the heavens, and he set the servant at variance with the master, and the master with his servant; rather he did not set them at variance, but attempted to indeed, but was not able, in order that whenever thou mayest set another servant at variance with his master, Adam with God, and believing the Devil's slander, thou mayest learn that he gained strength, not owing to his own power but from that man's slothfulness and carelessness. He is called the Devil therefore on that account. But to slander, and to refrain from slander is not natural, but an action which takes place and which ceases to take place, occurring and ceasing to occur. Now such things do not reach the rank of the nature or of the essence of a thing. I know that this consideration about essence and accident is hard to be grasped by many. But there are they who are able to lend a finer ear, wherefore also we have spoken these things. Do you wish that I should come to another name? You shall see that that also is not a name which belongs to his essence or nature. He is called wicked. But his wickedness is not from his nature, but from his choice. For even this at one time is present, at another time is absent. Do not thou then say this to me that it always remains with him. For it was not indeed with him at the beginning, but afterwards came upon him; wherefore he is called apostate. Although many men are wicked, he alone is called wicked by pre-eminence. Why then is he thus called? Because though in no way wronged by us, having no grudge whether small or great, when he saw mankind had in honor, he straightway envied him his good. What therefore could be worse than this wickedness, except when hatred and war exist, without having any reasonable cause. Let the Devil then be let alone, and let us bring forward the creation, in order that thou mayest learn that the Devil is not the cause of ills to us, if we would only take heed: in order that thou mayest learn that the weak in choice, and the unprepared, and slothful, even were there no Devil, falls, and casts himself into many a depth of evil. The Devil is evil. I know it myself and it is acknowledged by all, yet give heed strictly to the things which are now about to be said. For they are not ordinary matters, but those about which many words, many times, and in many places arise, about which there is many a fight and battle not only on the part of the faithful against unbelievers but also on the part of the faithful against the faithful. For this is that which is full of pain.

3. The Devil then is acknowledged, as I said, to be evil by all. What shall we say about this beautiful and wondrous creation? Pray is the creation too, wicked? and who is so corrupt, who so dull, and demented as to accuse the creation? what then shall we say about this? For it is not wicked, but is both beautiful and a token of the wisdom and power and lovingkindness of God. Hear at

least how the prophet marvels at it, saying, "How are thy works magnified O Lord! in wisdom Thou hast made them all." He did go through them one by one, but withdrew before the incomprehensible wisdom of God. And that he has made it thus beautiful and vast hear a certain one saying, "From the vastness and beauty of the creatures, the originator of them is proportionably seen." Hear too Paul saying, "For the invisible things of Him, since the creation of the world, are clearly seen, being perceived through the things that are made." For each of these by which he spoke declared that the creation leads us to the knowledge of God, because it causes us to know the Master fully. What then? If we see this beautiful and wondrous creation itself becoming a cause of impiety to many, shall we blame it? In no wise, but them who were unable to use the medicine rightly. Whence then is this which leads us to the knowledge of God, a cause of impiety? "The wise" saith he "were darkened in their understandings, and worshipped and served the creature more than the creator." The Devil is nowhere here, a Demon is nowhere here, but the creation alone is set before us, as the teacher of the knowledge of God. How then has it become the cause of impiety? Not owing to its own nature, but owing to the carelessness of those who do not take heed. What then? Shall we take away even the creation? tell me.

And why do I speak about the creation? Let us come to our own members. For even these we shall find to be a cause of destruction if we do not take heed, not because of their own nature, but because of our sloth. And look; an eye was given, in order that thou mayest behold the creation and glorify the Master. But if thou dost not use the eye well, it becomes to thee the minister of adultery. A tongue has been given, in order that thou mayest speak well, in order that thou mayest praise the Creator. But if thou gives not excellent heed, it becomes a cause of blasphemy to thee. And hands were given thee that thou mayest stretch them forth unto prayer. But if thou are not wary, thou stretches them out unto covetousness. Feet were given in order that thou mayest run unto good works, but if thou art careless thou wilt cause wicked works by means of them: Dost thou see that all things hurt the weak man? Do you see that even the medicines of salvation inflict death upon the weak, not because of their own nature but because of his weakness? God made the heaven in order that thou mayest wonder at the work and worship the master. But others, leaving the creator alone, have worshipped the heaven; and this from their own carelessness and senselessness. But why do I speak of the creation? assuredly what could be more conducive to salvation than the Cross? But this Cross has become an offence to the weak. "For the word of the Cross is to them that are perishing, foolishness: but to those which are being saved, it is the power of God." And again, "we preach Christ crucified, unto Jews a stumbling-block and unto Gentiles foolishness." What could be more fit for teaching than Paul, and the apostles? But the Apostles became a savor of death to many. He says at least, "to one a savor from death unto death: to the other a savor from life unto life." Do you see that the weak is hurt even by Paul, but the strong is injured not even by the Devil?

4. Do you wish that we should exercise the argument in the case of Jesus Christ? What is equal to that salvation? what more profitable than that presence? But this very saving presence, so profitable, became an

additional means of chastening to many. "For judgment" saith he "came I into this world, that they which see not may see, and that they which see may become blind." What dost thou say? The light became a cause of blindness? The light did not become a cause of blindness, but the weakness of the eyes of the soul was not able to entertain the light. Thou hast seen that a weak man is hurt on all sides, but the strong is benefited on all sides. For in every case, the purpose is the cause, in every case the disposition is master. Since the Devil, if thou would understand it, is even profitable to us, if we use him aright, and benefits us greatly, and we gain no ordinary advantages; and this, we shewed in a small degree from the case of Job. And it is possible also to learn this from Paul: for writing about the fornicator he thus speaks "Deliver such a one unto Satan for the destruction of the flesh, that the spirit may be saved." Behold even the Devil has become a cause of salvation, but not because of his own disposition, but because of the skill of the Apostle. For as the physicians taking serpents and cutting off their destructive members, prepare medicines for antidotes; so also did Paul. He took whatever was profitable of the chastening that proceeds from the Devil and left the rest alone; in order that you may learn that the Devil is not the cause of salvation, but that he hasted to destroy and devour mankind. But that the Apostle through his own wisdom cut his throat: hear in the second epistle to the Corinthians, what he saith about this very fornicator, "confirm your love towards him," "lest by any means such an one should be swallowed up by over much sorrow." And, "we be taken advantage of by Satan." We have snatched beforehand the man from the gullet of the wild beast, he saith. For the Apostle often used the Devil as an executioner. For the executioners punish those who have done wrong, not as they choose, but as the judges allow. For this is the rule for the executioner, to take vengeance, giving heed to the command of the judge. Do you see to what a dignity the Apostle mounted? He who was invested with a body, used the bodiless as an executioner; and that which their common master saith to the Devil, concerning Job: charging him thus, "Touch his flesh, but thou shalt not touch his life;" giving him a limit, and measure of vengeance, in order that the wild beast might not be impetuous and leap upon him too shamelessly; this too the Apostle does. For delivering the fornicator over to him he says, "For the destruction of the flesh," that is "thou shalt not touch his life." Do you see the authority of the servant? Fear not therefore the Devil, even if he be bodiless: for he has come in contact with him. And nothing is weaker than he who has come into such contact even though he be not invested with a body, as then nothing is stronger than he who has boldness even though he bear about a mortal body.

5. All these things have been now said by me, not in order that I may discharge the Devil from blame, but that I may free you from slothfulness. For he wishes extremely to attribute the cause of our sins to himself, in order that we being nourished by these hopes, and entering on all kinds of evil, may increase the chastening in our own case, and may meet with no pardon from having transferred the cause to him. Just as Eve met with none. But let us not do this. But let us know ourselves. Let us know our wounds. For thus shall we be able to apply the medicines. For he who does not know his disease, will give no care to his weakness. We have sinned much: I know this well. For we are all liable for

penalties. But we are not deprived of pardon; nor shall we fall away from repentance for we still stand in the arena and are in the struggles of repentance. Art thou old, and hast thou come to the last outlet of life? Do not consider even thus that thou hast fallen from repentance, nor despair of thine own salvation, but consider the robber who was freed on the cross. For what was briefer than that hour in which he was crowned? Yet notwithstanding even this was enough for him, for salvation. Art thou young? Do not be confident in thy youth, nor think that thou hast a very fixed term of life, "For the day of the Lord so cometh as a thief in the night." On this account he has made our end invisible, in order that we might make our diligence and our forethought plain. Dost thou not see men taken away prematurely day after day? On this account a certain one admonishes "make no tarrying to turn to the Lord and put not off from day to day," lest at any time, as thou delays, thou art destroyed. Let the old man keep this admonition, let the young man take this advice. Yea, art thou in security, and art thou rich, and dost thou abound in wealth, and does no affliction happen to thee? Still hear what Paul says, "when they say peace and safety, then sudden destruction cometh upon them." Affairs are full of much change. We are not masters of our end. Let us be masters of virtue. Our Master Christ is loving.

6. Do you wish that I shall speak of the ways of repentance? They are many, and various, and different, and all lead to heaven. The first way of repentance is condemnation of sins. "Declare thou first thy sins that thou mayest be justified." Wherefore also the prophet said, "I said, I will speak out, my transgression to the Lord, and thou remitted the iniquity of my heart."

Condemn thyself therefore for thy sins. This is enough for the Master by way of self-defense. For he who condemns his sins, is slower to fall into them again. Awake thy conscience, that inward accuser, in order that thou mayest have no accuser at the judgment seat of the Lord. This is one way of repentance, the best; and there is another not less than this, not to bear a grudge against thine enemies to overcome anger, to forgive the sins of our fellow-servants. For so will those which have been done against the master be forgiven us. See the second expiation of sins: "For if ye forgive" saith he, "your debtors, your Heavenly Father will also forgive you." Do you wish to learn a third way of repentance? Fervent and diligent prayer, and to do this from the bottom of the heart. Hast thou not seen that widow, how she persuaded the shameless judge? But thou hast a gentle Master, both tender, and kind. She asked, against her adversaries, but thou dost not ask against thine adversaries, but on behalf of thine own salvation. And if thou would learn a fourth way, I will say almsgiving. For this has a great power and unspeakable. For Daniel saith to Nebuchadnezzar when he had come to all kinds of evil, and had entered upon all impiety, "O King let my counsel be acceptable unto thee, redeem thy sins by almsgiving and thine iniquities by compassion on the poor." What could be compared with this loving kindness? After countless sins, after so many transgressions, he is promised that he will be reconciled with him he has come into conflict with if he will show kindness to his own fellow-servants. And modesty, and humility, not less than all words spoken, exhaust the nature of sins. And the publican is proof, being unable to declare his good deeds, in sight of all, bringing forward his humility, and laying aside the heavy burden of his sins. See we have shown five ways of repentance: first the condemnation of sins, next the forgiveness of our neighbors' sins, thirdly that which comes of prayer, fourth that which comes of almsgiving, fifth that which comes of humility. Do not thou then be lazy; but walk in all these day by day. For the ways are easy, nor canst thou plead poverty. And even if thou lives poorer than all, thou art able to leave thine anger, and be humble, and to pray fervently, and to condemn sins, and thy poverty is in no way a hindrance. And why do I speak thus, when not even in that way of repentance in which it is possible to spend money (I speak of almsgiving), not even there is poverty any hindrance to us from obeying the command? The widow who spent the two mites is a proof. Having learned then the healing of our wounds, let us constantly apply these medicines, in order that we may return to health and enjoy the sacred table with assurance; and with much glory, reach Christ the king of glory, and attain to everlasting good by the grace, and compassion, and lovingkindness of our Lord Jesus Christ, by whom and with whom be glory, power, honor, to the Father, together with the all holy, and good and quickening Spirit, now and always and for ever and ever. Amen.

Homily III.

That evil comes of sloth, and virtue from diligence, and that neither wicked men, nor the devil himself, are able to do the wary man any harm. The proof of this from many passages, and amongst others from those which relate to Adam and to Job.

1. The day before yesterday we set on foot our sermon concerning the Devil, out of our love for you. But others, the day before yesterday while these matters were being set on foot here, took their places in the theatre, and were looking on at the Devil's show. They were taking part in lascivious songs; ye were having a share in spiritual music. They were eating of the Devil's garbage: ye were feeding on spiritual unguents. Who pray decoyed them? Who pray separated them from the sacred flock? Did the Devil pray deceive them? How did he not deceive you? you and they are men alike; I mean as regards your nature. You and they have the same soul, you have the same desires, so far as nature is concerned. How is it then that you and they were not in the same place? Because you and they have not the same purpose. On this account they indeed are under deception, but you beyond deception. I do not say these things again as discharging the Devil from accusation, but as desiring earnestly to free you from sins. The Devil is wicked; I grant this indeed, but he is wicked for himself not towards us if we are wary. For the nature of wickedness is of this kind. It is destructive to those alone who hold to it. Virtue is the contrary. It is not only able to profit those who hold to it, but those nearest at hand too. And in order that thou mayest learn that evil is evil in itself, but good is also

good to others, I provide thee with proverbial evidence: "My son" saith he "if thou art become evil, thou shall bear thine evils alone, but if wise, for thyself and thy neighbor."

They were deceived in the theatre, but ye were not deceived. This is the greatest proof of things, a clear testimony, and unquestionable reasoning, that in every case, the purpose is master. Do thou accordingly use this method of proof, and if thou sees a man living in wickedness, and exhibiting all kinds of evil; then blaming the providence of God, and saying that by the necessity of fortune and fate and through tyranny of Demons He gave us our nature, and on all sides shifting the cause from himself indeed, and transferring it to the creator who provides for all; silence his speech not by word, but by deed, shewing him another fellow servant living in virtue and forbearance. There is no need of long speeches, no need of a complex plan, nor even of syllogisms. By means of deeds the proof is brought about. He said to him: thou art a servant, and he is a servant; thou art a man and he is a man. Thou lives in the same world: thou art nourished with the same nourishment under the same heaven: How is it that thou art living in wickedness, he in virtue? on this account God allowed the wicked to be mingled with the good; and did not give one law to the wicked indeed, and appointed another world as a colony for the good, but mixed these and those; conferring great benefit. For the good appear more thoroughly approved when they are in the midst of those who try to hinder them from living rightly, and who entice them to evil, and yet keep hold of virtue. "For there must" he saith "be also heresies among you that they which are approved may be made manifest among you."

Therefore also on this account he has left the wicked to be in the world, in order that the good may shine the brighter. Do you see how great is the gain? But the gain is not owing to the wicked but owing to the courage of the good. On this account also we admire Noe, not because he was righteous nor yet because he was perfect alone, but because in that perverse and wicked generation he preserved his virtue, when he had no pattern of virtue, when all men invited him to wickedness; and he went his whole way contrary to them, like some traveler, pursuing his way while the great multitude is being borne along vehemently. On this account he did not simply say "Noe was just, perfect," but added "in his generation" in that perverse, that desperate generation, when there was no acquisition of virtue. To the good indeed then this was the gain from the wicked. Thus at all events, also trees tossed about by contrary winds, become stronger. And there is a gain to the wicked from their mixing with the good. They feel confusion, they are ashamed, they blush in their presence; and even if they do not abstain from evil, yet nevertheless they dare what they dare with secrecy. And this is no small thing not to have transgression publicly committed. For the life of the others becomes the accuser of the wickedness of these. Hear at least what they say about the righteous man. "He is grievous to us, even when beheld," and it is no small beginning of amendment to be tormented at his presence. For if the sight of the righteous man did not torment them, this word would not have been uttered. But to be stung, and pinched in conscience at his presence, would be no little hindrance to indulging in wickedness with pleasure, Dost thou see how great is the gain both to the good from the wicked, and to the wicked from the good? On this account God has not set them apart but allowed them to be mingled together.

2. Let our argument also about the Devil be the same. For on this account He hath left him also to be here, in order that he might render thee the stronger, in order that he may make the athlete more illustrious, in order that the contests may be greater. When therefore any one says, why has God left the Devil here? say these words to him, because he not only does no harm to the wary and the heedful, but even profits them, not owing to his own purpose (for that is wicked), but owing to their courage who have used that wickedness aright. Since he even fixed upon Job not on this account that he might make him more illustrious, but in order that he might upset him. On this account he is wicked both because of such an opinion and such a purpose. But notwithstanding he did no harm to the righteous man, but he rather rejoiced in the conflict as we accordingly shewed. Both the Demon shewed his wickedness and the righteous man his courage. But he does upset many says one: owing to their weakness, not owing to his own strength: for this too has been already proved by many examples. Direct thine own intention aright then, and thou shalt never receive harm from any, but shall get the greatest gain, not only from the good but even from the wicked. For on this account, as I have before said, God has suffered men to be with one another, and especially the wicked with the good, in order that they may bring them over to their own virtue. Hear at least what Christ saith to his disciples, "The Kingdom of heaven is like unto a woman who took leaven and hid it in three measures of meal." So that the righteous have the power of leaven, in order that they may transfer the wicked to their own manner of conduct. But the righteous

are few, for the leaven is small. But the smallness in no way injures the lump, but that little quantity converts the whole of the meal to itself by means of the power inherent in it. So accordingly the power also of the righteous has its force not in the magnitude of their number, but in the grace of the Spirit. There were twelve Apostles. Do you see how little is the leaven? The whole world was in unbelief. Do you see how great is the lump? But those twelve turned the whole world to themselves. The leaven and the lump had the same nature but not the same manner of conduct. On this account he left the wicked in the midst of the good, that since they are of the same nature as the righteous, they may also become of the same purpose.

Remember these things. With these stop the mouths of the indolent, the dissolute, the slothful, the indisposed towards the labors of virtue, those who accuse their common Master. "Thou hast sinned" he saith "be still." "Do not add a second more grievous sin." It is not so grievous to sin, as after the sin to accuse the Master. Take knowledge of the cause of the sin, and thou wilt find that it is none other than thyself who hast sinned. Everywhere there is a need of a good intention. I have shown you this not from simple reasoning only, but from the case of fellow-servants living in the world itself. Do thou also use this proof. Thus too our common master will judge us. Learn this method of proof, and no one will be able to reason with you. Is any a fornicator? Show him another who is self-restrained. Is any covetous and rapacious? Show him one who gives alms. Does he live in jealousy and envy? Shew him one clean from passion. Is he overcome by anger? Bring into the midst one who is living in wisdom, for we must not only have recourse to ancient example but take our models from present times. For even to-day by the grace of God, good deeds are done not less than of old. Is a man incredulous? and does he think that the scriptures are false? Does he not believe that Job was such as he was? Shew him another man, emulating the life of that righteous person. Thus will the Master also judge us: He places fellow servants with fellow-servants, nor does he give sentence according to his own judgment, in order that no one may begin to say again, as that servant said, who was entrusted with the talent, and who instead of a talent brought the accusation. "Thou art an austere man." For he ought to mourn, because he did not double the talent, but rendered his sin the more grievous, by adding to his own idleness, his accusation against the Master. For what saith he? "I knew thee that thou art an austere man." O miserable, and wretched, ungrateful and lazy man! You ought to have accused thine own idleness, and to have taken away somewhat from thy former sin. But thou in bringing an account against the master hast doubled thy sin instead of doubling thy talent.

3. On this account God places together servants and servants in order that the one set may judge the other, and that some being judged by the others may not be able for the future to accuse the master. On this account, he saith "The Son of Man cometh in the glory of his Father." See the equality of the glory: he does not say in glory like to the glory of the Father, but in the glory of the Father, and will gather together all the nations. Terrible is the tribunal: terrible to the sinful, and the accountable. Since to those who are conscious to themselves of good works, it is desirable and mild. "And he will place the sheep on his right hand, and the kids on his left." Both these and

those are men. For what reason then are those indeed sheep but these kids? Not that thou mayest learn a difference in their nature, but the difference in their purpose. But for what reason are they who did not show compassion kids? Because that animal is unfruitful and is not able to contribute services, either by its milk, or by progeny, or by its hair, to those who possess it, being on all sides destitute of such a contribution as this, on account of the immaturity of its age. On this account he has called those who bear no fruit, by comparison, kids, but those on the right-hand sheep. For from these the offering is great, both of their natural wool, their progeny, and their milk. What then does he say to them? "Ye saw me hungering and ye fed me, naked and ye clothed me, a stranger and ye took me in." Again to those he says the contrary. And yet both these and those were alike men, both these and those received the same promises, the same rewards were assigned to both on doing right. The same person came both to these and to those, with the same nakedness: and to these and to those with the same hunger, and in the same way and a stranger. All things were alike to those and to these.

How then was the end not the same? Because the purpose did not permit it. For this alone made the difference. On this account the one set went to Gehenna, but the other to the Kingdom. But if the Devil were the cause to them of their sins, these would not be destined to be chastened, when another sinned and drove them on. Do you see here both those who sin, and those who do good works? Do you see how on seeing their fellow servants they were silenced? Come and let us bring our discourse to another example for thy benefit. There were ten virgins he says. Here again there are purposes which are upright, and purposes which are sinful, in order thou mayest see side by side, both the sins of the one and the good works of the others. For the comparison makes these things the plainer. And these and those were virgins; and these were five, and also those. All awaited the bridegroom. How then did some enter in, and others did not enter in? Because some indeed were churlish, and others were gentle and loving. Do you see again that the purpose determined the nature of the end, not the Devil? Do you see that the judgments were parallel, and that the verdict given proceeds from those who are like each other? Fellow servants will judge fellow-servants. Do you wish that I should shew thee a comparison arising from contrasts? for there is one also from contrasts so that the condemnation may become the greater. "The men of Nineveh" he saith "shall rise up, and shall condemn this generation." The judged are no longer alike, for the one are barbarians, the others are Jews. The one enjoyed prophetic teaching, the others were never partakers of a divine instruction. And this is not the only difference, but the fact that in that case a servant went to them, in this the master; and that man came and proclaimed an overthrow; but this man declared the glad tidings of a kingdom of heaven. Which of these was it the more likely, would believe? The barbarians, and ignorant, and they who had never partaken of divine teaching, or they who had from their earliest age been trained in prophetic books? To everyone, it is plain, that the Jews would be more likely to believe. But the contrary took place. And these disbelieved the Master when he preached a kingdom of heaven, but those believed their fellow-servant when he threatened an overthrow: in order that their goodness, and these men's folly might be manifested to a greater degree.

Is there a Demon? a Devil? chance? or Fate? has not each become the cause to himself both of evil, and of virtue? For if they themselves were not to be liable to account, he would not have said that they shall judge this generation. Nor would he have said that the Queen of the South would condemn the Jews. For then indeed not only will one people condemn another people, but one man will often judge a whole people, when they who, it is allowed, might readily have been deceived, are found to remain undeceived, and they who ought in every way to have the advantage, turn out to be worsted. On this account, we made mention of Adam and of Job, for there is necessity to revert to that subject, so as to put the finish to our discourse. He attacked Adam indeed by means of mere words, but Job by means of deeds. For the one he denuded of all his wealth, and deprived of his children. But from this man he took not away anything, great or little of his possessions. But let us rather examine the very words and the method of the plot. "The serpent came" saith he "and said to the woman, What is it that God hath said, ye shall not eat of every tree which is in the garden?" Here it is a serpent; there a woman, in the case of Job: mean while great is the difference between the counsellors. The one is a servant, the other a partner of the man's life. She is a helpmate, but the other is under subjection. Do you see how unpardonable this is? Eve indeed, the servant in subjection deceived: but him not even his partner, and helpmate could overthrow. But let us see what he saith. "What is this that God hath said, thou shalt not eat of every tree?" Assuredly indeed God did not say this but the opposite. See the villainy of the Devil. He said that which was not spoken, in order that he might learn what was spoken. What then did the woman?

She ought to have silenced him, she ought not to have exchanged a word with him. In foolishness she declared the judgment of the Master. Thereby she afforded the Devil a powerful handle.

4. See what an evil it is to commit ourselves rashly to our enemies, and to conspirators against us. On this account Christ used to say, "Give not holy things to the dogs, neither cast ye your pearls before the swine, lest they turn and rend you." And this happened in the case of Eve. She gave the holy things to the dog, to the swine. He trod underfoot the words: and turned and rent the woman. And see how he works evil. "Ye shall not die the death" saith he.

Give me your attention on this point, that the woman was able to understand the deceit. For he immediately announced his enmity, and his warfare against God, he immediately contradicted Him. Let it be so. Before this thou declares the judgment to one who wished to learn it. After this why did you follow one who said the opposite? God said "ye shall die the death." The Devil made answer to this and said "ye shall not die the death." What could be clearer than this warfare? From what other quarter ought one to learn the enemy and the foe, than from his answer returned to God? She ought then immediately to have fled from the bait, she ought to have started back from the snare. "Ye shall not die the death," saith he "for God knows, that on the day on which ye eat, your eyes shall be opened, and ye shall be as Gods. In hope of a greater promise she cast away the goods in her hand. He promised that he would make them Gods, and cast them down into the tyranny of death. Whence then O woman didst thou believe the Devil? What good didst thou discern? Was not the trustworthiness of the lawgiver sufficient to prove that the one was God, both creator and framer of the world, and the other the Devil and an enemy? And I do not say the Devil. You thought that he was a mere serpent. Ought a serpent to claim such equality that thou shouldest tell him the Master's judgment? Thou sees that it was possible to perceive the deceit, but she would not, and yet God gave many proofs of his own beneficence and shewed forth his care of his works. For he formed man, who had not existed before; and breathed a soul into him, and made him according to his image, making him ruler of all things upon the earth, and granted him a helpmate, planted Paradise, and having committed to him the use of the rest of the trees, refused him the taste of one only: and this very prohibition he made for man's advantage. But the Devil manifested no good things by his deed, whether little, or great: but exciting the woman with mere words and puffing her up with vain hopes, thus he deceived her. But nevertheless she considered the Devil to be more worthy of credit than God, although God shewed forth his good will by his works. The woman believed in one who professed mere words, and nothing else. Dost thou see how, from folly alone and sloth, and not from force, the deceit happened? and in order that thou mayest learn it more clearly hear how the scripture accuses the woman: For it does not say, being deceived, but "seeing the tree that it was fair, she ate." So that the blame belongs to her uncontrolled vision, not to the deceit alone which comes from the Devil. For she was defeated by yielding to her own desire, not by the wickedness. of the Demon. On this account she did not have the benefit of pardon, but though she said, "the serpent deceived me," she paid the uttermost penalty. For it was in her power not to have fallen. And in order that thou mayest understand this more clearly, come, let us conduct our discourse to the case of Job; from the defeated to the vanquisher, from the conquered to the conqueror. For this man will give us greater zeal, so that we may raise our hands against the Devil. There he who deceived and conquered was a serpent; here the tempter was a woman, and she did not prevail: and yet at least she was far more persuasive than he. For to Job after the destruction of his wealth, after the loss of his children, after being stripped bare of all his goods, her wiles were added. But in the other case there was nothing of this kind. Adam did not suffer the destruction of his children, nor did he lose his wealth: he did not sit upon a dunghill, but inhabited a Paradise of luxury and enjoyed all manner of fruits, and fountains and rivers, and every other kind of security. Nowhere was there labor or pain, or despair and cares, or reproaches, and insults, or the countless ills which assailed Job: but nevertheless, when nothing of this kind existed, he fell and was overthrown. Is it not evident that it was on account of sloth? Even so therefore as the other, when all these things beset him, and weighed upon him, stood nobly and did not fall, is it not evident that his steadfastness was owing to his vigilance of soul?

5. On both sides, beloved, reap the utmost gain, and avoid the imitation of Adam knowing how many ills are begotten of indolence: and imitate the piety of Job, learning how many glorious things spring from earnestness. Consider him, the conqueror throughout, and thou shalt have much consolation in all pain and peril. For as it were in the common theatre of the world that blessed and noble man stands forth, and by means of the sufferings which happened to him discourses to all to bear all things which befall them nobly, and never give in to

the troubles which come upon them. For verily, there is no human suffering which cannot receive consolation from thence. For the sufferings which are scattered over the whole world, these came together, and bore down upon one body, even his. What pardon then shall there be for him who is unable to bear with thankfulness his share of the troubles which are brought upon him? Since he appears not bearing a part only, but the entire ills of all men, and in order that thou mayest not condemn the extravagance of my words, come, and let us take in hand severally the ills that came upon him, and bring forward this fulfilment of them. And if thou wishes, let us first bring forward that which seems to be the most unendurable of all, I mean poverty, and the pain which arises from it. For everywhere all men bewail this. What was poorer then than Job, who was poorer than the outcasts at the baths, and those who sleep in the ashes of the furnace, poorer in fact than all men? For these indeed have one ragged garment, but he sat naked, and had only the garment which nature supplies, the clothing of the flesh, and this the Devil destroyed on all sides, with a distressing kind of decay. Again these poor folk are at least under the roof of the porches at the baths, and are covered with a shelter. But he continued always to pass his nights in the open air, not having even the consolation of a bare roof. And, what is still greater, the fact that these are conscious of many terrible evils within themselves, but he was conscious of nothing against himself. For this is to be noticed in each of the things which happened to him, a thing which caused him greater pain, and produced more perplexity; the ignorance of the reason of what took place. These persons then, as I said, would have many things with which to reproach themselves. And this contributes no little to consolation in calamity; to be conscious in oneself of being punished justly. But he was deprived of this consolation, and while exhibiting a conversation full of virtue, endured the fate of those who had dared to do extreme wickedness. And these folk who are with us, are poor from the outset, and from the beginning are versed in calamity. But he endured calamity in which he was unversed, experiencing the immense change from wealth. As then the knowledge of the cause of what takes place, is the greatest consolation; so it is not less than this, to have been versed in poverty from the beginning, and so to continue in it. Of both these consolations that man was deprived, and not even then, did he fall away. Do you see him indeed come to extreme poverty, even in comparison with which it is impossible to find a fellow? For what could be poorer than the naked who has not even a roof over him? Yea rather not even was it in his power to enjoy the bare ground, but he sat upon the dunghill. Therefore whenever thou sees thyself come to poverty, consider the suffering of the just one, and straightway thou shalt rise up, and shake off every thought of despondency. This one calamity therefore seems to men to be the groundwork of all sufferings together. And the second after it, yea rather before it, is the affliction of the body. Who then was even so disabled? Who endured such disease? Who received or saw anyone else receive so great an affliction? No one. Little by little his body was wasted, and a stream of worms on every side issued from his limbs, the running was constant, and the evil smell which surrounded him was strong, and the body being destroyed little by little, and decaying with such putrefaction, used to make food distasteful and hunger was to him strange and unusual.

For not even was he able to enjoy the nourishment which was given to him. For saith he "I see my food to be loathsome." Whenever then you fall into weakness, O man, remember that body and that saintly flesh. For it was saintly and pure, even when it had so many wounds. And if any one belong to the army, and then unjustly and without any reasonable pretext, be hanged upon the pillory, and has his sides rasped to pieces, let him not think the matter to be a reproach, nor let him give way to the pain when he thinks upon this saint. But this man, says one, has much comfort and consolation in knowing that God was bringing these sufferings upon him. This indeed especially troubled and disturbed him, to think that the just God who had in every way been served by him, was at war with him. And he was not able to find any reasonable pretext for what took place, since, when at least he afterwards learned the cause, see what piety he shewed, for when God said to him "Dost thou think that I have had dealings with thee in order that thou might appear righteous?" conscious-stricken he says "I will lay my hand upon my mouth, once have I spoken but to a second word I will not proceed," and again "as far as the hearing of the ear I have heard thee before, but now mine eye hath seen thee, wherefore I have held myself to be vile, and am wasted away, and I consider myself to be earth and ashes."

6. But if thou thinks that this is sufficient for consolation, thou wilt thyself also be able to experience this comfort. And even if thou dost not suffer any of these misfortunes at the hands of God but owing to the insolence of men; and yet gives thanks and dost not blaspheme him who is able to prevent them indeed, but who permits them for the sake of testing thee: just as they

who suffer at the hands of God are crowned, so also thou shalt obtain the same reward, because thou hast borne nobly the calamities which were brought upon thee from men, and didst give thanks to him who was able indeed to hinder them, but not willing.

    Behold then! thou hast seen poverty and disease, and both in the extremist degree brought upon this just man. Do you wish that I should shew thee the warfare at nature's hands, in such excessive degree waged then against this noble man? He lost ten children, the ten at one fell swoop, the ten in the very bloom of youth, ten who displayed much virtue, and that not by the common law of nature, but by a violent and pitiable death. Who could be able to recount so great a calamity? No one. Whenever therefore thou loses son and daughter together, have recourse to this just man, and thou shalt find altogether much comfort for thyself. Were these then the only misfortunes which happened to him? The desertion and treachery of his friends, and the gibes, and raillery, and the mockery and derision, and the tearing in pieces by all, was something intolerable. For the character of calamities is not of such a kind, that they who reproach us about our calamities are wont to vex our soul. Not only was there no one to soothe him but many even on many sides beset him with taunts. And thou sees him lamenting this bitterly and saying, "but even you too fell upon me." And he calls them pitiless, and says "My neighbors have rejected me, and my servants spoke against me, and I called the sons of my concubines, and they turned away from me." "And others" saith he "sport upon me, and I became the common talk of all. And my very raiment" saith he "abhorred me." These things at least are unbearable to hear, still more to endure in their reality, extreme poverty, and intolerable disease new and strange, the loss of children so many and so good, and in such a manner, reproaches and gibes, and insults from men. Some indeed mocked and some reproached and others despised; not only enemies, but even friends; not only friends, but even servants, and they not only mock and reproach, but even abhorred him, and this not for two or three, or ten days, but for many months; and (a circumstance which happened in that man's case alone) not even had he comfort by night, but the delusions of terrors by night were a greater aggravation of his misfortunes by day. For that he endured more grievous things in his sleep, hear what he says "why dost thou frighten me in sleep, and terrify me in visions?" What man of iron, what heart of steel could have endured so many misfortunes? For if each of these was unbearable in itself, consider what a tumult their simultaneous approach excited. But nevertheless he bore all these, and in all that happened to him he sinned not, nor was there guile in his lips.

7. Let the sufferings of that man then be the medicines for our ills, and his grievous surging sea the harbor of our sufferings, and in each of the accidents which befall us, let us consider this saint, and seeing one person exhausting the misfortunes of the universe, we shall conduct ourselves bravely in those which fall to our share, and as to some affectionate mother, stretching forth her hands on all sides, and receiving and reviving her terrified children, so let us always flee to this book, and even if the pitiable troubles of all men assail us, let us take sufficient comfort for all and so depart. And if thou sayest, he was Job, and for this reason bore all this, but I am not like him; thou supplies me with a greater accusation against thyself and fresh praise of him. For it is

more likely that thou shouldest be able to bear all this than he. Why pray? Because he indeed was before the day of grace and of the law, when there was not much strictness of life, when the grace of the Spirit was not so great, when sin was hard to fight against, when the curse prevailed and when death was terrible. But now our wrestling have become easier, all these things being removed after the coming of Christ; so that we have no excuse, when we are unable to reach the same standard as he, after so long a time, and such advantage, and so many gifts given to us by God. Considering therefore all these things, that misfortunes were greater for him, and that when the conflict was more grievous, then he stripped for the contest; let us bear all that comes upon us nobly, and with much thankfulness, in order that we may be able to obtain the same crown as he, by the grace and lovingkindness of Jesus Christ our Lord, with whom be glory to the Father together with the Holy Spirit, now and always and for ever and ever. Amen.

HOMILY

ON THE PASSAGE (MATT. XXVI. 19), "FATHER IF IT BE POSSIBLE LET THIS CUP PASS FROM ME," ETC., AND AGAINST MARCIONISTS AND MANICHÆANS.

TRANSLATED BY
REV. W. R. W. STEPHENS, M.A.,
PREBENDARY OF CHICHESTER CATHEDRAL,
AND RECTOR OF WOOLBEDING,
SUSSEX.

AGAINST MARCIONISTS AND MANICHÆANS.

On the passage "Father if it be possible let this cup pass from me, nevertheless not as I will but as thou wilt:" and against Marcionists and Manichæans: also, that we ought not to rush into danger, but to prefer the will of God before every other will.

1. I lately inflicted a severe stroke upon those who are grasping and wish to overreach others; I did this not in order to wound them but in order to correct them; not because I hate the men, but because I detest their wickedness. For so the physician also lances the abscess, not as making an attack upon the suffering body, but as a means of contending with the disorder and the wound. Well today let us grant them a little respite, that they may recover from their distress, and not recoil from the remedy by being perpetually afflicted. Physicians also act thus; after the use of the knife they apply plasters and drugs and let a few days pass whilst they devise things to allay the pain. Following their example let me today, devising means for them to derive benefit from my discourse, start a question concerning doctrine, directing my speech to the words which have been read. For I imagine that many feel perplexed as to the reason why these words were uttered by Christ: and it is probable also that any heretics who are present may pounce upon the words and thereby upset many of the more simple-minded brethren.

In order then to build a wall against their attack and to relieve those who are in perplexity from bewilderment and confusion, let us take in hand the words which have been cited, and dwell upon the passage, and dive into the depths of its meanings. For reading does not suffice unless knowledge also be added to it. Even as the eunuch of Candace read, but until one came who instructed him in the meaning of what he was reading he derived no great benefit from it. In order therefore that you may not be in the same condition attend to what is said, exert your understanding, let me have your mind disengaged from other thoughts, let your eye be quick-sighted, your intention earnest: let your soul be set free from worldly cares, that we may not sow our words upon the thorns, or upon the rock, or by the way side, but that we may till a deep and rich field, and so reap an abundant harvest. For if you thus attend to what is said you will render my labor lighter and facilitate the discovery of that which you are seeking.

What then is the meaning of the passage which has been read "Father if it be possible let this cup pass from me?" What does the saying mean? For we ought to unlock the passage by first giving a clear interpretation of the words. What then does the saying mean? "Father if it be possible take away the cross." How sayest thou? is he ignorant whether this be possible or impossible? Who would venture to say this? Yet the words are those of one who is ignorant: for the addition of the word "if," is indicative of doubt: but as I said we must not attend to the words merely, but turn our attention to the sense, and learn the aim of the speaker, and the cause and the occasion, and by putting all these things together turn out the hidden meaning. The unspeakable Wisdom then, who knows the Father even as the Father knows the Son, how should he have been ignorant of this? For this knowledge concerning His passion was not greater than the knowledge concerning His essential nature, which He alone accurately knew. "For as the Father knows me" He says, "even so know I the Father." And why do I speak of the only begotten Son of God? For even the prophets appear not to have been ignorant of this fact, but to have known it clearly, and to have declared beforehand with much assurance that so it must come to pass, and would certainly be.

 Hear at least how variously all announce the cross. First of all the patriarch Jacob: for directing his discourse to Him he says "Out of a tender shoot didst thou spring up:" by the word shoot signifying the Virgin and the undefiled nature of Mary. Then indicating the cross he said "Thou didst lie down and slumber as a lion, and as a lion's whelp; who shall raise him up?" Here he called death a slumbering and a sleep, and with death he combined the resurrection when he said, "who shall raise him up?" No one indeed save he himself—wherefore also Christ said, "I have power to lay down my life, and I have power to take it again," and again "Destroy this temple and in three days I will raise it up." And what is meant by the words "thou didst lie down and slumber as a lion?" For as the lion is terrible not only when he is awake but even when he is sleeping, so Christ also not only before the cross but also on the cross itself and in the very moment of death was terrible, and wrought at that time great miracles, turning back the light of the sun, cleaving the rocks, shaking the earth, rending the veil, alarming the wife of Pilate, convicting Judas of sin, for then he said "I have sinned in that I have betrayed the innocent blood;" and the wife of Pilate declared "Have nothing to do with that just man, for I have suffered many things in a dream because of Him." The darkness took possession of the earth, and night appeared at midday, then death was brought to nought, and his tyranny was destroyed: many bodies at least of the saints which slept arose. These things the patriarch declaring beforehand, and demonstrating that, even when crucified, Christ would be terrible, said "thou didst lie down and slumber as a lion." He did not say thou shalt slumber but thou didst slumber, because it would certainly come to pass. For it is the custom of the prophets in many places to predict things to come as if they were already past. For just as it is impossible that things which have happened should not have happened, so is it impossible that this should not happen, although it be future. On this account they predict things to come under the semblance of past time, indicating by this means the impossibility of their failure, the certainty of their coming to pass. So also spoke David, signifying the cross; "They pierced my hands and my feet." He did not say they "shall pierce" but "they pierced" "they counted all my bones." And not only does he say this, but he also describes the things which were done by the soldiers. "They parted my garments among themselves, and upon my vesture did they cast lots." And not only this but he also relates they gave Him gall to eat, and vinegar to drink. For he says, "they gave me gall for my food, and for my thirst they gave me vinegar to drink." And again another one says that they smote him with a spear, for "they shall look on Him whom they pierced." Esaias again in another fashion predicting the cross said, "He was led as a sheep to the slaughter, and as a lamb before his shearer is dumb, so opened he not his mouth." "In his humiliation his judgment was taken away."

2. Now observe I pray how each one of these writers speaks as if concerning things already past, signifying by the use of this tense the absolute inevitable certainty of the event. So also David, describing this tribunal, said, "Why did the heathen rage and the people imagine vain things? The Kings of the earth stood up, and the rulers were gathered together against the Lord and against his Christ." And not only does he mention the trial, and the cross, and the incidents on the cross, but also him who betrayed him, declaring that he was his familiar companion and guest. "For," he saith, "he that eats bread with me did magnify his heel against me." Thus also does he foretell the voice which Christ was to utter on the cross saying "My God, My God why hast thou forsaken me?" and the burial also does he describe: "They laid me in the lowest pit, in dark places, and in the shadow of death." And the resurrection: "thou shalt not leave my soul in hell, neither shalt thou suffer thy Holy One to see corruption;" and the ascension: "God has gone up with a merry noise, the Lord with the sound of the trump." And the session on the right hand: "The Lord said to my Lord sit thou on my right hand until I make thy foes thy footstool." But Esaias also declares the cause; saying, "for the transgressions of my people is He brought to death," and because all have strayed like sheep, therefore is he sacrificed." Then also he adds mention of the result, saying "by his stripes we have all been healed:" and "he hath borne the sins of many." The prophets then knew the cross, and the cause of the cross and that which was effected by it, and the burial and the resurrection, and the ascension, and the betrayal, and the trial, and described them all with accuracy: and is He who sent them and commanded them to speak these things ignorant of them

Himself? What reasonable man would say that? Seest thou that we must not attend merely to the words? For this is not the only perplexing passage, but what follows is more perplexing. For what does He say? "Father if it be possible let this cup pass from me." Here he will be found to speak not only as if ignorant, but as if deprecating the cross: For this is what He says. "If it be permissible let me not be subjected to crucifixion and death." And yet when Peter, the leader of the apostles, said this to Him, "Be it far from thee Lord, this shall not happen unto Thee," He rebuked him so severely as to say; "get thee behind me Satan, thou art an offence unto me, for thou savors not the things which be of God, but those which be of men:" although a short time before he had pronounced him blessed. But to escape crucifixion seemed to Him so monstrous a thing, that him who had received the revelation from the Father, him whom He had pronounced blessed, him who had received the keys of Heaven, He called Satan, and an offence, and accused him of not savoring the things which be of God because he said to Him, "Be it far from thee Lord, this shall never be unto Thee"—namely crucifixion. He then who thus vituperated the disciple, and poured such an invective upon him as actually to call him Satan (after having bestowed such great praise on him), because he said "avoid crucifixion," how could He desire not to be crucified? and how after these things when drawing the picture of the good shepherd could He declare this to be the special proof of his virtue, that he should be sacrificed for the sake of the sheep, thus saying, "I am the good shepherd; the good shepherd lays down his life for the sheep?" Nor did He even stop there, but also added, "but he that is a hireling and not the shepherd sees the wolf coming and leaves the sheep and flees." If then it is the sign of the good shepherd to sacrifice himself, and of the hireling to be unwilling to undergo this, how can He who calls Himself the good shepherd beseech that he may not be sacrificed? And how could He say, "I lay down my life of myself"? For if thou lays down thy life of thyself, how canst thou beseech another that thou mayest not lay it down? And how is it that Paul marvels at Him on account of this declaration, saying "Who being in the form of God counted it not a prize to be on an equality with God, but emptied Himself taking the form of a servant, being made in the likeness of men, and being found in fashion as a man he humbled himself, becoming obedient even unto death, yea, the death of the cross." And He Himself again speaks in this wise, "For this cause doth my Father love me, because I lay down my life that I may take it again." For if He does not desire to lay it down, but deprecates the act, and beseeches the Father, how is it that He is loved on this account? For love is of those who are like minded. And how does Paul say again, "Love one another even as Christ also loved us and gave Himself for us?" And Christ Himself when He was about to be crucified said "Father, the hour has come: glorify thy Son," speaking of the cross as glory: and how then does He deprecate it here when He urges it there? For that the cross is glory listen to what the evangelist says, "the Holy Ghost was not yet given, because Jesus was not yet glorified." Now the hearing of this expression is "grace was not yet given because the enmity towards men was not yet destroyed by reason that the cross had not yet done its work." For the cross destroyed the enmity of God towards man, brought about the reconciliation, made the earth Heaven, associated men with angels, pulled down the citadel of death, unstrung the force of the devil, extinguished the power of sin, delivered the world from error, brought back the truth, expelled the Demons, destroyed temples, overturned altars, suppressed the sacrificial offering, implanted virtue, founded the Churches. The cross is the will of the Father, the glory of the Son, the rejoicing of the Spirit, the boast of Paul, "for," he says, "God forbid that I should boast save in the cross of our Lord Jesus Christ." The cross is that which is brighter than the sun, more brilliant than the sunbeam: for when the sun is darkened then the cross shines brightly: and the sun is darkened not because it is extinguished, but because it is overpowered by the brilliancy of the cross. The cross has broken our bond, it has made the prison of death ineffectual, it is the demonstration of the love of God. "For God so loved the world that He gave His only begotten Son, that everyone who believes in Him should not perish." And again Paul says, "If being enemies we were reconciled to God by the death of His Son." The cross is the impregnable wall, the invulnerable shield, the safeguard of the rich, the resource of the poor, the defense of those who are exposed to snares, the armor of those who are attacked, the means of suppressing passion, and of acquiring virtue, the wonderful and marvelous sign. "For this generation seeks after a sign: and no sign shall be given it save the sign of Jonas;" and again Paul says, "for the Jews ask for a sign and the Greeks seek wisdom, but we preach Christ crucified." The cross opened Paradise, it brought in the robber, it conducted into the kingdom of Heaven the race of man, which was about to perish, and was not worthy even of earth. So great are the benefits which have sprung and do spring from the cross, and yet doth He not desire to be crucified I ask? Who would venture to say this? And if He did not desire it who compelled Him, who forced Him to it? and why did He send prophets beforehand announcing that He would be crucified, if He was not to be, and did not wish to undergo it? And for what reason does He call the cross a cup, if He did not desire to be crucified? For that is the word of one who signifies the desire which he has concerning the act. For as the cup is sweet to those who are thirsty so also was crucifixion to Him: wherefore also He said "With desire have I desired to eat this Passover with you," and this He meant not absolutely, but relatively, because after that evening the cross was awaiting Him.

3. He then who calls the thing glory, and rebukes the disciple because he was trying to hinder Him, and proves that what constitutes the good shepherd is his sacrificing himself on behalf of the sheep, and declares that he earnestly longs for this thing, and willingly goes to meet it, how is it that He beseeches it may not come to pass? And if He did not wish it what difficulty was there in hindering those who came for that purpose? But in fact you behold Him hastening towards the deed. At least when they came upon Him, He said "Whom seek ye?" and they replied "Jesus." Then He saith to them "Lo! I am He: and they went backward and fell to the ground." Thus having first crippled them and proved that He was able to escape their hands, He then surrendered Himself, that thou might learn that not by compulsion or force, or the tyrannical power of those who attacked Him, did He unwillingly submit to this, but willingly with purpose and desire, preparing for it a long time before. Therefore also were prophets sent beforehand, and patriarchs foretold the events, and by means of words and deeds the cross was prefigured. For the sacrifice of Isaac also signified the

cross to us: wherefore also Christ said, "Abraham your father rejoiced to see my glory, and he saw it and was glad." The patriarch then was glad beholding the image of the cross, and does He Himself deprecate it? Thus Moses also prevailed over Amalek when he displayed the figure of the cross: and one may observe countless things happening in the Old Testament descriptive by anticipation of the cross. For what reason then was this the case if He who was to be crucified did not wish it to come to pass? And the sentence which follows this is yet more perplexing. For having said "Let this cup pass from me He added "nevertheless not as I will but as Thou wilt." For herein as far as the actual expression is concerned we find two wills opposed to one another: if at least the Father desires Him to be crucified, but He Himself does not desire it. And yet we everywhere behold Him desiring and purposing the same things as the Father. For when He says, "grant to them, as I and Thou are one that they also may be one in us," it is equivalent to saying that the purpose of the Father and of the Son is one. And when He says, "The words which I speak I speak not myself, but the Father which dwelleth in me, He doeth these works," He indicates the same thing. And when He says "I have not come of myself" and "I can of my own self do nothing" he does not say this as signifying that He has been deprived of authority, either to speak or to act (away with the thought!), but as desiring to prove the concord of his purpose, both in words and deeds, and in every kind of transaction, to be one and the same with the Father, as I have already frequently demonstrated. For the expression "I speak not of myself" is not an abrogation of authority but a demonstration of agreement. How then does He say here, "Nevertheless not as I will but as Thou wilt"?

Perhaps I have excited a great conflict in your mind, but be on the alert: for although many words have been uttered I know well that your zeal is still fresh: for the discourse is now hastening on to the solution. Why then has this form of speech been employed? Attend carefully, The doctrine of the incarnation was very hard to receive. For the exceeding measure of His lovingkindness and the magnitude of His condescension were full of awe and needed much preparation to be accepted. For consider what a great thing it was to hear and to learn that God the ineffable, the incorruptible, the unintelligible, the invisible, the incomprehensible, in whose hand are the ends of the earth, who looked upon the earth, and causes it to tremble, who touches the mountains, and maketh them smoke, the weight of whose condescension not even the Cherubim were able to bear but veiled their faces by the shelter of their wings, that this God who surpasses all understanding, and baffles all calculation, having passed by angels, archangels, and all the spiritual powers above, deigned to become man, and to take flesh formed of earth and clay, and enter the womb of a virgin, and be borne there the space of nine months, and be nourished with milk, and suffer all things to which man is liable. Inasmuch then as that which was to happen was so strange as to be disbelieved by many even when it had taken place, He first of all sends prophets beforehand, announcing this very fact. For instance the patriarch predicted it saying "Thou didst spring from a tender shoot my son: thou didst lie down and slumber as a lion;" and Esaias saying "Behold the Virgin shall conceive and bear a son and they shall call His name Emmanuel;" and elsewhere again "We beheld Him as a young child, as a root in a dry ground;"679 and by the dry ground he means the virgin's womb. And again "unto us a child is born, unto us a son is given," and again "there shall come forth a rod out of the root of Jesse, and a flower shall spring out of his root." And Baruch in the book of Jeremiah says "this is our God: no other shall be reckoned by the side of Him: He found out every path of knowledge and gave it to Jacob His servant, and Israel his beloved. After these things also He appeared upon the earth and held converse with men." And David signifying His incarnate presence said "He shall come down like the rain into a fleece of wool, and like the drop which distills upon the earth" because He noiselessly and gently entered into the Virgin's womb.

4. But these proofs alone did not suffice, but even when He had come, lest what had taken place should be deemed an illusion, He warranted the fact not only by the sight but by duration of time and by passing through all the phases incident to man. For He did not enter once for all into a man matured and completely developed, but into a virgin's womb, so as to undergo the process of gestation and birth and suckling and growth, and by the length of the time and the variety of the stages of growth to give assurance of what had come to pass. And not even here were the proofs concluded, but even when bearing about the body of flesh He suffered it to experience the infirmities of human nature and to be hungry, and thirsty, and to sleep and feel fatigue; finally also when He came to the cross He suffered it to undergo the pains of the flesh. For this reason also streams of sweat flowed down from it and an angel was discovered strengthening it, and He was sad and down-cast: for before He uttered these words He said, "my soul is troubled, and exceeding sorrowful ever unto death." If then after all these things

have taken place the wicked mouth of the devil speaking through Marcion of Pontus, and Valentinus, and Manichæus of Persia and many more heretics, has attempted to overthrow the doctrine of the Incarnation and has vented a diabolical utterance declaring that He did not become flesh, nor was clothed with it, but that this was mere fancy, and illusion, a piece of acting and pretense, although the sufferings, the death, the burial, the thirst, cry aloud against this teaching; supposing that none of these things had happened would not the devil have sown these wicked doctrines of impiousness much more widely? For this reason, just as He hungered, as He slept, as He felt fatigue, as He ate and drank, so also did He deprecate death, thereby manifesting his humanity, and that infirmity of human nature which does not submit without pain to be torn from this present life. For had He not uttered any of these things, it might have been said that if He were a man He ought to have experienced human feelings. And what are these? in the case of one about to be crucified, fear and agony, and pain in being torn from present life: for a sense of the charm which surrounds present things is implanted in human nature: on this account wishing to prove the reality of the fleshly clothing, and to give assurance of the incarnation He manifests the actual feelings of man with full demonstration.

This is one consideration, but there is another no less important. And what is this? Christ having come to earth wished to instruct men in all virtue: now the instructor teaches not only by word, but also by deed: for this is the teacher's best method of teaching. A pilot for instance when he makes the apprentice sit by his side shows him how he handles the rudder, but he also joins speech to action, and does not depend upon words alone or example alone: in like manner also an architect when he has placed by his side the man who is intended to learn from him how a wall is constructed, shows him the way by means of action as well as by means of oral teaching; so also with the weaver, and embroiderer, and gold refiner, and coppersmith;—and every kind of art has teachers who instruct both orally and practically. Inasmuch then as Christ Himself came to instruct us in all virtue, He both tells us what ought to be done, and does it. "For," he says, "he who does and teaches the same shall be called great in the kingdom of heaven." Now observe; He commanded men to be lowly minded, and meek, and He taught this by His words: but see how He also teaches it by His deeds. For having said "Blessed are the poor in spirit, blessed are the meek," He shows how these virtues ought to be practiced. How then did He teach them? He took a towel and girded Himself and washed the disciples' feet. What can match this lowliness of mind? For He teaches this virtue no longer by His words only but also by His deeds. Again He teaches meekness and forbearance by His acts. How so? He was struck on the face by the servant of the high priest, and said "If I have spoken evil bear witness of the evil: but if well why smites thou me?" He commanded men to pray for their enemies: this also again He teaches by means of His acts: for when He had ascended the cross, He said "Father forgive them for they know not what they do." As therefore He commanded men to pray so does He Himself pray, instructing thee to do so by his own unflagging utterances of prayer. Again He commanded us to do good to those who hate us, and to deal fairly with those who treat us despitefully: and this He did by his own acts: for he cast devils out of the Jews, who said that He Himself was possessed by a devil, He bestowed benefits on His persecutors, He fed those who were forming designs against Him, He conducted into His kingdom those who were desiring to crucify Him. Again He said to His disciples "Get you no gold nor silver neither brass in your purses," thus training them for poverty: and this also He taught by His example, thus saying, "Foxes have holes, and the birds of the air have nests, but the Son of man hath not where to lay His head." And He had neither table nor dwelling nor anything else of that kind: not because He was at a loss to obtain them, but because He was instructing men to go in that path. After the same manner then he taught them also to pray. They said to Him "Teach us to pray." Therefore also He prays, in order that they may learn to pray. But it was necessary for them not merely to learn to pray but also how they ought to pray: for this reason He delivered to them a prayer in this form: "Our Father which art in Heaven hallowed be thy name, Thy kingdom come: Thy will be done, as in Heaven, so on earth. Give us this day our daily bread: and forgive us our debts as we also forgive our debtors: and lead us not into temptation:" that is into danger, into snares. Since then He commanded them to pray "lead us not into temptation," He instructs them in this very precept by putting it in practice Himself, saying "Father if it be possible, let this cup pass away from me," thus teaching all the saints not to plunge into dangers, not to fling themselves into them but to wait for their approach, and to exhibit all possible courage, only not to rush forwards themselves, or to be the first to advance against terrors. Why so, pray? Both to teach us lowliness of mind, and also to deliver us from the charge of vainglory. On this account it is said also in this passage that when He had spoken these words "He went away and prayed:" and after He had prayed, He speaks thus to His disciples "Could ye not watch with me one hour? Watch and pray that ye enter not into temptation." Seest thou He not only prays but also admonishes? "For the Spirit indeed is willing," He said, "but the flesh is weak." Now this He said by way of emptying their soul of vanity, and delivering them from pride, teaching them self-restraint, training them to practice moderation. Therefore the prayer which He wished to teach them, He Himself also offered, speaking after the manner of men, not according to His Godhead (for the divine nature is impassable) but according to His manhood. And He prayed as instructing us to pray, and even to seek deliverance from distress; but, if this be not permitted, then to acquiesce in what seems good to God. Therefore He said "Nevertheless not as I will but as Thou wilt:" not because He had one will and the Father another; but in order that He might instruct men even if they were in distress and trembling, even if danger came upon them, and they were unwilling to be torn from present life, nevertheless to postpone their own will to the will of God: even as Paul also when he had been instructed practically exhibited both these principles; for he besought that temptations might be removed from him, thus saying "For this thing I besought the Lord thrice:" and yet since it did not please God to remove it, he says "Wherefore I take pleasure in infirmities, in insults, in persecutions." But perhaps what I have said is not quite clear: therefore I will make it clearer. Paul incurred many dangers and prayed that he might not be exposed to them. Then he heard Christ saying, "my grace is sufficient for thee, for my strength is made perfect in weakness." As soon then as he saw what the will of God was, he in future submitted his will to God's will. By means of this prayer then Christ taught both these truths, that we should not plunge into dangers, but rather pray that we may not fall into them; but if they come upon us we should bear them bravely, and postpone our own will to the will of God. Knowing these things then let us pray that we may never enter into temptation: but if we do enter it let us beseech God to give us patience and courage, and let us honor His will in preference to every will of our own. For then we shall pass through this present life with safety, and shall obtain the blessings to come: which may we all receive by the favor and lovingkindness of our Lord Jesus Christ, with Whom be to the Father, together with the Holy Ghost, glory, might, honor, now and forever world without end. Amen.

HOMILY
ON THE PARALYTIC LET DOWN THROUGH THE ROOF:

AND CONCERNING THE EQUALITY OF THE DIVINE FATHER AND THE SON.

TRANSLATED BY
REV. W. R. W. STEPHENS, M.A.,
PREBENDARY OF CHICHESTER CATHEDRAL,
AND RECTOR OF WOOLBEDING,
SUSSEX.

HOMILY ON THE PARALYTIC LET DOWN THROUGH THE ROOF.

1. Having lately come across the incident of the paralytic who lay upon his bed beside the pool, we discovered a rich and large treasure, not by delving in the ground, but by diving into his heart: we found a treasure not containing silver and gold and precious stones, but endurance, and philosophy, and patience and much hope towards God, which is more valuable than any kind of jewel or source of wealth. For material riches are liable to the designs of robbers, and the tales of false accusers, and the violence of housebreakers, and the villainy of servants, and when they have escaped all these things, they often bring the greatest ruin upon those who possess them by exciting the eyes of the envious, and consequently breeding countless storms of trouble. But the spiritual riches escape all these occasions of mischief and are superior to all abuse of this kind, laughing to scorn both robbers, and housebreakers, and slanderers, and false accusers and death itself. For they are not parted from the possessor by death, but on the contrary the possession becomes then more especially secured to the owners, and they accompany them on their journey to the other world, and are transplanted with them to the future life, and become marvelous advocates of those with whom they depart hence, and render the judge propitious to them.

This wealth we found in great abundance stored in the soul of the paralytic. And you are witnesses who with great zeal drew up draughts of this treasure yet without exhausting it. For such is the nature of spiritual wealth; it resembles fountains of water, or rather exceeds their plenteousness, being most abundant when it has many to draw upon it. For when it enters into any man's soul it is not divided, not diminished, but coming in its entireness to each remains continually unconsumed, being incapable of ever failing which was just what took place at that time. For although so many have applied to the treasure, and all are drawing upon it as much as they can—but why do I speak of you, seeing that it has made countless persons rich from that time to the present day, and yet abides in its original perfection? Let us not then grow weary in having recourse to this source of spiritual wealth: but as far as possible let us now also draw forth draughts from it, and let us gaze upon our merciful Lord, gaze upon His patient servant. He had been thirty and eight years struggling with an incurable infirmity and was perpetually plagued by it, yet he did not repine, he did not utter a blasphemous word, he did not accuse his Maker but endured his calamity bravely and with much meekness. And whence is this manifest? you say: for Scripture has not told us anything clearly concerning his former life, but only that he had been thirty-eight years in his infirmity; it has not added a word to prove that he did not show discontent, or anger or petulance. And yet it has made this plain also, if anyone will pay careful attention to it, not looking at it curiously and carelessly. For when you hear that on the approach of Christ who was a stranger to him, and regarded merely as a man, he spoke to him with such great meekness, you may be able to perceive his former wisdom. For when Jesus said to him "Wilt thou be made whole?" he did not make the natural reply "thou sees me who have been this long time lying sick of the palsy, and dost thou ask me if I wish to be made whole? hast thou come to insult my distress, to reproach me and laugh me to scorn and make a mock of my calamity? He did not say or conceive anything of this kind but meekly replied "Yea Lord." Now if after thirty-eight years he was thus meek and gentle, when all the vigor and strength of his reasoning faculties was broken down, consider what he is likely to have been at the outset of his trouble. For be assured that invalids are not so hard to please at the beginning of their disorder, as they are after a long lapse of time: they become most intractable, most intolerable to all, when the malady is prolonged. But as he, after so many years, was so wise, and replied with so much forbearance, it is quite clear that during the previous time also he had been bearing that calamity with much thankfulness.

Considering these things then let us imitate the patience of our fellow-servant: for his paralysis is sufficient to brace up our souls: for no one can be so supine and indolent after having observed the magnitude of that calamity as not to endure bravely all evils which may befall him, even if they are more intolerable than all that were ever known. For not only his soundness but also his sickness has become a cause of the greatest benefit to us: for his cure has stimulated the souls of the hearers to speak the praise of the Lord, and his sickness and infirmity has encouraged you to patience, and urged you to match his zeal; or rather it has exhibited to you the lovingkindness of God. For the actual deliverance of the man to such a malady, and the protracted duration of his infirmity is a sign of the greatest care for his welfare. For as a gold refiner having cast a piece of gold into the furnace suffers it to be proved by the fire until such time as he sees it has become purer: even so God permits the souls of men to be tested by troubles until they become pure and transparent and have reaped much profit from this process of sifting: wherefore this is the greatest species of benefit.

2. Let us not then be disturbed, neither dismayed, when trials befall us. For if the gold refiner sees how long he ought to leave the piece of gold in the furnace, and when he ought to draw it out, and does not allow it to remain in the fire until it is destroyed and burnt up: much more does God understand this, and when He sees that we have become more pure, He releases us from our trials so that we may not be overthrown and cast down by the multiplication of our evils. Let us then not be repining, or faint-hearted, when some unexpected thing befalls us; but let us suffer Him who knows these things accurately, to prove our hearts by fire as long as He pleases: for He does this for a useful purpose and with a view to the profit of those who are tried.

On this account a certain wise man admonishes us saying "My Son, if thou come to serve the Lord prepare thy soul for temptation, set thy heart aright and constantly endure and make not haste in time of trouble;" "yield to Him" he says, "in all things," for He knows exactly when it is right to pluck us out of the furnace of evil. We ought therefore everywhere to yield to Him and always to give thanks, and to bear all things contentedly, whether He bestows benefits or chastisement upon us, for this also is a species of benefit. For the physician, not only when he bathes and nourishes the patient and conducts him into pleasant gardens, but also when he uses cautery and the knife, is a physician all the same: and a father not only when he caresses his son, but also when he expels him from his house, and when he chides and scourges him, is a father all the same, no less than when he praises him.

Knowing therefore that God is more tenderly loving than all physicians, do not enquire too curiously concerning His treatment nor demand an account of it from Him, but whether He is pleased to let us go free or whether He punishes, let us offer ourselves for either alike; for He seeks by means of each to lead us back to health, and to communion with Himself, and He knows our several needs, and what is expedient for each one, and how and in what manner we ought to be saved, and along that path He leads us. Let us then follow whithersoever He bids us and let us not too carefully consider whether He commands us to go by a smooth and easy path, or by a difficult and rugged one: as in the case of this paralytic. It was one species of benefit indeed that his soul should be purged by the long duration of his suffering, being delivered to the fiery trial of affliction as to a kind of furnace; but it was another benefit no less than this that God was present with him in the midst of the trials, and afforded him great consolation. He it was who strengthened him, and upheld him, and stretched forth a hand to him, and suffered him not to fall. But when you hear that it was God Himself do not deprive the paralytic of his need of praise, neither him nor any other man who is tried and yet steadfastly endures. For even if we be infinitely wise, even if we are mightier and stronger than all men, yet in the absence of His grace we shall not be able to withstand even the most ordinary temptation. And why do I speak of such insignificant and abject beings as we are? For even if one were a Paul, or a Peter, or a James, or a John, yet if he should be deprived of the divine help he would easily be put to shame, overthrown, and laid prostrate. And on behalf of these I will read you the words of Christ Himself: for He saith to Peter "Behold

Satan hath asked to have you that he may sift you as wheat, but I have prayed for thee that thy faith fail not." What is the meaning of "sift"? to turn and twist, and shake and stir and shatter, and worry, which is what takes place in the case of things which are winnowed: but I he says have restrained him, knowing that you are not able to endure the trial, for the expression "that thy faith fail not" is the utterance of one who signifies that if he had permitted it his faith would have failed. Now if Peter who was such a fervent lover of Christ and exposed his life for Him countless times and sprang into the foremost rank in the Apostolic band, and was pronounced blessed by his Master, and called Peter on this account because he kept a firm and inflexible hold of the faith, would have been carried away and fallen from profession if Christ had permitted the devil to try him as much as he desired, what other man will be able to stand, apart from His help? Therefore also Paul saith "But God is faithful, who will not suffer you to be tempted above that ye are able, but will with the temptation also make the way of escape that ye may be able to bear it." For not only does He say that He does not suffer a trial to be inflicted beyond our strength, but even in that which is proportioned to our strength He is present carrying us through it, and bracing us up, if only we ourselves first of all contribute the means which are at our disposal, such as zeal, hope in Him, thanksgiving, endurance, patience. For not only in the dangers which are beyond our strength, but in those which are proportioned to it, we need the divine assistance, if we are to make a brave stand; for elsewhere also it is said "even as the sufferings of Christ abound to us, even so our comfort also abounded through Christ, that we may be able to comfort those who are in any trouble, by the comfort wherewith we ourselves are comforted of God." So then he who comforted this man is the same who permitted the trial to be inflicted upon him. And now observe after the cure what tenderness He displays. For He did not leave him and depart, but having found him in the temple he saith "behold! thou art made whole; sin no more lest some worse thing happen unto thee." For had He permitted the punishment because He hated him He would not have released him, He would not have provided for his future safety: but the expression "lest some worse thing happen unto thee" is the utterance of one who would check coming evils beforehand. He put an end to the disease but did not put an end to the struggle: He expelled the infirmity but did not expel the dread of it, so that the benefit which had been wrought might remain unmoved. This is the part of a tender-hearted physician, not only to put an end to present pains, but to provide for future security, which also Christ did, bracing up his soul by the recollection of past events. For seeing that when the things which distress us have departed, the recollection of them oftentimes departs with them, He wishing it to abide continually, saith "sin no more lest some worse thing happen unto thee."

3. Moreover it is possible to discern His forethought and consideration not only from this, but also from that which seems to be a rebuke. For He did not make a public exposure of his sins, but yet He told him that he suffered what he did suffer on account of his sins, but what those sins were He did not disclose; nor did He say "thou hast sinned" or "thou hast transgressed," but He indicated the fact by one simple utterance "sin no more;" and having said so much as just to remind him of it He put him more on the alert against future events, and at the

same time He made manifest to us all his patience and courage and wisdom, having reduced him to the necessity of publicly lamenting his calamity, and having displayed his own earnestness on the man's behalf, "for while I am coming," he says, "another stepped down before me:" yet he did not publicly expose his sins. For just as we ourselves desire to draw a veil over our sins even so does God much more than we: on this account He wrought the cure in the presence of all, but He gives the exhortation or the advice privately. For He never makes a public display of our sins, except at any time He sees men insensible to them. For when He says "ye saw me hungry and fed me not: and thirsty and gave me no drink," He speaks thus at the present time in order that we may not hear these words in time to come. He threatens, He exposes us in this world, that He may not have to expose us in the other: even as He threatened to overthrow the city of the Ninevites for the very reason that He might not overthrow it. For if He wished to publish our sins He would not announce beforehand that He would publish them: but as it is He does make this announcement in order that being sobered by the fear of exposure, if not also by the fear of punishment we may purge ourselves from them all. This also is what takes place in the case of baptism: for He conducts the man to the pool of water without disclosing his sins to any one; yet He publicly presents the boon and makes it manifest to all, while the sins of the man are known to no one save God Himself and him who receives the forgiveness of them. This also was what took place in the case of this paralytic, He makes the reproof without the presence of witnesses, or rather the utterance is not merely a reproof but also a justification; He justifies Himself as it were for evil-entreating him so long, telling him and proving to him that it was not without cause and purpose that He had suffered him to be so long afflicted, for He reminded him of his sins, and declared the cause of his infirmity. "For having found him," we read, "in the temple, He said unto him, sin no more lest some worse thing happen unto thee."

And now since we have derived so much profit from the account of the former paralytic let us turn to the other who is presented to us in St. Matthew's Gospel. For in the case of mines where any one happens to find a piece of gold he makes a further excavation again in the same place: and I know that many of those who read without care imagine that one and the same paralytic is presented by the four evangelists: but it is not so. Therefore you must be on the alert and pay careful attention to the matter. For the question is not concerned with ordinary matters, and this discourse when it has received its proper solution will be serviceable against both Greeks and Jews and many of the heretics. For thus all find fault with the evangelists as being at strife and variance: yet this is not the fact, Heaven forbid! but although the outward appearance is different, the grace of the Spirit which works upon the soul of each is one, and where the grace of the Spirit is, there is love, joy, and peace; and there war and disputation, strife and contention are not. How then shall we make it clear that this paralytic is not the same as the other, but a different man? By many tokens, both of place and time, and season, and day, and from the manner of the cure, and the coming of the physician and the loneliness of the man who was healed. And what of this? someone will say: for have not many of the evangelists given diverse accounts of other signs? Yes, but it is one thing to make statements which are diverse, and another, statements which are contradictory; for the former causes no discord or strife: but that which is now presented to us is a strong case of contradiction unless it be proved that the paralytic at the pool was a different man from him who is described by the other three evangelists. Now that you may understand what is the difference between statements which are diverse and contradictory, one of the evangelists has stated that Christ carried the cross, another that Simon the Cyrenian carried it: but this causes no contradiction or strife. "And how," you say, "is there no contradiction between the statements that he carried and did not carry?" Because both took place. When they went out of the Prætorium Christ was carrying it: but as they proceeded Simon took it from Him and bore it. Again in the case of the robbers, one says that the two blasphemed: another that one of them checked him who was reviling the Lord. Yet in this again there is no contradiction: because here also both things took place, and at the beginning both the men behaved ill: but afterwards when signs occurred, when the earth shook and the rocks were rent, and the sun was darkened, one of them was converted, and became more chastened, and recognized the crucified one and acknowledged his kingdom. For to prevent your supposing that this took place by some constraining force of one impelling him from within, and to remove your perplexity, he exhibits the man to you on the cross while he is still retaining his former wickedness in order that you may perceive that his conversion was effected from within and out of his own heart assisted by the grace of God and so he became a better man.

4. And it is possible to collect many other instances of this kind from the Gospels, which seem to

have a suspicion of contradiction, where there is no real contradiction, the truth being that some incidents have been related by this writer, others by that; or if not occurring at the same hour one author has related the earlier event, another the later; but in the present case there is nothing of this kind, but the multitude of the evidences which I have mentioned proves to those who pay any attention whatever to the matter, that the paralytic was not the same man in both instances. And this would be no slight proof to demonstrate that the evangelists were in harmony with each other and not at variance. For if it were the same man the discord is great between the two accounts: but if it be a different one all material for dispute has been destroyed.

Well then let me now state the actual reasons why I affirm that this man is not the same as that. What are they? The one is cured in Jerusalem, the other in Capernaum; the one by the pool of water, the other in some house; there is the evidence from place: the former during the festival: there is the evidence from the special season: the former had been thirty and eight years suffering from infirmity: concerning the other the evangelist relates nothing of that kind: there is the evidence from time: the former was cured on the Sabbath: there is the evidence from the day: for had this man also been cured on the Sabbath Matthew would not have passed by the fact in silence nor would the Jews who were present have held their peace: for they who found fault for some other reason even when a man was not cured on the Sabbath would have been yet more violent in their accusation against Christ if they had got an additional handle from the argument of the special day. Moreover this man was brought to Christ: to the other Christ

Himself came, and there was no man to assist him. "Lord," said he, "I have no man:" whereas this man had many who came to his aid, who also let him down through the roof. And He healed the body of the other man before his soul: for after he had cured the paralysis He then said "Behold thou art made whole, sin no more:" but not so in this case, but after He had healed his soul, for He said to him "Son be of good cheer thy sins be forgiven thee," He then cured his paralysis. That this man then is not the same as the other has been clearly demonstrated by these proofs, but it now remains for us to turn to the beginning of the narrative and see how Christ cured the one and the other, and why differently in each case: why the one on the Sabbath and the other not on the Sabbath, why He came Himself to the one but waited for the other to be brought to Him, why He healed the body of the one and the soul of the other first. For He does not these things without consideration and purpose seeing that He is wise and prudent. Let us then give our attention and observe Him as He performs the cure. For if in the case of physicians when they use the knife or cautery or operate in any other way upon a maimed and crippled patient, and cut off a limb, many persons crowd round the invalid and the physician who is doing these things, much more ought we to act thus in this case, in proportion as the physician is greater and the malady more severe, being one which cannot be corrected by human art, but only by divine grace. And in the former case we have to see the skin being cut, and matter discharging, and gore set in motion, and to endure much discomfort produced by the spectacle, and great pain and sorrow not merely from the sight of the wounds, but also from the suffering undergone by those who are subjected to this burning or cutting: for no one is so stony-hearted as to stand by those who are suffering these things, and hear them shrieking, without being himself overcome and agitated, and experiencing much depression of spirit; but yet we undergo all this owing to our desire to witness the operation. But in this case nothing of that kind has to be seen, no application of fire, no plunging in of an instrument, no flowing of blood, no pain or shrieking of the patient; and the reason of this is, the wisdom of the healer, which needs none of these external aids, but is absolutely self-sufficient. For it is enough that He merely utters a command and all distress ceases. And the wonder is not only that He effects the cure with so much ease, but also without pain, causing no trouble to those who are being healed.

Seeing then that the marvel is greater and the cure more important, and the pleasure afforded to the spectators unalloyed by any kind of sorrow, let us now carefully contemplate Christ in the act of healing. "And He entered into a boat and crossed over and came into His own city: and behold they brought to him a man sick of the palsy lying on a bed: and Jesus seeing their faith said unto the sick of the palsy "Son! be of good cheer: thy sins are forgiven." Now they were inferior to the centurion in respect of their faith, but superior to the impotent man by the pool. For the former neither invited the physician nor brought the sick man to the physician; but approached Him as God and said, "Speak the word only and my servant shall be healed." Now these men did not invite the physician to the house, and so far they are on an equality with the centurion: but they brought the sick man to the physician and so far they are inferior, because they did not say "speak the word only." Yet they are far better than the man lying by the pool. For he said "Lord I have no man when the water is troubled to put me into the pool:" but these men knew that Christ had no need either of water, or pool, or anything else of that kind: nevertheless Christ not only released the servant of the centurion but the other two men also from their maladies, and did not say: "because thou hast proffered a smaller degree of faith the cure which thou receives shall be in proportion;" but He dismissed the man who displayed the greater faith with eulogy and honor, saying "I have not found so great faith, no, not in Israel." On the man who exhibited less faith than this one he bestowed no praise yet He did not deprive him of a cure, no! not even him who displayed no faith at all. But just as physicians when curing the same disorder receive from some person a hundred gold pieces, from others half, from others less and from some nothing at all: even so Christ received from the centurion a large and unspeakable degree of faith, but from this man less and from the other not even an ordinary amount, and yet He healed them all. For what reason then did He deem the man who made no deposit of faith worthy of the benefit? Because his failure to exhibit faith was not owing to indolence, or to insensibility of soul, but to ignorance of Christ and having never heard any miracle in which He was concerned either small or great. On this account therefore the man obtained indulgence: which in fact the evangelist obscurely intimates when he says, "for he wist not who it was," but he only recognized Him by sight when he lighted upon Him the second time.

5. There are indeed some who say that this man was healed merely because they who brought him believed; but this is not the fact. For "when He saw their faith" refers not merely to those who brought the man but also to the man who was brought. Why so? "Is not one

man healed," you say, "because another has believed?" For my part I do not think so unless owing to immaturity of age or excessive infirmity he is in some way incapable of believing. How then was it you say that in the case of the woman of Canaan the mother believed but the daughter was cured? and how was it that the servant of the centurion who believed rose from the bed of sickness and was preserved. Because the sick persons themselves were not able to believe. Hear then what the woman of Canaan says: "My daughter is grievously vexed with a devil and sometimes she falleth into the water and sometimes into the fire:" now how could she believe whose mind was darkened and possessed by a devil, and was never able to control herself, not in her sound senses? As then in the case of the woman of Canaan so also in the case of the centurion; his servant lay ill in the house, not knowing Christ, himself, nor who He was. How then was he to believe in one who was unknown to him, and of whom he had never yet obtained any experience? But in the case before us we cannot say this: for the paralytic believed. Whence is this manifest? From the very manner of his approach to Christ. For do not attend simply to the statement that they let the man down through the roof: but consider how great a matter it is for a sick man to have the fortitude to undergo this. For you are surely aware that invalids are so faint-hearted and difficult to please as often to decline the treatment administered to them on their sick bed, and to prefer bearing the pain which arises from their maladies to undergoing the annoyance caused by the remedies. But this man had the fortitude to go outside the house, and to be carried into the midst of the marketplace, and to exhibit himself in the presence of a crowd. And it is the habit of sick folk to die under their disorder rather than disclose their personal calamities. This sick man however did not act thus, but when he saw that the place of assembly was filled, the approaches blocked, the haven of refuge obstructed, he submitted to be let down through the roof. So ready in contrivance is desire, so rich in resource is love. "For he also that seeks finds, and to him that knocks it shall be opened." The man did not say to his friends "What is the meaning of this? why make this ado? why push on? Let us wait until the house is cleared and the assembly is dissolved: the crowds will withdraw, we shall then be able to approach him privately and confer about these matters. Why should you expose my misfortunes in the midst of all the spectators, and let me down from the roof-top, and behave in an unseemly manner?" That man said none of these things either to himself or to his bearers, but regarded it as an honor to have so many persons made witnesses of his cure. And not from this circumstance only was it possible to discern his faith but also from the actual words of Christ. For after he had been let down and presented Christ said to him, "Son! be of good cheer, thy sins are forgiven thee." And when he heard these words he was not indignant, he did not complain, he did not say to the physician "What mean you by this? I came to be healed of one thing and you heal another. This is an excuse and a pretense and a screen of incompetence. Do you forgive sins which are invisible?" He neither spoke nor thought any of these things, but waited, allowing the physician to adopt the method of healing which He desired. For this reason also Christ did not go to him, but waited for him to come, that He might exhibit his faith to all. For could He not have made the entrance easy? But He did none of these things; in order that He might exhibit the man's zeal and fervent faith to all. For as He went to the man who had been suffering thirty and eight years because he had no one to aid him, so did He wait for this man to come to him because he had many friends that He might make his faith manifest by the man being brought to Him, and inform us of the other man's loneliness by going to him, and disclose the earnestness of the one and the patience of the other to all and especially to those who were present. For some envious and misanthropical Jews were accustomed to grudge the benefits done to their neighbors and to find fault with His miracles, sometimes on account of the special season, saying that He healed on the sabbath day; sometimes on account of the life of those to whom the benefit was done, saying "if this man were a prophet He would have known who the woman was who touched Him:" not knowing that it is the special mark of a physician to associate with the infirm and to be constantly seen by the side of the sick, not to avoid them, or hurry from their presence—which in fact was what He expressly said to those murmurers; "They that are whole have no need of a physician but they that are sick." Therefore in order to prevent their making the same accusations again He proves first of all that they who come to Him are deserving of a cure on account of the faith which they exhibit. For this reason He exhibited the loneliness of one man, and the fervent faith and zeal of the other: for this reason He healed the one on the Sabbath, the other not on the Sabbath: in order that when you see them accusing and rebuking Christ on another day you may understand that they accused him on the former occasion also not because of their respect for the law, but because they could not contain their own malice. But why did He not first address Himself to the cure of the paralytic, but said, "Son! be of good cheer, thy sins are forgiven thee?" He did this very wisely. For it is a habit with physicians to destroy the originating cause of the malady before they remove the malady itself. Often for example when the eyes are distressed by some evil humor and corrupt discharge, the physician, abandoning any treatment of the disordered vision, turns his attention to the head, where the root and origin of the infirmity is: even so did Christ act: He represses first of all the source of the evil. For the source and root and mother of all evil is the nature of sin. This it is which enervates our bodies: this it is which brings on disease: therefore also on this occasion He said, "Son! be of good cheer, thy sins are forgiven thee." And on the other He said, "Behold! thou art made whole, sin no more lest some worse thing happen unto thee," intimating to both that these maladies were the offspring of sin. And in the beginning and outset of the word disease as the consequence of sin attacked the body of Cain. For after the murder of his brother, after that act of wickedness, his body was subject to palsy. For trembling is the same thing as palsy. For when the strength which regulates a living creature becomes weakened, being no longer able to support all the limbs, it deprives them of their natural power of direction and then having become unstrung they tremble and turn giddy.

6. Paul also demonstrated this: for when he was reproaching the Corinthians with a certain sin he said, "For this cause many are weak and sickly among you." Therefore also Christ first removes the cause of the evil, and having said "Son! be of good cheer, thy sins are forgiven thee," He uplifts the spirit and rouses the downcast soul: for the speech became an efficient cause and having entered into the conscience it laid hold of the

soul itself and cast out of it all distress. For nothing creates pleasure and affords confidence so much as freedom from self-reproach. For where remission of sins is there is sonship. Even so at least we are not able to call God Father until we have washed away our sins in the pool of the sacred water. It is when we have come up from thence, having put off that evil load, that we say, "Our Father which art in Heaven." But in the case of the man who was infirm thirty and eight years why did He not act thus, but cured his body first of all? Because by that long period of time his sins had been exhausted: for the magnitude of a trial can lighten the load of sins; as indeed we read was the case with Lazarus, that he received his evil things in full, and thereupon was comforted: and again in another place we read, "Comfort ye my people, say ye to the heart of Jerusalem, that she hath received of the Lord's hand double for her sins." And again the prophet says, "O Lord give us peace, for thou hast requited all things to us," indicating that penalties and punishments work forgiveness of sins; and this we might prove from many passages. It seems to me then that the reason why He said nothing to that man about remission of sins, but only secured him against the future, was because the penalty for his sins had been already worked out by the long duration of his sickness: or if this was not the reason, it was because he had not yet attained any high degree of belief concerning Christ that the Lord first addressed Himself to the lesser need, and one which was manifest and obvious, the health of the body; but in the case of the other man He did not act thus, but inasmuch as this man had more faith, and a loftier soul, He spoke to him first of all concerning the more dangerous disease: with the additional object of exhibiting his equality of rank with the Father. For just as in the former case He healed on the Sabbath day because He wished to lead men away from the Jewish mode of observing it, and to take occasion from their reproaches to prove Himself equal with the Father: even so in this instance also, knowing beforehand what they were going to say, He uttered these words that He might use them as a starting-point and a pretext for proving His equality of rank with the Father. For it is one thing when no one brings an accusation or charge to enter spontaneously upon a discourse about these things, and quite another when other persons give occasion for it, to set about the same work in the order and shape of a defense. For the nature of the former demonstration was a stumbling block to the hearers: but the other was less offensive, and more acceptable, and everywhere we see Him doing this, and manifesting His equality not so much by words as by deeds. This at any rate is what the Evangelist implied when he said that the Jews persecuted Jesus not only because He broke the Sabbath but also because He said that God was His Father, making Himself equal with God, which is a far greater thing, for He effected this by the demonstration of His deeds. How then do the envious and wicked act, and those who seek to find a handle in every direction? "Why does this man blaspheme?" they say for "no man can forgive sins save God alone." As they persecuted Him there because He broke the Sabbath, and took occasion from their reproaches to declare His equality with the Father in the form of a defense, saying "my Father worketh hitherto and I work," so here also starting from the accusations which they make He proves from these His exact likeness to the Father. For what was it they said? "No man can forgive sins save God alone."

Inasmuch then as they themselves laid down this definition, they themselves introduced the rule, they themselves declared the law, He proceeds to entangle them by means of their own words. "You have confessed," He says, "that forgiveness of sins is an attribute of God alone: my equality therefore is unquestionable." And it is not these men only who declare this but also the prophet thus saying: "who is God as thou?" and then, indicating His special attribute he adds "taking away iniquity and passing over unrighteousness." If then anyone else appears thus doing the same thing He also is God, God even as that one is God. But let us observe how Christ argues with them, how meekly and gently, and with all tenderness. "And behold some of the scribes said within themselves: this man blasphemes." They did not utter the word, they did not proclaim it through the tongue but reasoned in the secret recesses of their heart. How then did Christ act? He made public their secret thoughts before the demonstration which was concerned with the cure of the paralytic's body, wishing to prove to them the power of His Godhead. For that it is an attribute of God alone, a sign of His deity to shew the secrets of His mind, the Scripture saith "Thou alone knowest men's hearts." Seest thou that this word "alone," is not used with a view of contrasting the Son with the Father. For if the Father alone knows the heart, how does the Son know the secrets of the mind? "For He Himself" it is said, "knew what was in man;" and Paul when proving that the knowledge of secret things is a special attribute of God says, "and He that searches the heart," shewing that this expression is equivalent to the appellation "God." For just as when I say "He who causes rain said," I signify none other than God by mentioning the deed, since it is one which belongs to Him alone: and when I say "He who maketh the sun to rise," without adding the word God, I yet signify Him by mentioning the deed: even so when Paul said "He who searches the hearts," he proved that to search the heart is an attribute of God alone. For if this expression had not been of equal force with the name "God" for pointing out Him who was signified, he would not have used it absolutely and by itself. For if the power were shared by Him in common with some created being, we should not have known who was signified, the community of power causing confusion in the mind of the hearers. Inasmuch then as this appears to be a special attribute of the Father, and yet is manifested of the Son whose equality becomes thence unquestionable, therefore we read "why think ye evil in your hearts? For whether is easier: to say: Thy sins are forgiven thee or to say arise and walk?"

    7. See moreover, He makes a second proof of His power of forgiving sins. For to forgive sins is a very much greater act than to heal the body, greater in proportion as the soul is greater than the body. For as paralysis is a disease of the body, even so sin is a disease of the soul: but although this is the greater it is not palpable: whereas the other although it be less is manifest. Since then He is about to use the less for a demonstration of the greater proving that He acted thus on account of their weakness, and by way of condescension to their feeble condition He says "whether is easier? to say thy sins are forgiven thee or to say arise and walk?" For what reason then should He address Himself to the lesser act on their account? Because that which is manifest presents the proof in a more distinct form. Therefore He did not enable the man to rise until He had said to them "But that ye may know

that the Son of man hath power on earth to forgive sins, (then saith He to the sick of the palsy) arise and walk:" as if He had said: forgiveness of sins is indeed a greater sign: but for your sakes I add the less also since this seems to you to be a proof of the other. For as in another case when He praised the centurion for saying "speak the word only and my servant shall be healed: for I also say to this man go and he goes and to the other come and he comes," He confirmed his opinion by the eulogy which He pronounced: and again when He reproved the Jews for finding fault with Him on the Sabbath day saying that He transgressed the law, He proved that He had authority to alter laws: even so in this instance also when some said "He maketh Himself equal with God by promising that which belongs only to the Father," He having upbraided and accused them and proved by His deeds that He did not blaspheme supplied us with indisputable evidence that He could do the same things as the Father who begat Him. Observe at least the manner in which He pleases to establish the fact that what belongs to the Father only, belongs also to Himself: for He did not simply enable the paralytic to get up, but also said "but that ye may know that the Son of man hath power on earth to forgive sins:" thus it was his endeavor and earnest desire to prove above all things that He had the same authority as the Father.

8. Let us then carefully hold fast all these things, both those which were spoken yesterday and the day before that, and let us beseech God that they may abide immovably in our heart, and let us contribute zeal on our side, and constantly meet in this place. For in this way we shall preserve the truths which have been formerly spoken, and we shall add others to our store; and if any of them slip from our memory through the lapse of time we

shall easily be able to recover them by the aid of continual teaching. And not only will the doctrines abide sound and uncorrupt, but our course of life will have the benefit of much diligent care and we shall be able to pass through this present state of existence with pleasure and cheerfulness. For whatever kind of suffering is oppressing our soul when we come here will easily be got rid of seeing that now also Christ is present, and he who approaches Him with faith will readily receive healing from Him. Suppose someone is struggling with perpetual poverty, and at a loss for necessary food, and often goes to bed hungry, if he has come in here, and heard Paul saying that he passed his time in hunger and thirst and nakedness, and that he experienced this not on one or two or three days, but constantly (this at least is what he indicates when he says "up to the present hour we both hunger and thirst and are naked"), he will receive ample consolation, learning by means of these words that God has not permitted him to be in poverty because He hated him or abandoned him: for if this were the effect of hatred, He would not have permitted it in the case of Paul who was of all men especially dear to Him: but He permitted it out of His tender love and providential care, and by way of conducting him to a higher degree of spiritual wisdom. Has some other man a body which is beset with disease and countless sufferings? The condition of these paralytics may be an ample source of consolation and besides these the blessed and brave disciple of Paul who was continually suffering from disorders, and never had any respite from prolonged infirmity, even as Paul also said "Use a little wine for thy stomach's sake and thine often infirmities," where he does not speak merely of infirmities as such. Or another having been subjected to false accusation has acquired a bad reputation with the public, and this is continually vexing and gnawing his soul: he enters this place and hears "Blessed are ye when men shall reproach you and say all manner of evil against you falsely: rejoice ye and be exceeding glad for great is your reward in Heaven:" then he will lay aside all despondency and receive every kind of pleasure: for it is written "leap for joy, and be exceeding glad when men cast out your name as evil." In this manner then God comforts those that are evil spoken of, and them that speak evil He puts in fear after another manner saying, "every evil word which men shall speak they shall give an account thereof whether it be good or evil."

Another perhaps has lost a little daughter or a son, or one of his kinsfolk, and he also having come here listens to Paul groaning over this present life and longing to see that which is to come, and oppressed by his sojourn in this world, and he will go away with a sufficient remedy for his grief when he has heard him say "Now concerning them that are asleep I would not have you ignorant brethren that ye sorrow not even as others who have no hope." He did not say concerning the dying, but "concerning them that are asleep" proving that death is a sleep. As then if we see anyone sleeping we are not disturbed or distressed, expecting that he will certainly get up: even so when we see anyone dead, let us not be disturbed or dejected for this also is a sleep, a longer one indeed, but still a sleep. By giving it the name of slumber He comforted the mourners and overthrew the accusation of the unbelievers. If you mourn immoderately over him who has departed, you will be like that unbeliever who has no hope of a resurrection. He indeed does well to mourn, inasmuch as he cannot exercise any spiritual wisdom concerning things to come: but thou who hast received such strong proofs concerning the future life, why dost thou sink into the same weakness with him? Therefore it is written "now concerning them that are asleep we would not have you ignorant that ye sorrow not even as others who have no hope."

And not only from the New Testament but from the Old also it is possible to receive abundant consolation. For when you hear of Job after the loss of his property, after the destruction of his herds, after the loss not of one, or two, or three, but of a whole troop of sons in the very flower of their age, after the great excellence of soul which he displayed, even if thou art the weakest of men, thou wilt easily be able to repent and regain thy courage. For thou, O man, hast constantly attended thy sick son, and hast seen him laid upon the bed, and hast heard him uttering his last words, and stood beside him whilst he was drawing his last breath and hast closed his eyes, and shut his mouth: but he was not present at the death struggle of his sons, he did not see them breathing their last gasp, but the house became the common grave of them all, and on the same table brains and blood were poured forth, and pieces of wood and tiles, and dust, and fragments of flesh, and all these things were mingled together in like manner. Nevertheless after such great calamities of this kind he was not petulant, but what does he say—"The Lord gave, the Lord hath taken away; as it seemed good unto the Lord even so has it come to pass, blessed be the name of the Lord forever." Let this speech be our utterance also over each event which befalls us; whether it be loss of property, or infirmity of body, or insult, or false accusation or any other form of evil incident to mankind, let us say these words "The Lord gave, the Lord hath taken away; as it seemed good to the Lord so has it come to pass; blessed be the name of the Lord forever." If we practice this spiritual wisdom, we shall never experience any evil, even if we undergo countless sufferings, but the gain will be greater than the loss, the good will exceed the evil: by these words thou wilt cause God to be merciful unto thee, and wilt defend thyself against the tyranny of Satan. For as soon as thy tongue has uttered these words forthwith the Devil hastens from thee: and when he has hastened away, the cloud of dejection also is dispelled and the thoughts which afflict us take to flight, hurrying off in company with him, and in addition to all this thou wilt win all manner of blessings both here and in Heaven. And you have a convincing example in the case of Job, and of the Apostle, who having for God's sake despised the troubles of this world, obtained the everlasting blessings. Let us then be trustful and in all things which befall us let us rejoice and give thanks to the merciful God, that we may pass through this present life with serenity, and obtain the blessings to come, by the grace and lovingkindness of our Lord Jesus Christ to whom be glory, honor and might always, now and ever, world without end. Amen.

HOMILY
TO THOSE WHO HAD NOT ATTENDED THE ASSEMBLY:

AND ON THE APOSTOLIC SAYING, "IF THINE ENEMY HUNGER, FEED HIM, ETC. (ROM. XII. 20),

AND CONCERNING RESENTMENT OF INJURIES.

TRANSLATED BY
REV. W. R. W. STEPHENS, M.A.,
PREBENDARY OF CHICHESTER CATHEDRAL, AND RECTOR OF WOOLBEDING, SUSSEX.

TO THOSE WHO HAD NOT ATTENDED THE ASSEMBLY.

To those who had not attended the assembly; on the apostolic saying, "If thy enemy hunger feed him," and concerning resentment of injuries.

1. I did no good as it seems by the prolonged discourse which I lately addressed to you with a view to kindling your zeal for the assemblies here: for again our Church is destitute of her children. Wherefore also I am again compelled to seem vexatious and burdensome, reproving those who are present, and finding fault with those who have been left behind: with them because they have not put away their sloth, and with you because you have not given a helping hand to the salvation of your brethren. I am compelled to seem burdensome and vexatious, not on behalf of myself, or my own possessions, but on your behalf and for your salvation, which is more precious to me than anything else. Let him who pleases take it in bad part, and call me insolent and impudent, yet will I not cease continually annoying him for the same purpose; for nothing is better for me than this kind of impudence. For it may be, it may be, that this at least if nothing else, will put you to shame, and that to avoid being perpetually importuned concerning the same things, ye will take part in the tender care of your brethren. For what profit is there to me in praise when I do not see you making advances in virtue? and what harm is there from the silence of the hearers when I behold your piety increasing? For the praise of the speaker does not consist in applause, but in the zeal of the hearers for godliness: not in noise made just at the time of hearing,

but in lasting earnestness. As soon as applause has issued from the lips it is dispersed in air and perishes; but the moral improvement of the hearers brings an imperishable and immortal reward both to him who speaks and to them who obey. The praise of your cheers makes the speaker illustrious here, but the piety of your soul affords the teacher much confidence before the judgment-seat of Christ. Wherefore if anyone loves the speaker, let him not desire the applause but the profit of the hearers. To neglect our brethren is no ordinary wrong, but one which brings extreme punishment, and an inexorable penalty. And the case of the man who buried the talent proves this: he was not reproached at least on account of his own life: for as regarded the deposit itself he did not turn out a bad man, since he restored it intact: nevertheless he did turn out a bad man as regarded his management of the deposit. For he did not double that which was entrusted to him; and so was punished. Whence it is manifest that even if we are earnest and well trained, and have much zeal about hearing the holy scriptures this does not suffice for our salvation. For the deposit must be doubled, and it becomes doubled when together with our own salvation we undertake to make some provision for the good of others. For the man in the parable said "Lo! there thou hast that is thine:" but this did not serve him for a defense: for it was said to him "thou ought to have put the money to the exchangers."

And observe I pray how easy the commands of the Master are: for men indeed make those who lend out capital sums at interest answerable for recalling them; "you have made the deposit," one says, "you must call it in: I have no concern with the man who has received it." But God does not act thus; He only commands us to make the deposit and does not render us liable for the recall. For the speaker has the power of advising, not of persuading. Therefore he says: "I make thee answerable for depositing only, and not for the recall." What can be easier than this? And yet the servant called the master hard, who was thus gentle and merciful. For such is the wont of the ungrateful and indolent; they always try to shift the blame of their offences from themselves to their master. And therefore the man was thrust out with torture and bonds into the outer darkness. And lest we should suffer this penalty let us deposit our teaching with the brethren, whether they be persuaded by it, or not. For if they be persuaded they will profit both themselves and us: and if they are not, they involve themselves indeed in inevitable punishment, but will not be able to do us the slightest injury. For we have done our part, by giving them advice: but if they do not listen to it no harm will result to us from that. For blame would attach to us not for failing to persuade, but for failing to advise: and after prolonged and continual exhortation and counsel they and not we, have to reckon henceforth with God.

  I have been anxious at any rate to know clearly, whether you continue to exhort your brethren, and if they remain all the time in the same condition of indolence: otherwise I would never have given you any trouble: as it is, I have fears that they may remain uncorrected in consequence of your neglect and indifference. For it is impossible that a man who continually has the benefit of exhortation and instruction should not become better and more diligent. The proverb which I am about to cite is certainly a common one, nevertheless it confirms this very truth. For "a perpetual dropping of water" it says, "wears a rock," yet what is softer than water? and what is harder than a rock? Nevertheless perpetual action conquers nature: and if it conquers nature much more will it be able to prevail over the human will. Christianity is no child's play, my beloved: no matter of secondary importance. I am continually saying these things, and yet I affect nothing.

2. How am I distressed, think you, when I call to mind that on the festival days the multitudes assembled resemble the broad expanse of the sea, but now not even the smallest part of that multitude is gathered together here? Where are they now who oppress us with their presence on the feast days? I look for them, and am grieved on their account when I mark what a multitude are perishing of those who are in the way of salvation, how large a loss of brethren I sustain, how few are reached by the things which concern salvation, and how the greater part of the body of the Church is like a dead and motionless carcass. "And what concern is that to us?" you say. The greatest possible concern if you pay no attention to your brethren, if you do not exhort and advise, if you put no constraint on them, and do not forcibly drag them hither, and lead them away out of their deep indolence. For that one ought not to be useful to himself alone, but also to many others, Christ declared plainly, when He called us salt, and leaven, and light: for these things are useful and profitable to others. For a lamp does not shine for itself, but for those who are sitting in darkness: and thou art a lamp not that thou mayest enjoy the light by thyself, but that thou mayest bring back yonder man who has gone astray. For what profit is a lamp if it does not give light to him who sits in darkness? and what profit is a Christian when he benefits no one, neither leads any one back to virtue? Again salt is not an

astringent to itself but braces up those parts of the body which have decayed and prevents them from falling to pieces and perishing. Even so do thou, since God has appointed thee to be spiritual salt, bind and brace up the decayed members, that is the indolent and sordid brethren, and having rescued them from their indolence as from some form of corruption, unite them to the rest of the body of the Church. And this is the reason why He called you leaven: for leaven also does not leaven itself, but, little though it is, it affects the whole lump however big it may be. So also do ye: although ye are few in number, yet be ye many and powerful in faith, and in zeal towards God. As then the leaven is not weak on account of its littleness, but prevails owing to its inherent heat, and the force of its natural quality, so ye also will be able to bring back a far larger number than yourselves, if you will, to the same degree of zeal as your own. Now if they make the summer season their excuse: for I hear of their saying things of this kind, "the present stifling heat is excessive, the scorching sun is intolerable, we cannot bear being trampled and crushed in the crowd, and to be steaming all over with perspiration and oppressed by the heat and confined space:" I am ashamed of them, believe me: for such excuses are womanish: indeed even in their case who have softer bodies, and a weaker nature, such pretexts do not suffice for justification. Nevertheless, even if it seems a disgrace to make a reply to a defense of this kind, yet is it necessary. For if they put forward such excuses as these and do not blush, much more does it behoove us not to be ashamed of replying to these things. What then am I to say to those who advance these pretexts? I would remind them of the three children in the furnace and the flame, who when they saw the fire

St. John Chrysostom

encircling them on all sides, enveloping their mouth and their eyes and even their breath, did not cease singing that sacred and mystical hymn to God, in company with the universe, but standing in the midst of the pyre sent up their song of praise to the common Lord of all with greater cheerfulness than they who abide in some flowery field: and together with these three children I should think it proper to remind them also of the lions which were in Babylon, and of Daniel and the den: and not of this one only but also of another den, and the prophet Jeremiah, and the mire in which he was smothered up to the neck. And emerging from these dens, I would conduct these persons who put forward heat as an excuse into the prison and exhibit Paul to them there, and Silas bound fast in the stocks, covered with bruises and wounds lacerated all over their body with a mass of stripes, yet singing praises to God at midnight and celebrating their holy vigil. For is it not a monstrous thing that those holy men, both in the furnace and the fire, and the den, and amongst wild beasts, and mire, and in a prison and the stocks, and amidst stripes and jailers, and intolerable sufferings, never complained of any of these things, but were continually uttering prayers and sacred songs with much energy and fervent zeal, whilst we who have not undergone any of their innumerable sufferings small or great, neglect our own salvation on account of a scorching sun and a little short lived heat and toil, and forsaking the assembly wander away, depraving ourselves by going to meetings which are thoroughly unwholesome? When the dew of the divine oracles is so abundant dost thou make heat thy excuse? "The water which I will give him," saith Christ "shall be in him a well of water springing up into everlasting life;" and again; "He that believeth on me as the Scripture hath said, out of his belly shall flow rivers of living water." Tell me; when thou hast spiritual wells and rivers, art thou afraid of material heat? Now in the marketplace where there is so much turmoil and crowding, and scorching wind, how is it that you do not make suffocation and heat an excuse for absenting yourself? For it is impossible for you to say that there you can enjoy a cooler temperature, and that all the heat is concentrated here with us:—the truth is exactly the reverse; here indeed owing to the pavement floor, and to the construction of the building in other respects (for it is carried up to a vast height), the air is lighter and cooler: whereas there the sun is strong in every direction, and there is much crowding, and vapor and dust, and other things which add to discomfort far more than these. Whence it is plain that these senseless excuses are the offspring of indolence and of a supine disposition, destitute of the fire of the Holy Spirit.

3. Now these remarks of mine are not so much directed to them, as to you who do not bring them forward, do not rouse them from their indolence, and draw them to this table of salvation. Household slaves indeed when they have to discharge some service in common, summon their fellow slaves, but you when you are going to meet for this spiritual ministry suffer your fellow servants to be deprived of the advantage by your neglect. "But what if they do not desire it?" you say. Make them desire it by your continual importunity: for if they see you insisting upon it they certainly will desire it. Nay these things are a mere excuse and pretense. How many fathers at any rate are there here who have not their sons standing with them? Was it so difficult for thee to bring hither some of thy children? Whence it is clear that

the absence of all the others who remain outside is due not only to their own indolence, but also to your neglect. But now at least, if never before, rouse yourselves up, and let each person enter the Church accompanied by a member of his family: let them incite and urge one another to the assembly here, the father his son, the son his father, the husbands their wives, and the wives their husbands, the master his slave, brother his brother, friend his friend: or rather let us not summon friends only but also enemies to this common treasury of good things. If thy enemy sees thy care for his welfare, he will undoubtedly relinquish his hatred.

Say to him: "art thou not ashamed and dost thou not blush before the Jews who keep their sabbath with such great strictness, and from the evening of it abstain from all work? And if they see the sun verging towards setting on the day of the Preparation they break off business, and cut short their traffic: and if anyone who has been making a purchase from them, before the evening, comes in the evening bringing the price, they do not suffer themselves to take it, or to accept the money." And why do I speak of the price of market wares and transaction of business? Even if it were possible to receive a treasure they would rather lose the gain than trample on their law. Are the Jews then so strict, and this when they keep the law out of due season, and cling to an observance of it which does not profit them, but rather does them harm: and wilt thou, who art superior to the shadow, to whom it has been vouchsafed to see the Sun of Righteousness, who art ranked as a citizen of the Heavenly commonwealth, wilt thou not display the same zeal as those who unseasonably cleave to what is wrong, thou who hast been entrusted with the truth, but although thou art summoned here for only a short part of the day, canst thou not endure to spend even this upon the hearing of the divine oracles? and what kind of indulgence, pray, could you obtain? and what answer will you have to make which is reasonable and just? It is utterly impossible that one who is so indifferent and indolent should ever obtain indulgence, even if he should allege the necessities of worldly affairs ten thousand times over as an excuse. Do you not know that if you come and worship God and take part in the work which goes on here, the business you have on hand is made much easier for you? Have you worldly anxieties? Come here on that account that by the time you spend here you may win for yourself the favor of God, and so depart with a sense of security; that you may have Him for your ally, that you may become invincible to the demons because you are assisted by the heavenly hand. If you have the benefit of prayers uttered by the fathers, if you take part in common prayer, if you listen to the divine oracles, if you win for yourself the aid of God, if, armed with these weapons, you then go forth, not even the devil himself will be able henceforth to look you in the face, much less wicked men who are eager to insult and malign you. But if you go from your house to the marketplace, and are found destitute of these weapons, you will be easily mastered by all who insult you. This is the reason why both in public and private affairs, many things occur contrary to our expectation, because we have not been diligent about spiritual things in the first place, and secondarily about the secular, but have inverted the order. For this reason also the proper sequence and right arrangement of things has been upset, and all our affairs are full of much confusion. Can you imagine what distress and grief I suffer when I observe, that if a public holy day and festival is at hand there is a concourse of all the inhabitants of the city, although there is no one to summon them; but when the holy day and festival are past, even if we should crack our voice by continuing to call you all day long there is no one who pays any heed? For often when turning these things over in my mind I have groaned heavily, and said to myself: What is the use of exhortation or advice, when you do everything merely by the force of habit, and do not become a whit more zealous in consequence of my teaching? For whereas in the festivals you need no exhortation from me, but, when they are past you profit nothing by my teaching, do you not show that my discourse, so far as you are concerned, is superfluous?

4. Perhaps many of those who hear these things are grieved. But such is not the sentiment of the indolent: else they would put away their carelessness, like ourselves, who are daily anxious about your affairs. And what gain do you make by your secular transactions in proportion to the damage you sustain? It is impossible to depart from any other assembly, or gathering, in the possession of so much gain as you receive from the time spent here, whether it be the law court, or council-chamber, or even the palace itself. For we do not commit the administration of nations or cities nor the command of armies to those who enter here, but another kind of government more dignified than that of the empire itself; or rather we do not ourselves commit it, but the grace of the spirit.

What then is the government, more dignified than that of the empire, which they who enter here receive? They are trained to master untoward passions, to rule wicked lusts, to command anger, to regulate ill-will, to subdue vainglory. The emperor, seated on the imperial throne, and wearing his diadem, is not so dignified as the man who has elevated his own inward right reason to the throne of government over base passions, and by his dominion over them has bound as it were a glorious diadem upon his brow. For what profit is there, pray, in purple, and raiment wrought with gold, and a jeweled crown, when the soul is in captivity to the passions? What gain is there in outward freedom when the ruling element within us is reduced to a state of disgraceful and pitiable servitude. For just as when a fever penetrates deep, and inflames all the inward parts, there is no benefit to be got from the outward surface of the body, although it is not affected in the same way: even so when our soul is violently carried away by the passion within, no outward government, not even the imperial throne, is of any profit, since reason is deposed from the throne of empire by the violent usurpation of the passions, and bows and trembles beneath their insurrectionary movements. Now to prevent this taking place prophets and apostles concur on all sides in helping us, repressing our passions, and expelling all the ferocity of the irrational element within us, and committing a mode of government to us far more dignified than the empire. This is why I said that they who deprive themselves of this care receive a blow in the vital parts, sustaining greater damage than can be inflicted from any other quarter inasmuch as they who come here get greater gain than they could derive from any other source: even as Scripture has declared. The law said "Thou shalt not appear before the Lord empty;" that is, enter not into the temple without sacrifices. Now if it is not right to go into the house of God without sacrifices, much more ought we to enter the assembly accompanied by our brethren: for this sacrifice and offering is better than that, when thou brings a soul with thee into the Church. Do you not see doves which have been trained, how they hunt for others when they are let out? Let us also do this. For what kind of excuse shall we have, if irrational creatures are able to hunt for an animal of their own species, while we who have been honored with reason and so much wisdom neglect this kind of pursuit? I exhorted you in my former discourse with these words: "Go, each of you to the houses of your neighbors, wait for them to come out, lay hold of them, and conduct them to their common mother: and imitate those who are mad upon theatre going, who diligently arrange to meet each other and so wait at early dawn to see that iniquitous spectacle." Yet I have not affected anything by this exhortation. Therefore I speak again and shall not cease speaking, until I have persuaded you. Hearing profits nothing unless it is accompanied by practice. It makes our punishment heavier, if we continually hear the same things and do none of the things which are spoken. That the chastisement will be heavier, hear the statement of Christ. "If I had not come and spoken to them they had not sin: but now they have no cloak for their sin." And the Apostle says, "for not the hearers of the law shall be justified." These things He says to the hearers; but when He wishes to instruct the speaker also, that even he will not gain anything from his teaching unless his behavior is in close correspondence with his doctrine, and his manner of life is in harmony with his speech, hear how the Apostle and the prophet address themselves to him: for the latter says "but to the sinner said God, why dost thou preach my laws and takes my covenant in thy mouth, whereas thou hast hated instruction?" And the Apostle, addressing himself to these same again who thought great things of their teaching, speaks on this wise: "Thou art confident that thou thyself art a leader of the blind, a light of those who are in darkness, an instructor of the foolish, a teacher of babes: thou therefore that teaches another teaches thou not thyself?" Inasmuch then as it could neither profit me the speaker to speak, nor you the hearers to hear, unless we comply with the things which are spoken, but rather would increase our condemnation, let us not limit the display of our zeal to hearing only, but let us observe what is said, in our deeds. For it is indeed a good thing to spend time continually in hearing the divine oracles: but this good thing becomes useless when the benefit to be derived from hearing is not linked with it.

Therefore that you may not assemble here in vain I shall not cease beseeching you with all earnestness, as I have often besought you before, "conduct your brethren to us, exhort the wanderers, counsel them not by word only but also by deed." This is the more powerful teaching—that which comes through our manners and behavior—Even if you do not utter a word, but yet, after you have gone out of this assembly, by your mien, and your look, and your voice and all the rest of your demeanor you exhibit to the men who have been left behind the gain which you have brought away with you, this is sufficient for exhortation and advice. For we ought to go out from this place as it were from some sacred shrine, as men who have descended from heaven itself, who have become sedate, and philosophical, who do and say everything in proper measure: and when a wife sees her husband returning from the assembly, and a father his son, and a friend his friend, and an enemy his enemy, let them all receive an impression of the benefit which you have derived from coming here: and they will receive it, if they perceive that you have become milder, more philosophical, more devout. Consider what privileges you enjoy who hast been initiated into the mysteries, with what company thou offers up that mystic hymn, with what company thou cries aloud the "Ter Sanctus." Teach "them that are without" that thou hast joined the chorus of the Seraphim, that thou art ranked as a citizen of the commonwealth above, that thou hast been enrolled in the choir of Angels, that thou hast conversed with the Lord, that thou hast been in the company of Christ. If we regulate ourselves in this way we shall not need to say anything when we go out to those who are left behind: but from our advantage they will perceive their own loss and will hasten hither, so as to enjoy the same benefits themselves. For when, merely by the use of their senses, they see the beauty of your soul shining forth, even if they are the most stupid of men, they will become enamored of your goodly appearance. For if corporeal beauty excites those who behold it, much more will symmetry of soul be able to move the spectator and stimulate him to equal zeal. Let us then adorn our inward man, and let us be mindful of the things which are said here, when we go out: for there especially is it a proper time to remember them; and just as an athlete displays in the lists the things which he has learned in the training school: even so ought we to display in our transactions in the world without the things which we have heard here.

5. Bear in mind then the things which are said here, that when you have gone out and the devil lays hold of you either by means of anger or vainglory, or any other passion, you may call to remembrance the teaching which you have received here and may be able easily to shake

off the grasp of the evil one. Do you not see the wrestling-masters in the practicing grounds, who, after countless contests having obtained exemption from wrestling on account of their age, sit outside the lines by the side of the dust and shout to those who are wrestling inside, telling one to grasp a hand, or drag a leg, or seize upon the back, and by many other directions of that kind, saying, "if you do so and so you will easily throw your antagonist," they are of the greatest service to their pupils? Even so do thou look to thy training master, the blessed Paul, who after countless victories is now sitting outside the boundary, I mean this present life, and cries aloud to us who are wrestling, shouting out by means of his Epistles, when he sees us overcome by wrath and resentment of injuries, and choked by passion; "if thy enemy hunger feed him, if he thirst give him drink;"—a beautiful precept full of spiritual wisdom, and serviceable both to the doer and the receiver. But the reminder of the passage causes much perplexity and does not seem to correspond to the sentiment of him who uttered the former words. And what is the nature of this? the saying that "by so doing thou shalt heap coals of fire on his head." For by these words he does a wrong both to the doer and the receiver: to the latter by setting his head on fire, and placing coals upon it; for what good will he get from receiving food and drink in proportion to the evil he will suffer from the heaping of coals on his head? Thus then the recipient of the benefit is wronged, having a greater vengeance inflicted on him, but the benefactor also is injured in another way. For what can he gain from doing good to his enemies when he acts in the hope of revenge? For he who gives meat and drink to his enemy for the purpose of heaping coals of fire on his head would not become merciful and kind, but cruel and harsh, having inflicted an enormous punishment by means of a small benefit. For what could be more unkind than to feed a person for the purpose of heaping coals of fire on his head? This then is the contradiction: and now it remains that the solution should be added, in order that by those very things which seem to do violence to the letter of the law you may clearly see all the wisdom of the lawgiver. What then is the solution?

That great and noble-minded man was well aware of the fact that to be reconciled quickly with an enemy is a grievous and difficult thing; grievous and difficult, not on account of its own nature, but of our moral indolence. But he commanded us not only to be reconciled with our enemy, but also to feed him, which was far more grievous than the former. For if some are infuriated by the mere sight of those who have annoyed them, how would they be willing to feed them when they were hungry? And why do I speak of the sight infuriating them? If anyone makes mention of the persons, and merely introduces their name in society, it revives the wound in our imagination and increases the heat of passion. Paul then being aware of all these things and wishing to make what was hard and difficult of correction smooth and easy, and to persuade one who could not endure to see his enemy, to be ready to confer that benefit already mentioned upon him, added the words about coals of fire, in order that a man prompted by the hope of vengeance might hasten to do this service to one who had annoyed him. And just as the fisherman surrounding the hook on all sides with the bait presents it to the fishes in order that one of them hastening to its accustomed food may be captured by means of it and easily held fast: even so Paul also wishing to lead on the man who has been wronged to bestow a benefit on the man who has wronged him does not present to him the bare hook of spiritual wisdom, but having covered it as it were with a kind of bait, I mean the "coals of fire," invites the man who has been insulted, in the hope of inflicting punishment, to confer this benefit on the man who has annoyed him; but when he has come he holds him fast in future, and does not let him make off, the very nature of the deed attaching him to his enemy; and he all but says to him: "if thou art not willing to feed the man who has wronged thee for piety's sake: feed him at least from the hope of punishing him." For he knows that if the man once sets his hand to the work of conferring this benefit, a starting point is made and a way of reconciliation is opened for him. For certainly no one would have the heart to regard a man continually as his enemy to whom he has given meat and drink, even if he originally does this in the hope of vengeance. For time as it goes on relaxes the tension of his anger. As then the fisherman, if he presented the bare hook would never allure the fish, but when he has covered it gets it unawares into the mouth of the creature who comes up to it: so also Paul if he had not advanced the expectation of inflicting punishment would never have persuaded those who were wronged to undertake to benefit those who had annoyed them. Wishing then to persuade those who recoiled in disgust, and were paralyzed by the very sight of their enemies, to confer the greatest benefits upon them, he made mention of the coals of fire, not with a view of thrusting the persons in question into inexorable punishment, but in order that when he had persuaded those who were wronged to benefit their enemies in the expectation of punishing them, he might afterwards in time persuade them to abandon their anger altogether.

6. Thus then did he encourage the man who has been wronged; but observe also how he unites again the man who has done the wrong to him who has been provoked. First of all by the very manner of the benefit: (for there is no one so degraded and unfeeling as to be unwilling, when he receives meat and drink, to become the servant and friend of him who does this for him): and in the second place through the dread of vengeance. For the passage, "by so doing thou shalt heap coals of fire on his head" seems indeed to be addressed to the person who gives the food; but it more especially touches him who has caused the annoyance, in order that through fear of this punishment he may be deterred from remaining continually in a state of enmity, and being aware that the reception of food and drink might do him the greatest mischief if he constantly retains his animosity, may suppress his anger. For thus he will be able to quench the coals of fire. Wherefore the proposed punishment and vengeance both induces the one who has been wronged to benefit him who has annoyed him, and it deters and checks him who has given the provocation and impels him to reconciliation with the man who gives him meat and drink. Paul therefore linked the two persons by a twofold bond, the one depending on a benefit, the other on an act of vengeance. For the difficulty is to make a beginning and to find an opening for the reconciliation: but when that has once been cleared in whatever way it may be, all which follows will be smooth and easy. For even if at first the man who has been annoyed feeds his enemy in the hope of punishing him, yet becoming his friend by the act of giving him food he will be able to

expel the desire of vengeance. For when he has become a friend he will no longer feed the man who has been reconciled to him, with an expectation of this kind. Again he who has given the provocation, when he sees the man who has been wronged electing to give him meat and drink, casts out all his animosity, both on account of this deed, and also of his fear of the punishment which is in store for him, even if he be excessively hard and harsh and stony hearted, being put to shame by the benevolence of him who gives him food, and dreading the punishment reserved for him, if he continues to be an enemy after accepting the food.

For this reason Paul did not stop even here in his exhortation, but when he has emptied each side of wrath, he proceeds to correct their disposition, saying, "be not overcome of evil." "For if," he says, "you continue to bear resentment and to seek revenge you seem indeed to conquer your enemy, but in reality you are being conquered by evil, that is, by wrath: so that if you wish to conquer, be reconciled, and do not make an attack upon your adversary;" for a brilliant victory is that in which by means of good, that is to say by forbearance, you overcome evil, expelling wrath and resentment. But the injured man, when inflamed with passion would not have borne these words. Therefore when he had satisfied his wrath, he proceeded to conduct him to the best reason for reconciliation and did not permit him to remain permanently animated by the wicked hope of vengeance. Do you perceive the wisdom of the lawgiver? And that you may learn that he introduced this law only on account of the weakness of those who would not otherwise be content to make terms amongst themselves, hear how Christ, when He ordained a law on this same subject did not propose the same reward, as the Apostle; but, having said "Love your enemies, do good to them that hate you," which means give them food and drink, He did not add "for in so doing ye shall heap coals of fire on their heads:" but what did He say? "that ye may become like your Father who is in Heaven." Naturally so, for He was discoursing to Peter, James, and John and the rest of the apostolic band: therefore He proposed that reward. But if you say that even on this understanding the precept is onerous you improve once more the defense which I am making for Paul, but you deprive yourself of every plea of indulgence. For I can prove to you that this which seems to you onerous was accomplished under the Old Dispensation when the manifestation of spiritual wisdom was not so great as it is now. For this reason also Paul did not introduce the law in his own words, but used the very expressions which were employed by him who originally brought it in, that he might leave no room for excuse to those who do not observe it: for the precept "if thine enemy hunger feed him, if he thirst give him drink" is not the utterance of Paul in the first instance, but of Solomon. For this reason he quoted the words that he might persuade the hearer that for one who has been advanced to such a high standard of wisdom to regard an old law as onerous and grievous which was often fulfilled by the men of old time, is one of the basest things possible. Which of the ancients, you ask, fulfilled it? There were many, but amongst others David especially did so more abundantly. He did not indeed merely give food or drink to his enemy, but also rescued him several times from death, when he was in jeopardy; and when he had it in his power to slay him he spared him once, twice, yea many times. As for Saul he hated and abhorred him so much after the countless good services which he had done, after his brilliant triumphs, and the salvation which he had wrought in the matter of Goliath, that he could not bear to mention him by his own name, but called him after his father. For once when a festival was at hand, and Saul, having devised some treachery against him, and contrived a cruel plot, did not see him arrive—"where," said he, "is the son of Jesse?" He called him by his father's name, both because on account of his hatred he could not endure the recollection of his proper name, and also because he thought to damage the distinguished position of that righteous man by a reference to his low birth;—a miserable and despicable thought: for certainly, even if he had some accusation to bring against the father this could in no wise injure David. For each man is answerable for his own deeds, and by these he can be praised and accused. But as it was, not having any evil deed to mention, he brought forward his low birth, expecting by this means to throw his glory into the shade, which in fact was the height of folly. For what kind of offence is it to be the child of insignificant and humble men, "the son of Jesse," but when David found him sleeping inside the cave, he did not call him the "son of Kish," but by his title of honor: "for I will not lift up my hand," he said, "against the Lord's anointed." So purely free was he from wrath and resentment of injuries: he calls him the Lord's anointed who had done him such great wrongs, who was thirsting for his blood, who after his countless good services had many times attempted to destroy him. For he did not consider how Saul deserved to be treated, but he considered what was becoming for himself both to do and to say, which is the greatest stretch of moral wisdom. How so? When thou hast got thy enemy in a prison, made fast by a twofold, or rather by a triple chain, confinement of space, dearth of assistance, and necessity of sleep, dost thou not demand a penalty and punishment of him? "No," he says; "for I am not now regarding what he deserves to suffer, but what it behooves me to do." He did not look to the facility for slaying, but to the accurate observance of the moral wisdom which was becoming to him. And yet which of the existing circumstances was not sufficient to prompt him to the act of slaughter? Was not the fact that his enemy was delivered bound into his hands a sufficient inducement? For you are aware I suppose that we hasten more eagerly to deeds for which facilities abound, and the hope of success increases our desire to act, which was just what happened then in his case.

Well! did the captain who then counselled and urged him to the deed, did the memory of past events induce him to slay? no one of these things moved him: in fact the very facility for slaughter averted him from it: for he bethought him that God had put Saul in his hands for the purpose of furnishing ample ground and opportunity for the exercise of moral wisdom. You then perhaps admire him, because he did not cherish the memory of any of his past evils: but I am much more astonished at him for another reason. And what is this? That the fear of future events did not impel him to lay violent hands on his enemy. For he knew clearly that if Saul escaped his hands, he would again be his adversary; yet he preferred exposing himself to danger by letting go the man who had wronged him, to providing for his own security by laying violent hands upon his foe. What could equal then the great and generous spirit of this man, who, when the law commanded eye to be plucked out for eye, and tooth for tooth, and retaliation on equal terms, not only abstained from doing this, but exhibited a far greater measure of moral wisdom? At least if he had slain Saul at that time he would have retained credit for moral wisdom unimpaired, not merely because he had acted on the defensive, not being himself the originator of violence, but also because by his great moderation he was superior to the precept "an eye for an eye." For he would not have inflicted one slaughter in return for one; but, in return for many deaths, which Saul endeavored to bring on him, having attempted to slay him not once or twice but many times, he would have brought only one death on Saul; and not only this, but if he had proceeded to avenge himself out of fear of the future, even this, combined with the things already mentioned, would procure him the reward of forbearance without any deduction. For he who is angry on account of the things which have been done to him, and demands satisfaction would not be able to obtain the praise of forbearance: but when a man dismisses the consideration of all past evils, although they are many and painful, but is compelled to take steps for self-defense from fear of the future, and by way of providing for his own security, no one would deprive him of the rewards of moderation.

7. Nevertheless David did not act even thus, but found a novel and strange form of moral wisdom: and neither the remembrance of things past, nor the fear of things to come, nor the instigation of the captain, nor the solitude of the place, nor the facility for slaying, nor anything else incited him to kill; but he spared the man who was his enemy, and had given him pain just as if he was some benefactor, and had done him much good. What kind of indulgence then shall we have, if we are mindful of past transgressions, and avenge ourselves on those who have given us pain, whereas that innocent man

who had undergone such great sufferings and expected more and worse evils to befall him in consequence of saving his enemy, is seen to spare him, so as to prefer incurring danger himself and to live in fear and trembling, rather than put to a just death the man who would cause him endless troubles?

His moral wisdom then we may perceive, not only from the fact that he did not slay Saul, when there was so strong a compulsion, but also that he did not utter an irreverent word against him, although he who was insulted would not have heard him. Yet we often speak evil of friends when they are absent, he on the contrary not even of the enemy who had done him such great wrong. His moral wisdom then we may perceive from these things: but his lovingkindness and tender care from what he did after these things. For when he had cut off the fringe of Saul's garment, and had taken away the bottle of water he withdrew afar off and stood and shouted, and exhibited these things to him whose life he had preserved, doing so not with a view to display and ostentation, but desiring to convince him by his deeds that he suspected him without a cause as his enemy, and aiming therefore at winning him into friendship. Nevertheless when he had even thus failed to persuade him, and could have laid hands on him, he again chose rather to be an exile from his country and to sojourn in a strange land, and suffer distress every day, in procuring necessary food than to remain at home and vex his adversary. What spirit could be kinder than his? He was indeed justified in saying "Lord remember David and all his meekness." Let us also imitate him and let us neither say nor do evil to our enemies, but benefit them according to our power: for we shall do more good to ourselves than to them. "For if ye forgive your enemies," we are told "ye shall be forgiven." Forgive base offences that thou mayest receive a royal pardon for thy offences; but if anyone has done thee great wrongs, the greater the wrongs you forgive, the greater will be the pardon which you will receive. Therefore we have been instructed to say, "Forgive us, as we forgive," that we may learn that the measure of our forgiveness takes its beginning in the first place from ourselves. Wherefore in proportion to the severity of the evil which the enemy does to us is the greatness of the benefit which he bestows. Let us then be earnest and eager to be reconciled with those who have vexed us, whether their wrath be just or unjust. For if thou art reconciled here, thou art delivered from judgment in the other world; but if in the interval while the hatred is still going on, death interrupting steps in and carries the enmity away with it, it follows of necessity that the trial of the case should be brought forward in the other world. As then many men when they have a dispute with one another, if they come to a friendly understanding together outside the law court save themselves loss, and alarm, and many risks, the issue of the case turning out in accordance with the sentiment of each party; but if they severally entrust the affair to the judge the only result to them will be loss of money, and in many cases a penalty, and the permanent endurance of their hatred; even so here if we come to terms during our present life we shall relieve ourselves from all punishment; but if while remaining enemies we depart to that terrible tribunal in the other world we shall certainly pay the utmost penalty at the sentence of the judge there, and shall both of us undergo inexorable punishment: he who is unjustly wroth because he is thus unjustly disposed, and he who is justly wroth, because he has, however justly, cherished resentment. For even if we have been unjustly ill-treated, we ought to grant pardon to those who have wronged us. And observe how he urges and incites those who have unjustly given pain to reconciliation with those whom they have wronged. "If thou offers thy gift before the altar, and there remembers that thy brother hath ought against thee, go thy way; first be reconciled to thy brother." He did not say, "assemble, and offer thy sacrifice" but "be reconciled and then offer it." Let it lie there, he says, in order that the necessity of making the offering may constrain him who is justly wroth to come to terms even against his will. See how he again prompts us to go to the man who has provoked us when he says, "Forgive your debtors in order that your Father may also forgive your trespasses." For He did not propose a small reward, but one which far exceeds the magnitude of the achievement. Considering all these things then and counting the recompense which is given in this case and remembering that to wipe away sins does not entail much labor and zeal, let us pardon those who have wronged us. For that which others scarcely accomplish, I mean the blotting out of their own sins by means of fasting and lamentations, and prayers, and sackcloth, and ashes, this it is possible for us easily to effect without sackcloth and ashes and fasting if only we blot out anger from our heart, and with sincerity forgive those who have wronged us. May the God of peace and love, having banished from our soul all wrath and bitterness, and anger, deign to grant that we being closely knit one to another according to the proper adjustment of the parts, may with one accord, one mouth and one soul continually offer up our hymns of thanksgiving due to

Him: for to Him be glory and power for ever and ever. Amen.

St. John Chrysostom

HOMILY
AGAINST PUBLISHING THE ERRORS OF THE BRETHREN,
AND UTTERING IMPRECATIONS UPON ENEMIES.

TRANSLATED BY
R. BLACKBURN, M.A.,

AGAINST PUBLISHING THE ERRORS OF THE BRETHREN.

HOMILY.
Upon the not publishing the errors of the Brethren, nor uttering imprecations upon enemies.

1. I account you happy for the zeal, beloved, with which you flock into the Father's house. For from this zeal I have ground for feeling confidence about your health also with respect to the soul; for indeed the school of the Church is an admirable surgery—a surgery, not for bodies, but for souls. For it is spiritual, and sets right, not fleshly wounds, but errors of the mind, and of these errors and wounds the medicine is the word. This medicine is compounded, not from the herbs growing on the earth, but from the words proceeding from heaven—this no hands of physicians, but tongues of preachers have dispensed. On this account it lasts right through; and neither is its virtue impaired by length of time, nor defeated by any strength of diseases. For certainly the medicines of physicians have both these defects; for while they are fresh they display their proper strength, but when much time has passed; just as those bodies which have grown old; they become weaker; and often too the difficult character of maladies is wont to baffle them; since they are but human. Whereas the divine medicine is not such as this; but after much time has intervened, it still retains all its inherent virtue. Ever since at least Moses was born (for from thence dates the beginning of the Scripture) it has healed so many human beings; and not only has it not lost its proper power, but neither has any disease ever yet

overcome it. This medicine it is not possible to get by payment of silver; but he who has displayed sincerity of purpose and disposition goes his way having it all. On account of this both rich and poor alike obtain the benefit of this healing process. For where there is a necessity to pay down money the man of large means indeed shares the benefit; but the poor man often has to go away deprived of the gain, since his income does not suffice him for the making up of the medicine. But in this case, since it is not possible to pay down silver coin, but it is needful to display faith and a good purpose, he who has paid down these with forwardness of mind, this is he who most reaps the advantage; since indeed these are the price paid for the medicinal treatment. And the rich and the poor man share the benefit alike; or rather it is not alike that they share the benefit, but often the poor man goes away in the enjoyment of more. Whatever can be the reason? It is because the rich man, possessed beforehand by many thoughts, having the pride and puffed-up temper belonging to wealthiness; living with carelessness and lazy ease as companions, receives the medicine of the hearing of the Scriptures not with much attention, nor with much earnestness; but the poor man, far removed from delicate living and gluttony and indolence; spending all his time in handicraft and honest labors; and gathering hence much love of wisdom for the soul; becomes thereby more attentive and free from slackness, and is wont to give his mind with more accurate care to all that is said: whence also, inasmuch as the price he has paid is higher, the benefit which he departs having reaped is greater.

2. It is not as absolutely bringing an accusation against those who are wealthy that I say all this; nor as praising the poor without reference to circumstances: for

neither is wealth an evil, but the having made a bad use of wealth; nor is poverty a virtue, but the having made a virtuous use of poverty. That rich man who was in the time of Lazarus was punished, not because he was rich, but because he was cruel and inhuman. And that poor man who rested in the bosom of Abraham was praised, not because he was poor, but because he had borne his poverty with thankfulness.

For of things—(now attend carefully to this saying; for it will avail to put into you sufficient religious knowledge, and to cast out all unsound reasoning, and to bring about your having your judgment right concerning the truth of things)—well, of things some are by nature morally good, and others the contrary; and others neither good nor evil, but they occupy the intermediate position. A good thing piety is by nature, impiety an evil thing; a good thing virtue, an evil thing wickedness; but wealth and poverty in themselves are neither the one nor the other; but from the will of those who use them they become either the one or the other. For if thou hast used thy wealth for purposes of philanthropy, the thing becomes to thee a foundation of good; but if for rapine and grasping and insolence, thou hast turned the use of it to the direct opposite; but for this wealth is not chargeable, but he who has used his wealth for insolence. So also we may say of poverty: if thou have borne it nobly by giving thanks to the Master, what has been done becomes to thee a cause and ground for receiving crowns; but if on account of this thou blaspheme thy Creator, and accuse Him for His providence, thou hast again used the thing to an evil purpose. But just as in that case it is not wealth that is responsible for the avarice, but the person who has made a bad use of wealth, so also here we are not to lay the blame of the blasphemy on poverty, but on him who did not choose to bear the thing in a sober spirit. For in every case both the praise and the blame belong to our own will and choice. Good is wealth, yet not absolutely, but to him only to whom it is not sin; and again poverty is wicked, but not absolutely, but only in the mouth of the impious, because he is discontented, because he blasphemes, because he is indignant, because he accuses Him who has made him.

3. Let us not therefore accuse riches, nor revile poverty absolutely, but those who do not will to use these virtuously; for the things themselves lie in the middle. But as I was saying (for it is good to return to the former subject), both rich and poor enjoy the benefit of the medicines administered here with the same boldness and freedom; and often the poor with more earnestness. For the special excellence of the medicines is not this only, that they heal souls, that their virtue is not destroyed by length of time, that they are not worsted by any disease, that the benefit is publicly offered gratuitously, that the healing treatment is on a footing of equality both for rich and poor—but they have another quality also not inferior to these good points. Pray of what character is this? It is that we do not publicly expose those who come to this surgery. For they who go off to the surgeries of the outside world, have many who examine their wounds, and unless the physician have first uncovered the sore, he does not apply the dressing; but here not so, but seeing as we do innumerable patients, we go through the medical treatment of them in a latent manner. For not by dragging into publicity those who have sinned do we thus noise abroad the sins committed by them; but after putting forth our teaching, as common to all, we leave it entirely to the

conscience of the hearers; so that each may draw to himself from what is said the suitable medicine for his own wound. For there proceeds the word of doctrine from the tongue of the speaker, containing accusation of wickedness, praise of virtue, blame of lewdness, commendation of chasteness, censure of pride, praise of gentleness, just as a medicine of varied and manifold ingredients, compounded from every kind; and to take what is applicable to himself and salutary is the part of each of the hearers. The word then issues openly, and settling into the conscience of each, secretly both affords the healing treatment which comes from it, and before the malady has been divulged, has often restored health.

4. You at all events heard yesterday how I extolled the power of prayer, how I reproached those who pray with listlessness; without having publicly exposed one of them. Those then who were conscious to themselves of earnestness, accepted that commendation of prayer, and became still more earnest by the praises, while those who were conscious to themselves of listlessness, accepted on the other hand the rebuking, and put off their carelessness. But neither these nor those do we know; and this ignorance is serviceable to both—how, I now tell you. He who has heard the commendations of prayer and is conscious to himself of earnestness, were he to have many witnesses of the commendations, would have lapsed towards pride; but, as it is, by having secretly accepted the praise, he is removed from all arrogance. On the other hand he who is conscious to himself of listlessness, having heard the accusation, has become better from the accusation, as having no one of men a witness of the rebuking; and this was of no ordinary profit to him. For on account of the being flurried at the opinion of the

vulgar, so long as we may think that we escape notice in our wickedness, we exert ourselves to become better; but when we have become notorious to all, and have lost the consolation derived from the escaping notice, we grow more shameless and remiss rather. And just as sores become more painful by being unbandaged and frequently exposed to cold air, so also the soul after having sinned, if in the presence of many it be rebuked for what it has done amiss, grows thereby more shameless. In order therefore that this might not take place, the word administered its medicine to you covertly. And that you may understand that the gain which this covert treatment has is great, hear what the Christ says. "If thy brother have committed a fault against thee convince him of it," and he did not say "between him and the whole town," nor, "between thee and the whole people," but "only between thee and him." Let the accusation, he says, be unwitnessed to, in order that the change to amendment may be made easy of digestion. A great good surely, the making the advice unpublished. Sufficient is the conscience, sufficient that incorruptible judge. It is not so much thou who rebukes him who has done wrong as his own conscience (that accuser is the sharper), nor dost thou do it with the more exact knowledge of the faults committed. Add not therefore wound to wound by exposing him who has done wrong; but administer for thyself the counsel unwitnessed. This therefore we are doing now—the very thing that Paul also did, framing the indictment against him who among the Corinthians had sinned without citing of witnesses. And hear how. "On this account," he says, "brethren, I have applied these figures of speech to myself and Apollos." And yet not he himself nor Apollos were they who had rent the people in schism and divided the

Church; but all the same he concealed the accusation, and just as by some masks, by hiding the countenances of the defendants by his own and Apollos' names, he afforded them power to amend of that wickedness. And again, "Lest in some way after I have come God humble me, and I may have to mourn many of those who have before sinned and have not repented over the uncleanness and lasciviousness which they had committed." See how here also he indefinitely mentions those who had sinned, in order that he might not, by openly bringing the accusation, render the soul of those who had sinned more shameless. Therefore, just as we administer our reproof with so much sparing of your feelings, so do ye also with all seriousness receive the correction; and attend with carefulness to what is said.

5. We discoursed to you yesterday about the power which is in prayer. I pointed out how the devil then lies in wait, deceiver that he is. For since he sees very great gain accruing to us from prayer, then most he assails us, in order that he may disable us from our defense; that he may send us off home empty-handed. And just as before magistrates, when the officers of the court who are about the person of the magistrate have a hostile feeling toward those who come before him, they by their staves drive them away to a distance, preventing their coming near and resorting to lamentation and so obtaining compassion; so also the devil, when he has seen us coming to the judge, drives us away to a distance, not by any staff, but through our own slackness. For he knows, he knows clearly, that if they have come to him in a sober spirit, and have told the sins committed, and have mourned with their soul fervent, they will depart having received full forgiveness; for God loves mankind; and on

this account he is beforehand with them, and debars them from access, in order that they may obtain no one of the things which they need. But the soldiers of magistrates with violence scare away those who are coming to them; but he with no compulsion, but by deceiving us, and throwing us into security. On this account we are not deserving even of allowance, since we voluntarily deprive ourselves of the good things. Prayer with earnestness is a light of the understanding and soul—a light unquenchable and perpetual. On this account he throws into our minds countless rubbish-heaps of imaginations; and things which we never had imagined, these collecting together at the very moment of prayer he pours down upon our souls. And just as winds often rushing from an opposite quarter by a violent gust extinguish a lamp's flame as it is being lighted, so also the devil, when he has seen the flame of our prayer being kindled, blowing it on every side with the blasts of countless thoughts, does not desist before and until he has quenched the light. But the very thing which they who are kindling those lamps do, this let us also do. And what do they do? When they see a violent wind coming, by laying their finger upon the opening of the lamp they bar the entrance against the wind. For so long as he assails from without we shall be able to stand against him; but when we have opened to him the doors of the mind, and have received the enemy inside; after that we are no longer able to withstand even a little; but, having on all sides completely extinguished the memory, just as a smoking lamp, he allows our mouth to utter empty words. But just as they put their finger upon the opening of the lamp, so let us lay consideration upon our mind: let us close off from the wicked spirit the entrance, in order that he may not quench our light of prayer.

Remember both those illustrations, both that of the soldiers and the magistrate, and that respecting the lamp. For with this purpose we adduce to you these illustrations; with which we are conversant, in which we live, in order that, after we have departed hence and have returned home, we may from things of familiar occurrence receive a reminder of what has been said.

6. Prayer is a strong piece of armor and a great security. You heard yesterday how the three children, fettered as they were, destroyed the power of the fire; how they trampled down the blaze; how they overcame the furnace, and conquered the operation of the element. Hear today again how the noble and great Isaac overcame the nature itself of bodies through prayer. They destroyed the power of fire, this man to-day loosed the bonds of incapacitated nature. And learn how he affected this. "Isaac," it says, "prayed concerning his wife, because she was barren." This has to-day been read to you; yesterday the sermon was about prayer; and today again there is a demonstration of the power of prayer. See how the grace of the Spirit has ordered that what has been read today harmonizes with what was said yesterday. "Isaac," it says, "prayed concerning Rebecca his wife, because she was barren." This first is worth inquiring into, for what cause she was barren. She was of a life admirable and replete with much chastity—both herself and her husband. We cannot lay hold of the life of those just ones and say that the barrenness was the work of sin. And not only was she herself barren, but also his mother Sarah, who had borne him; not only was his mother barren and his wife, but also his daughter-in-law, the wife of Jacob, Rachel. What is the meaning of this band of barren ones? All were righteous, all living in virtue, all were witnessed to by

God. For it was of them that He said, "I am the God of Abraham, and the God of Isaac, and the God of Jacob." Of the same persons Paul also thus speaks. "For which cause God is not ashamed to call himself their God." Many are the commendations of them in the New, many the praises of them in the Old Testament. On all sides they were bright and illustrious, and yet they all had barren wives, and continued in childlessness until an advanced period. When therefore thou sees man and wife living with virtue; when thou sees them beloved of God, caring for piety, and yet suffering the malady of childlessness; do not suppose that the childlessness is at all a retribution for sins. For many are God's reasons for the dispensation, and to us inexplicable; and for all we must be heartily thankful and think those only wretched who live in wickedness; not those who do not possess children. Often God does it expediently, though we know not the cause of events. On this account in every case it is our duty to admire His wisdom, and to glorify His unspeakable love of man.

7. Well, this consideration indeed is able to school us in moral character, but it is necessary also to state the cause for which those women were barren. What then was the cause? It was in order that when thou hast seen the Virgin bringing forth our common Master, thou might not disbelieve. Wherefore exercise thy mind in the womb of the barren; in order that when thou hast seen the womb, disabled and bound as it is, being opened to the bearing of children from the grace of God, thou might not marvel at hearing that a virgin has brought forth. Or rather even marvel and be astounded; but do not disbelieve the marvel. When the Jew says to thee, "how did the virgin bear?" say to him "how did she bear who was barren and

enfeebled by old age?" There were then two hindrances, both the unseasonableness of her age and the unserviceableness of nature; but in the case of the Virgin there was one hindrance only, the not having shared in marriage. The barren one therefore prepares the way for the virgin. And that thou mayest learn that it was on this account that the barren ones had anticipated it, in order that the Virgin's childbirth might be believed, hear the words of Gabriel which were addressed to her—For when he had come and said to her, "thou shalt conceive in the womb and bear a son, and thou shalt call his name Jesus;" the Virgin was astonished and marveled, and said, "how will this be to me, since I know not a man." What then said the Angel? "The Holy Ghost shall come upon thee." Seek not the sequence of nature, he says, when that which takes place is above nature; look not round for marriage and throes of childbirth, when the manner of the birth is too grand for marriage. "And how will this be," she says, "since I know not a husband." And verily on this account shall this be, since thou knowest no husband. For didst thou know a husband, thou would not have been deemed worthy to serve this ministry. So that, for the reason why thou disbelieves, for this believe. And thou would not have been deemed worthy to serve this ministry, not because marriage is an evil; but because virginity is superior; and right it was that the entry of the Master should be more august than ours; for it was royal, and the king enters through one more august. It was necessary that He should both share as to birth and be diverse from ours. Wherefore both these things are managed.

For the being born from the womb is common in respect to us, but the being born without marriage is a thing greater than on a level with us. And the gestation and conception in the belly belongs to human nature; but that the pregnancy should take place without sexual intercourse is too august for human nature. And for this purpose both these things took place, in order that thou mayest learn both the pre-eminence and the fellowship with thee of Him who was born.

8. And pray consider the wisdom of all that was done. Neither did the pre-eminence injure the likeness and kinship to us, nor did the kinship to us dim the pre-eminence; but both were displayed by all the circumstances; and the one had our condition in its entirety, and the other what was diverse compared with us. But just as I was saying, on this account the barren ones went before, in order that the Virgin's child-birth might be believed, that she might be led by the hand to faith in that promise and undertaking which she heard from the angel, saying, "The Holy Ghost shall come upon thee, and the miraculous power of the Most High shall overshadow thee"—thus, he says, thou art able to bear. Look not to the earth; it is from the heavens that the operation will come. That which takes place is a grace of the Spirit; pray inquire not about nature and laws of marriage. But since those words were too high for her, he wills to afford also another demonstration. But do thou, pray, observe how the barren one leads her on the way to the belief in this. For since that demonstration was too high for the Virgin's intelligence, hear how he brought down what he said to lower things also, leading her by the hand by sensible facts. For "behold," he says, "Elizabeth thy kinswoman—she also has conceived a son in her old age; and this month is the sixth to her who was called barren." Seest thou that the barren one was for the sake of the Virgin? since with what object did he adduce to her

the child-bearing of her kinswoman? with what object did he say, "in her old age?" with what object did he add, "who was called barren?" It was by way of inducing her by all these things, manifestly, to the believing the glad annunciation. For this cause he spoke of both the age and the disabling effect of nature; for this cause he awaited the time also which had elapsed from the conception; for he did not tell to her the glad tidings immediately from the beginning, but awaited for a six-months period to have passed to the barren one, in order that the puerperal swelling might, for the rest, be a pledge of the pregnancy, and an indisputable demonstration might arise of the conception. And pray again, look at the intelligence of Gabriel. For he neither reminded her of Sarah, nor of Rebecca, nor of Rachel; and yet they also were barren, and they had grown old, and that which took place was a marvel; but the stories were ancient. Now things new and recent and occurring in our generation are wanting to induce us into the belief of marvels more than those which are old. On this account having let those women alone, that she should understand from her kinswoman Elizabeth herself what was coming upon her, he brought it forward; so as from her to lead her to her own—that most awful and august childbirth. For the childbirth of the barren one lay between ours and that of the Master less indeed than that of the Virgin, but greater than ours. On this account it was by Elizabeth lying between, just as by some bridge, that he lifted up the mind of the Virgin from the travail, which is according to nature, to that which is above nature.

  9. I did desire to say more, and to teach you other reasons for which Rebecca, and Rachel, were barren; but the time does not permit; urging on the discourse to the

power of prayer. For on this account indeed I have mooted all these points, that ye might understand how the prayer of Isaac unbound the barrenness of his wife; and that prayer for so long a time. "Isaac," it says, "continually prayed about Rebecca his wife, and God listened to him." For do not suppose that he invoked God and had immediately been listened to; for he had spent much time in praying to God. And if you desire to learn how much, I will tell you this too with exactness. He had spent the number of twenty years in praying to God. Whence is this manifest? from the sequence itself. For the Scripture, desiring to point out the faith and the endurance and the love of wisdom of that righteous man, did not break off and leave untold even the time, but made it also clear to us, covertly indeed, so as to rouse up our indolence; but nevertheless did not allow it to be uncertain. Hear then how it covertly indicated to us the time. "Now Isaac was forty years old when he took Rebecca, a daughter of Bethuel the Syrian." You hear how many years old he was when he brought home his wife: "Forty years old," it says, "he was when he took Rebecca." But since we have learnt how many years old he was when he married his wife, let us learn also when he after all became a father, and how many years old he was then, when he begat Jacob; and we shall be able to see how long a time his wife had remained barren; and that during all that time he continued to pray to God. How many years old then was he when he begat Jacob? "Jacob," it says, "came forth laying hold with his right hand of his brother's heel: on this account he called him Jacob, and him Esau. Now Isaac was sixty years old when he begat them." If therefore when he brought Rebecca home he was forty years old, and when he begat the sons sixty, it is very plain that his wife had remained barren for twenty years between, and during all this time Isaac continued to pray to God.

10. After this do we not feel shame, and hide our faces, at seeing that righteous man for twenty years persevering and not desisting; we ourselves after a first or second petition often fainting and indignant? And yet he indeed had in large measure liberty of speech towards God, and all the same he felt no discontent at the delay of the giving, but remained patient, whereas we, laden with countless sins, living with an evil conscience, displaying no good will towards the Master; if we are not heard before having spoken, are bewildered, impatiently recoil, desist from asking—on this account we always retire with empty hands. Who has for twenty years besought God for one thing, as this righteous man did? or rather who for twenty months only? Yesterday I was saying that they are many who pray with slackness, and yawning, and stretching themselves, and continually shifting their attitude, and indulging in every carelessness in their prayers—but to-day I have found also another damage attaching itself to their prayers more destructive than that one. For many, throwing themselves prostrate, and striking the ground with their forehead, and pouring forth hot tears, and groaning bitterly from the heart and stretching out their hands, and displaying much earnestness, employ this warmth and forwardness against their own salvation. For it is not on behalf of their own sins that they beseech God; nor are they asking forgiveness of the offences committed by them; but they are exerting this earnestness against their enemies entirely, doing just the same thing as if one, after whetting his sword, were not to use the weapon against his

enemies, but to thrust it through his own throat. So these also use their prayers not for the remission of their own sins, but about revenge on their enemies; which is to thrust the sword against themselves. This too the wicked one has devised, in order that on all sides we may destroy ourselves, both through slackness and through earnestness. For the one class by their carelessness in their prayers exasperate God, by displaying contempt through their slackness; and the others, when they display earnestness, display the earnestness on the other hand against their own salvation. "A certain person," he (the devil) says, "is slack: that is sufficient for me with a view to his obtaining nothing; this man is earnest and thoroughly aroused; what then must be done to accomplish the same result? I cannot slacken his earnestness, nor throw him into carelessness; I will contrive his destruction in the other way. How so? I will manage that he use his earnestness for transgressing the law:" (for the praying against one's personal enemies is a transgression of law). "He shall depart therefore not only having gained nothing by his earnestness, but also having endured the hurt which is greater than that caused through slackness." Such as these are the injuries of the devil: the one sort he destroys through their remissness; and the other through their earnestness itself, when it is shown not according to God's laws.

11. But it is also worth hearing the very words of their prayer, and how the words are of a puerile mind; of how infantile a soul. I am ashamed in truth when about to repeat them; but it is absolutely necessary to repeat them, and to imitate that coarse tongue. What then are the words? "Avenge me of my enemies, show them that I too have God (on my side)." They do not then learn, man, that

we have God, when we are indignant and angry and impatient; but when we are gentle and meek and subdued, and practice all love of wisdom. So also God said, "Let your light shine before men, that they may see your good works, and glorify your Father who is in the heavens." Perceives thou not that it is an insult to God, the making a request to God against thine enemies? And how is it an insult? one will say. Because He Himself said, "pray for your enemies;" and brought in this divine law. When therefore thou claims that the legislator should relax his own laws; and calls upon him to legislate in opposition to himself; and supplicates him who had forbidden thee to pray against thine enemies to hear thee praying against thine enemies; thou art not praying in doing this, nor calling upon him; but thou art insulting the lawgiver, and acting with drunken violence towards him, who is sure to give to thee the good things which result from prayer. And how is it possible to be heard when praying, tell me, when thou exasperates him who is sure to hear? For by doing these things thou art pushing thine own salvation into a pit, and art rushing down a precipice, by striking thine enemy before the king's eyes. For even if thou does not this with the hands, with thy words thou strikes him, the thing which thou dares not do even in the case of thy fellow-slaves. At least dare to do this in a ruler's presence, and though thou hast done countless public services, thou wilt straightway surely be led away to execution. Then (I ask) in the presence of a ruler dost thou not dare to insult thine equal, but when doing this in God's presence, tell me, dost thou not shudder, nor fear when in the time of entreaty and prayer being so savage and turning thyself into a wild beast; and displaying greater want of feeling than he who demanded payment of the hundred pence? For that thou art more insolent than he, listen to the story itself. A certain man owed ten thousand talents to his master; then, not having (wherewith) to pay, he entreated him to be long-suffering, in order that, his wife having been sold and his house and his children, he might settle his master's claim. And the master seeing him lamenting had compassion on him, and remitted the ten thousand talents. He having gone out and found another servant owing him a hundred pence, seizing his throat demanded them with great cruelty and inhumanity. The Master having heard this threw him into the prison, and laid on him again the debt of the ten thousand talents which he had before remitted; and he paid the penalty of the cruelty shown towards his fellow-servant.

12. Now do thou consider in how much more unfeeling and insensible in a way thou hast acted even than he, praying against thine enemies. He did not beg his master to demand, but he himself demanded, the hundred pence; whereas thou even calls on the Master for this shameless and forbidden demand. And he seized his fellow-servant's throat not before his lord's eyes, but outside; while thou in the very moment of prayer, standing in the King's presence, does this. And if he, for doing this without either having urged his master to the demand, and after going forth, met with no forgiveness; thou, both stirring up the Master to (exacting) this forbidden payment, and doing this before his eyes, what sort of penalty will thou have to pay? tell me. But thy mind is inflamed by the memory of the enmity, and swells, and thy heart rises, and when recurring in memory to him who has caused pain, thou art unable to reduce the swelling of thy thought. But set against this inflammation

the memory resulting from thine own sins committed the fear resulting from the punishment to come. Recall to memory for how many things thou art accountable to thy master, and that for all those things thou owes Him satisfaction; and this fear will surely overcome that anger; since indeed this is far more powerful than that passion. Recall the memory of hell and punishment and vengeance during the time of thy prayer; and thou wilt not be able even to receive thine enemy into thy mind. Make thy mind contrite, humble thy soul by the memory of the offences committed by thee, and wrath will not be able even to trouble thee. But the cause of all these evils is this, that we scrutinize the sins of all others with great exactitude; while we let our own pass with great remissness. Whereas we ought to do the contrary—to keep our own faults unforgotten; but never even to admit a thought of those of others. If we do this we shall both have God propitious, and shall cease cherishing immortal anger against our neighbors, and we shall never have any one as an enemy; and even if we should have at any time we shall both quickly put an end to his enmity, and should obtain speedy pardon for our own sins. For just as he who treasures up the memory of wrong against his neighbor does not permit the punishment upon his own sins to be done away; so he who is clear of anger will speedily be clear of sins also. For if we, wicked as we are and enslaved to passion, on account of the commandment of God overlook all the faults committed against us, much more will He who is a lover of mankind, and good, and free from any passion, overlook our delinquencies, rendering to us the recompense of our kindly spirit towards our neighbor in the forgiveness of our own sins: which God grant that we may attain, by the grace and lovingkindness of our Lord Jesus Christ, to whom is the glory and the dominion, to the ages of the ages. Amen.

TWO HOMILIES ON EUTROPIUS

I. WHEN HE HAD TAKEN REFUGE IN THE CHURCH.

II. WHEN HE HAD QUITTED THE ASYLUM OF THE CHURCH, AND HAD BEEN TAKEN CAPTIVE.

TRANSLATED BY
REV. W. R. W. STEPHENS, M.A.,
PREBENDARY OF CHICHESTER CATHEDRAL,
AND RECTOR OF WOOLBEDING,
SUSSEX.

St. John Chrysostom

INTRODUCTION TO THE TWO HOMILIES ON EUTROPIUS.

The interest of the two following discourses depends not only on their intrinsic value as specimens of Chrysostom's eloquence, but also on the singular and dramatic character of the incidents which gave occasion to them.
Arcadius the Emperor of the East like his brother Honorius the Emperor of the West was a man of feeble intellect. The history of the Empire under his reign is a melancholy record of imbecility on the part of the nominal rulers: of faithlessness and unscrupulous ambition on the part of their ministers. The chief administrator of affairs in the beginning of the reign of Arcadius was Rufinus, an Aquitanian Gaul; the very model of an accomplished adventurer. His intrigues, his arrogance, his rapacious avarice excited the indignation of the people, and he was at last assassinated by the troops to whom he was making an oration in the presence of the Emperor. His place in the favor and confidence of Arcadius was soon occupied by the eunuch Eutropius. The career of this person was a strange one. Born a slave, in the region of Mesopotamia, he had passed in boyhood and youth through the hands of many owners, performing the most menial offices incident to his position. At length Arnithus, an old military officer who had become his master, presented him to his daughter on her marriage; and in the words of the poet Claudian, "the future consul of the East was made over as part of a marriage dowry." But the young lady after a time grew tired of the slave who was becoming elderly and wrinkled, and without trying to sell him turned him out of her household. He

picked up a precarious living in Constantinople and was often in great want until an officer of the court took pity on him and procured him a situation in the lower ranks of the imperial chamberlains. This was the beginning of his rise. By the diligence with which he discharged his humble duties, by occasional witty sayings, and the semblance of a fervent piety he attracted the notice of the great Emperor Theodosius (the father of Arcadius), and gradually won his confidence so as to be employed on difficult and delicate missions. On the death of Theodosius he became in the capacity of grand chamberlain the intimate adviser and constant attendant of Arcadius and the most subtle and determined rival of Rufinus. It was by his contrivance that the scheme of Rufinus for marrying his own daughter to the Emperor was defeated: and that Eudoxia the daughter of a Frankish general was substituted for her. After the murder of Rufinus the government was practically in his hands; but he exercised his power more craftily than the vain and boastful Gaul. He contrived at first to discharge all the duties which fell to his lot as chamberlain with humble assiduity and sought no other title than he already possessed. Slowly but surely, however, he climbed to the summit of power by the simple process of putting out of the way on various pretexts all dangerous competitors. He deprived his victims of their last hope of escape by abolishing the right of the Church to afford shelter to fugitives. He sold the chief offices of the State, and the command of the provinces to the highest bidders. By surrounding the Emperor with a crowd of frivolous companions, by dissipating his mind with a perpetual round of amusements, by taking him every spring to Ancyra in Phrygia where he was subjected to the enervating influence of a soft climate and luxurious style of living he made the naturally feeble intellect of Arcadius more feeble still and withdrew it from the power of every superior mind but his own. From the pettiest detail of domestic life to the most important affairs of state, the wily minister at length ruled supreme. Arcadius was little more than a magnificently dressed puppet, and the eunuch slave was the real master of half the Roman world. It was by his advice that on the death of Nectarius in 397 that Chrysostom had been appointed, very much against his own will, to the vacant See of Constantinople. If Eutropius expected to find a complaisant courtier in the new Archbishop, he certainly sustained a severe disappointment. Some little pretenses which he made of assisting the work of the Church by patronizing Chrysostom's missionary projects could not blind the Archbishop to the gross venality of his administration, or exempt him from the censure and warning of one who was too honest and bold to be any respecter of persons. In fact when the Archbishop declaimed against the cupidity and oppressions of the rich it was obvious to all that Eutropius was the most signal example of these vices. At last the minister, not content to remain as he was—enjoying the reality of power without the name—prepared the way for his own ruin by inducing the Emperor to bestow on him the titles of Patrician and Consul. The acquisition of these venerable names by the eunuch slave caused a profound sensation of shame and indignation throughout the Empire, but especially in the Western capital, where they were bound up with all the noblest and most glorious memories in the history of the Roman people. The name of Eutropius was omitted from the Fasti or catalogue of consuls inscribed in the Capitol at Rome.

Amidst the general decadence and degeneracy of public spirit in the Empire the West did not descend, could not have descended, to those depths of servile adulation to which the Byzantines stooped at the inauguration of Eutropius as Consul. The senate, and all the great officials military and civil poured into the palace of the Cæsars to offer their homage and emulated each other in the honor of kissing the hand and even the wrinkled visage of the eunuch. They saluted him as the bulwark of the laws, and the second father of the Emperor. Statues of bronze or marble were placed in various parts of the city representing him in the costume of warrior or judge, and the inscriptions on them styled him third founder of the city, after Byzas, and Constantine. No wonder that Claudian declaimed with bitter sarcasm against "a Byzantine nobility and Greek divinities" and invokes Neptune by a stroke of his trident to unseat and submerge the degenerate city which had inflicted such a deep disgrace on the Empire. A blow indeed was about to fall upon the eastern capital, directed not by the hand of a mythic deity, but of a stout barbarian soldier. The consequences of it were averted from the city only by the sacrifice of the new consul upon whom it fell with crushing effect. He sank never to rise again. Tribigild, a distinguished gothic soldier who had been raised to the rank of Tribune in the Roman army, had demanded higher promotion for himself and higher pay for a body of military colonists in Phrygia of which he had the command. His petition had been coldly dismissed by Eutropius; Tribigild resent the affront and with the troops which he commanded broke into revolt. Eutropius entrusted the conduct of an expedition against him to one of his favorites, who suffered a most ignominious defeat in which he perished, and the greater part of his army was cut to pieces. Constantinople was convulsed with terror and indignation. Gäinas another Goth in command of the city troops declared that he could do nothing to check the progress of the revolt unless Eutropius was banished, the principal author of all the evils of the State. His demand was backed by the Empress Eudoxia, who had experienced much insolence from the minister. Eutropius was deprived of his official dignity, his property was declared confiscated, and he was commanded to quit the palace instantly under pain of death. Whither could the poor wretch fly who was thus in a moment hurled from the pinnacle of power into the lowest depths of degradation and destitution. There was but one place to which he could naturally turn in his distress—the sanctuary of the Church; but by the cruel irony of his fate, a law of his own devising here barred his entrance. Yet he knew that the law prohibiting asylum had been resented and resisted by the Church and it might be that the Archbishop would connive at the violation of the obnoxious measure by the very person who had passed it. He resolved to make the experiment. In the humblest guise of a suppliant, tears streaming down his puckered cheeks, his scant grey hairs smeared with dust, he crept into the Cathedral, drew aside the curtain in front of the altar and clung to one of the columns which supported it. Here he was found by Chrysostom in a state of pitiable and abject terror, for soldiers in search of him had entered the Church, and the clattering of their arms could be heard on the other side of the thin partition which concealed the fugitive. With quivering lips he craved the asylum of the church, and he was not repulsed as the destroyer of the refuge which he now sought. Chrysostom rejoiced in the opportunity afforded to the church of taking a noble revenge on her adversary. He concealed Eutropius in the sacristy, confronted his pursuers, and refused to surrender him. "None shall violate the sanctuary save over my body: the church is the bride of Christ who has entrusted her honor to me and I will never betray it." He desired to be conducted to the Emperor and taken like a prisoner between two rows of spearmen from the Cathedral to the palace where he boldly vindicated the church's right of asylum in the presence of the Emperor. Arcadius promised to respect the retreat of the fallen minister, and with difficulty persuaded the angry troops to accept his decision. The next day was Sunday, and the Cathedral was thronged with a vast multitude eager to hear what the golden mouth of the Archbishop would utter who had dared in defense of the Church's right to defy the law and confront the tide of popular feeling. But few probably were prepared to witness such a dramatic scene as was actually presented. The Archbishop had just taken his seat in the "Ambon" or high reading desk a little westward of the chancel from which he was wont to preach on the account of his diminutive stature, and a sea of faces was upturned to him waiting for the stream of golden eloquence when the curtain of the sanctuary was drawn aside and disclosed the cowering form of the miserable Eutropius clinging to one of the columns of the Holy Table. Many a time had the Archbishop preached to unheeding ears on the vain and fleeting character of worldly honor, prosperity, luxury, and wealth: now he would force attention, and drive home his lesson to the hearts of his vast congregation by pointing to a visible example of fallen grandeur in the poor wretch who lay groveling behind him.

Eutropius remained for some days within the precincts of the Church and then suddenly departed. Whether he mistrusted the security of his shelter and hoped to make his escape in disguise, or whether he surrendered himself on the understanding that exile would be substituted for capital punishment cannot be certainly known. Chrysostom declared that if he had not abandoned the Church, the Church would never have given him up. Anyhow he was captured and conveyed to Cyprus, but soon afterwards he was tried at Constantinople on various charges of high crimes and misdemeanors against the State and condemned to suffer capital punishment. He was taken to Chalcedon and there beheaded. The second of the two following discourses was delivered a few days after Eutropius had quit the sanctuary of the Church.

EUTROPIUS, PATRICIAN AND CONSUL.

Homily I.

On Eutropius, the eunuch, Patrician and Consul

1. "Vanity of vanities, all is vanity"—it is always seasonable to utter this but more especially at the present time. Where are now the brilliant surroundings of thy consulship? Where are the gleaming torches? Where is the dancing, and the noise of dancers' feet, and the banquets and the festivals? where are the garlands and the curtains of the theatre? where is the applause which greeted thee in the city, where the acclamation in the hippodrome and the flatteries of spectators? They are gone—all gone: a wind has blown upon the tree shattering down all its leaves, and showing it to us quite bare, and shaken from its very root; for so great has been the violence of the blast, that it has given a shock to all these fibers of the tree and threatens to tear it up from the roots. Where now are your feigned friends? Where are your drinking parties, and your suppers? where is the swarm of parasites, and the wine which used to be poured forth all day long, and the manifold dainties invented by your cooks? where are they who courted your power and did and said everything to win your favor? They were all mere visions of the night, and dreams which have vanished with the dawn of day: they were spring flowers, and when the spring was over they all withered: they were a shadow which has passed away—they were a smoke which has dispersed, bubbles which have burst, cobwebs which have been rent in pieces. Therefore we chant continually this spiritual song—"Vanity of vanities, all is

vanity." For this saying ought to be continually written on our walls, and garments, in the marketplace, and in the house, on the streets, and on the doors and entrances, and above all on the conscience of each one, and to be a perpetual theme for meditation. And inasmuch as deceitful things, and masking and pretense seem to many to be realities it behooves each one every day both at supper and at breakfast, and in social assemblies to say to his neighbor and to hear his neighbor say in return "vanity of vanities, all is vanity." Was I not continually telling thee that wealth was a runaway? But you would not heed me. Did I not tell thee that it was an unthankful servant? But you would not be persuaded. Behold actual experience has now proved that it is not only a runaway, and ungrateful servant, but also a murderous one, for it is this which has caused thee now to fear and tremble. Did I not say to thee when you continually rebuked me for speaking the truth, "I love thee better than they do who flatter thee?" "I who reprove thee care more for thee than they who pay thee court?" Did I not add to these words by saying that the wounds of friends were more to be relied upon than the voluntary kisses of enemies. If you had submitted to my wounds their kisses would not have wrought thee this destruction: for my wounds work health, but their kisses have produced an incurable disease. Where are now thy cupbearers, where are they who cleared the way for thee in the marketplace, and sounded thy praises endlessly in the ears of all? They have fled, they have disowned thy friendship, they are providing for their own safety by means of thy distress. But I do not act thus, nay in thy misfortune I do not abandon thee, and now when thou art fallen I protect and tend thee. And the Church which you treated as an enemy has opened her bosom and received thee into it; whereas the theatres which you courted, and about which you were oftentimes indignant with me have betrayed and ruined thee. And yet I never ceased saying to thee "why does thou these things?" "thou art exasperating the Church, and casting thyself down headlong," yet thou didst hurry away from all my warnings. And now the hippodromes, having exhausted thy wealth, have whetted the sword against thee, but the Church which experienced thy untimely wrath is hurrying in every direction, in her desire to pluck thee out of the net.

2. And I say these things now not as trampling upon one who is prostrate, but from a desire to make those who are still standing more secure; not by way of irritating the sores of one who has been wounded, but rather to preserve those who have not yet been wounded in sound health; not by way of sinking one who is tossed by the waves, but as instructing those who are sailing with a favorable breeze, so that they may not become overwhelmed. And how may this be affected? by observing the vicissitudes of human affairs. For even this man had he stood in fear of vicissitude would not have experienced it; but whereas neither his own conscience, nor the counsels of others wrought any improvement in him, do ye at least who plume yourselves on your riches profit by his calamity: for nothing is weaker than human affairs. Whatever term therefore one may employ to express their insignificance it will fall short of the reality; whether he calls them smoke, or grass, or a dream or spring flowers, or by any other name; so perishable are they, and more naught than nonentities; but that together with their nothingness they have also a very perilous element we have a proof before us. For who was more

exalted than this man? Did he not surpass the whole world in wealth? had he not climbed to the very pinnacle of distinction? did not all tremble and fear before him? Yet lo! he has become more wretched than the prisoner, more pitiable than the menial slave, more indigent than the beggar wasting away with hunger, having every day a vision of sharpened swords and of the criminal's grave, and the public executioner leading him out to his death; and he does not even know if he once enjoyed past pleasure, nor is he sensible even of the sun's ray, but at mid-day his sight is dimmed as if he were encompassed by the densest gloom. But even let me try my best I shall not be able to present to you in language the suffering which he must naturally undergo, in the hourly expectation of death. But indeed what need is there of any words from me, when he himself has clearly depicted this for us as in a visible image? For yesterday when they came to him from the royal court intending to drag him away by force, and he ran for refuge to the holy furniture, his face was then, as it is now, no better than the countenance of one dead: and the chattering of his teeth, and the quaking and quivering of his whole body, and his faltering voice, and stammering tongue, and in fact his whole general appearance were suggestive of one whose soul was petrified.

3. Now I say these things not by way of reproaching him, or insulting his misfortune, but from a desire to soften your minds towards him, and to induce you to compassion, and to persuade you to be contented with the punishment which has already been inflicted. For since there are many inhuman persons amongst us who are inclined, perhaps, to find fault with me for having admitted him to the sanctuary, I parade his sufferings

from a desire to soften their hardheartedness by my narrative.

For tell me, beloved brother, wherefore art thou indignant with me? You say it is because he who continually made war upon the Church has taken refuge within it. Yet surely we ought in the highest degree to glorify God, for permitting him to be placed in such a great strait as to experience both the power and the lovingkindness of the Church:—her power in that he has suffered this great vicissitude in consequence of the attacks which he made upon her: her lovingkindness in that she whom he attacked now casts her shield in front of him and has received him under her wings, and placed him in all security not resenting any of her former injuries, but most lovingly opening her bosom to him. For this is more glorious than any kind of trophy, this is a brilliant victory, this puts both Gentiles and Jews to shame, this displays the bright aspect of the Church: in that having received her enemy as a captive, she spares him, and when all have despised him in his desolation, she alone like an affectionate mother has concealed him under her cloak, opposing both the wrath of the king, and the rage of the people, and their overwhelming hatred. This is an ornament for the altar. A strange kind of ornament, you say, when the accused sinner, the extortioner, the robber is permitted to lay hold of the altar. Nay! say not so: for even the harlot took hold of the feet of Jesus, she who was stained with the most accursed and unclean sin: yet her deed was no reproach to Jesus, but rather redounded to His admiration and praise: for the impure woman did no injury to Him who was pure, but rather was the vile harlot rendered pure by the touch of Him who was the pure and spotless one. Grudge not then,

O man. We are the servants of the crucified one who said, "Forgive them for they know not what they do." But, you say, he cut off the right of refuge here by his ordinances and divers kinds of laws. Yes! yet now he has learned by experience what it was he did, and he himself by his own deeds has been the first to break the law, and has become a spectacle to the whole world, and silent though he is, he utters from thence a warning voice to all, saying "do not such things as I have done, that ye suffer not such things as I suffer." He appears as a teacher by means of his calamity, and the altar emits great luster, inspiring now the greatest awe from the fact that it holds the lion in bondage; for any figure of royalty might be very much set off if the king were not only to be seen seated on his throne arrayed in purple and wearing his crown, but if also prostrate at the feet of the king barbarians with their hands bound behind their backs were bending low their heads. And that no persuasive arguments have been used, ye yourselves are witnesses of the enthusiasm, and the concourse of the people. For brilliant indeed is the scene before us today, and magnificent the assembly, and I see as large a gathering here to-day as at the Holy Paschal Feast. Thus the man has summoned you here without speaking and yet uttering a voice through his actions clearer than the sound of a trumpet: and ye have all thronged hither to-day, maidens deserting their boudoirs, and matrons the women's chambers, and men the market place that ye may see human nature convicted, and the instability of worldly affairs exposed, and the harlot-face which a few days ago was radiant (such is the prosperity derived from extortion) looking uglier than any wrinkled old woman, this face I say you may see denuded of its enamel and pigments by the action of adversity as by a sponge.

4. Such is the force of this calamity: it has made one who was illustrious and conspicuous appear the most insignificant of men. And if a rich man should enter the assembly he derives much profit from the sight: for when he beholds the man who was shaking the whole world, now dragged down from so high a pinnacle of power, cowering with fright, more terrified than a hare or a frog, nailed fast to yonder pillar, without bonds, his fear serving instead of a chain, panic-stricken and trembling, he abates his haughtiness, he puts down his pride, and having acquired the kind of wisdom concerning human affairs which it concerns him to have he departs instructed by example in the lesson which Holy Scripture teaches by precept:—"All flesh is grass and all the glory of man as the flower of grass: the grass withered and the flower failed" or "They shall wither away quickly as the grass, and as the green herb shall they quickly fail" or "like smoke are his days," and all passages of that kind. Again the poor man when he has entered and gazed at this spectacle does not think meanly of himself, nor bewail himself on account of his poverty, but feels grateful to his poverty, because it is a place of refuge to him, and a calm haven, and secure bulwark; and when he sees these things he would many times rather remain where he is, than enjoy the possession of all men for a little time and afterwards be in jeopardy of his own life. Seest thou how the rich and poor, high and low, bond and free have derived no small profit from this man's taking refuge here? Seest thou how each man will depart hence with a remedy, being cured merely by this sight? Well! have I softened your passion, and expelled your wrath? have I

extinguished your cruelty? have I induced you to be pitiful? Indeed I think I have; and your countenances and the streams of tears you shed are proofs of it. Since then your hard rock has turned into deep and fertile soil let us hasten to produce some fruit of mercy, and to display a luxuriant crop of pity by falling down before the Emperor or rather by imploring the merciful God so to soften the rage of the Emperor, and make his heart tender that he may grant the whole of the favor which we ask. For indeed already since that day when this man fled here for refuge no slight change has taken place; for as soon as the Emperor knew that he had hurried to this asylum, although the army was present, and incensed on account of his misdeeds, and demanded him to be given up for execution, the Emperor made a long speech endeavoring to allay the rage of the soldiers, maintaining that not only his offences, but any good deed which he might have done ought to be taken into account, declaring that he felt gratitude for the latter, and was prepared to forgive him as a fellow creature for deeds which were otherwise. And when they again urged him to avenge the insult done to the imperial majesty, shouting, leaping, and brandishing their spears, he shed streams of tears from his gentle eyes, and having reminded them of the Holy Table to which the man had fled for refuge he succeeded at last in appeasing their wrath.

5. Moreover let me add some arguments which concern ourselves. For what pardon could you deserve, if the Emperor bears no resentment when he has been insulted, but ye who have experienced nothing of this kind display so much wrath? and how after this assembly has been dissolved will ye handle the holy mysteries, and repeat that prayer by which we are commanded to say

"forgive us as we also forgive our debtors" when ye are demanding vengeance upon your debtor? Has he inflicted great wrongs and insults on you? I will not deny it. Yet this is the season not for judgment but for mercy; not for requiring an account, but for showing loving kindness: not for investigating claims but for conceding them; not for verdicts and vengeance, but for mercy and favor. Let no one then be irritated or vexed, but let us rather beseech the merciful God to grant him a respite from death, and to rescue him from this impending destruction, so that he may put off his transgression, and let us unite to approach the merciful Emperor beseeching him for the sake of the Church, for the sake of the altar, to concede the life of one man as an offering to the Holy Table. If we do this the Emperor himself will accept us, and even before his praise we shall have the approval of God, who will bestow a large recompense upon us for our mercy. For as he rejects and hates the cruel and inhuman, so does He welcome and love the merciful and humane man; and if such a man be righteous, all the more glorious is the crown which is wreathed for him: and if he be a sinner, He passes over his sins granting this as the reward of compassion shown to his fellow-servant. "For" He saith "I will have mercy and not sacrifice," and throughout the Scriptures you find Him always enquiring after this, and declaring it to be the means of release from sin. Thus then we shall dispose Him to be propitious to us, thus we shall release ourselves from our sins, thus we shall adorn the Church, thus also our merciful Emperor, as I have already said, will commend us, and all the people will applaud us, and the ends of the earth will admire the humanity and gentleness of our city, and all who hear of these deeds throughout the world will extol us. That we then may enjoy these good things, let us fall down in prayer and supplication, let us rescue the captive, the fugitive, the suppliant from danger that we ourselves may obtain the future blessings by the favor and mercy of our Lord Jesus Christ, to whom be glory and power, now and for ever, world without end. Amen.

Homily II.

After Eutropius having been found outside the Church had been taken captive.

1. Delectable indeed are the meadow, and the garden, but far more delectable the study of the divine writings. For there indeed are flowers which fade, but here are thoughts which abide in full bloom; there is the breeze of the zephyr, but here the breath of the Spirit: there is the hedge of thorns, but here is the guarding providence of God; there is the song of cicadæ, but here the melody of the prophets: there is the pleasure which comes from sight, but here the profit which comes from study. The garden is confined to one place, but the Scriptures are in all parts of the world; the garden is subject to the necessities of the seasons, but the Scriptures are rich in foliage, and laden with fruit alike in winter and in summer. Let us then give diligent heed to the study of the Scriptures: for if thou does this the Scripture will expel thy despondency, and engender pleasure, extirpate vice, and make virtue take root, and in the tumult of life it will save thee from suffering like those who are tossed by troubled waves. The sea rages but thou sails on with calm weather; for thou hast the study of the Scriptures for thy pilot; for this is the cable which the trials of life do not break asunder. Now that I lie not events themselves bear witness. A few days ago the Church was besieged: an army came, and fire issued from their eyes, yet it did not scorch the olive tree; swords were unsheathed, yet no one received a wound; the imperial gates were in distress, but the Church was in security. And yet the tide of war

flowed hither; for here the refugee was sought, and we withstood them, not fearing their rage. And wherefore prithee? because we held as a sure pledge the saying "Thou art Peter, and upon this rock I will build my Church: and the gates of hell shall not prevail against it." And when I say the Church I mean not only a place but also a plan of life: I mean not the walls of the Church but the laws of the Church. When thou takes refuge in a Church, do not seek shelter merely in the place but in the spirit of the place. For the Church is not wall and roof but faith and life.

Do not tell me that the man having been surrendered was surrendered by the Church; if he had not abandoned the Church he would not have been surrendered. Do not say that he fled here for refuge and then was given up: the Church did not abandon him but he abandoned the Church. He was not surrendered from within the Church but outside its walls. Wherefore did he forsake the Church? Didst thou desire to save thyself? Thou shouldst have held fast to the altar. There were no walls here, but there was the guarding providence of God. Wast thou a sinner? God does not reject thee: for "He came not to call the righteous but sinners to repentance." The harlot was saved when she clung to His feet. Have ye heard the passage read today? Now I say these things that thou mayest not hesitate to take refuge in the Church. Abide with the Church, and the Church does not hand thee over to the enemy: but if thou flies from the Church, the Church is not the cause of thy capture. For if thou art inside the fold the wolf does not enter: but if thou goes outside, thou art liable to be the wild beast's prey: yet this is not the fault of the fold, but of thy own pusillanimity. The Church hath no feet. Talk not to me of walls and arms: for walls wax old with time, but the Church has no old age. Walls are shattered by barbarians, but over the Church even demons do not prevail. And that my words are no mere vaunt there is the evidence of facts. How many have assailed the Church, and yet the assailants have perished while the Church herself has soared beyond the sky? Such might hath the Church: when she is assailed she conquers: when snares are laid for her she prevails: when she is insulted her prosperity increases: she is wounded yet sinks not under her wounds; tossed by waves yet not submerged; vexed by storms yet suffers no shipwreck; she wrestles and is not worsted, fights but is not vanquished. Wherefore then did she suffer this war to be? That she might make more manifest the splendor of her triumph. Ye were present on that day, and ye saw what weapons were set in motion against her, and how the rage of the soldiers burned more fiercely than fire, and I was hurried away to the imperial palace. But what of that? By the grace of God none of those things dismayed me.

2. Now I say these things in order that ye too may follow my example. But wherefore was I not dismayed? Because I do not fear any present terrors. For what is terrible? Death? nay this is not terrible: for we speedily reach the unruffled haven. Or spoliation of goods? "Naked came I out of my mother's womb, and naked shall I depart;" or exile? "The earth is the Lord's and the fulness thereof;" or false accusation? "Rejoice and be exceeding glad, when men shall say all manner of evil against you falsely, for great is your reward in Heaven." I saw the swords and I meditated on Heaven; I expected death, and I bethought me of the resurrection; I beheld the sufferings of this lower world, and I took account of the heavenly prizes; I observed the devices of the enemy, and

I meditated on the heavenly crown: for the occasion of the contest was sufficient for encouragement and consolation. True! I was being forcibly dragged away, but I suffered no insult from the act; for there is only one real insult, namely sin: and should the whole world insult thee, yet if thou dost not insult thyself thou art not insulted. The only real betrayal is the betrayal of the conscience: betray not thy own conscience, and no one can betray thee. I was being dragged away and I saw the events—or rather I saw my words turned into events, I saw my discourse which I had uttered in words being preached in the marketplace through the medium of actual events. What kind of discourse? the same which I was always repeating. The wind has blown and the leaves have fallen. "The grass has withered and the flower has faded." The night has departed and the day has dawned; the shadow has been proved vain and the truth has appeared. They mounted up to the sky, and they came down to the level of earth: for the waves which were swelling high have been laid low by means of merely human events. How? The things which were taking place were a lesson. And I said to myself will posterity learn self-control? or before two days have passed by will these events have been abandoned to oblivion? The warnings were sounding in their ears. Again let me utter, yet again I will speak. What profit will there be? Certainly there will be profit. For if all do not hearken, the half will hearken; and if not the half, the third part: and if not the third the fourth: and if not the fourth, perhaps ten: and if not ten, perhaps five: and if not five perhaps one: and if not one, I myself have the reward prepared for me. "The grass withered and the flower faded; but the word of God abides forever."

3. Have ye seen the insignificance of human affairs? have ye seen the frailty of power? Have ye seen the wealth which I always called a runaway and not a runaway only, but also a murderer. For it not only deserts those who possess it, but also slaughters them; for when anyone pays court to it then most of all does it betray him. Why dost thou pay court to wealth which to-day is for thee, and to-morrow for another? Why dost thou court wealth which can never be held fast? Do you desire to court it? dost thou desire to hold it fast? Do not bury it but give it into the hands of the poor. For wealth is a wild beast: if it be tightly held it runs away: if it be let loose it remains where it is; "For," it is said, "he hath dispersed abroad and given to the poor; his righteousness remained forever." Disperse it then that it may remain with thee; bury it not lest it run away. Where is wealth? I would gladly enquire of those who have departed. Now I say these things not by way of reproach, God forbid, nor by way of irritating old sores, but as endeavoring to secure a haven for you out of the shipwreck of others. When soldiers and swords were threatening, when the city was in a blaze of fury, when the imperial majesty was powerless, and the purple was insulted, when all places were full of frenzy, where was wealth then? where was your silver plate? Where were your silver couches? where your household slaves? they had all betaken themselves to flight; where were the eunuchs? they all ran away; where were your friends? they changed their masks. Where were your houses? they were shut up. Where was your money? The owner of it fled: and the money itself, where was that? it was buried. Where was it all hidden? Am I oppressive and irksome to you in constantly declaring that wealth betrays those who use it badly? The occasion has

now come which proves the truth of my words. Why dost thou hold it so tightly, when in the time of trial it profited thee nothing? If it has power when thou falls into a strait, let it come to thy aid, but if it then runs away what need hast thou of it? events themselves bear witness. What profit was there in it? The sword was whetted, death was impending, an army raging: there was apprehension of imminent peril; and yet wealth was nowhere to be seen. Where did the runaway flee? It was itself the cause which brought about all these evils, and yet in the hours of necessity it runs away. Nevertheless many reproach me saying continually thou fastened upon the rich: while they on the other hand fasten upon the poor. Well I do fasten upon the rich: or rather not the rich, but those who make a bad use of their riches. For I am continually saying that I do not attack the character of the rich man, but of the rapacious. A rich man is one thing, a rapacious man is another: an affluent man is one thing, a covetous man is another. Make clear distinctions, and do not confuse things which are diverse. Art thou a rich man? I forbid thee not. Art thou a rapacious man? I denounce thee. Hast thou property of thy own? enjoy it. Do you take the property of others? I will not hold my peace. Would you stone me for this? I am ready to shed my blood: only I forbid thy sin. I heed not hatred, I heed not war: one thing only do I heed, the advancement of my hearers. The rich are my children, and the poor also are my children: the same womb has travailed with both, both are the offspring of the same travail-pangs. If then thou fastens reproaches on the poor man, I denounce thee: for the poor man does not suffer so much loss as the rich. For no great wrong is inflicted on the poor man, seeing that in his case the injury is confined to money; but in thy case the injury touches the soul. Let him who wills cast me off, let him who wills stone me, let him who wills hate me: for the plots of enemies are the pledges to me of crowns of victory, and the number of my rewards will be as the number of my wounds.

4. So then I fear not an enemy's plots: one thing only do I fear, which is sin. If no one convicts me of sin, then let the whole world make war upon me. For this kind of war only renders me more prosperous. Thus also do I wish to teach you a lesson. Fear not the devices of a potentate but fear the power of sin. No man will do thee harm, if thou dost not deal a blow to thyself. If thou hast not sin, ten thousand swords may threaten thee, but God will snatch thee away out of their reach: but if thou hast sin, even shouldest thou be in paradise thou wilt be cast out. Adam was in paradise, yet he fell; Job was on a dung hill, yet he was crowned victorious. What profit was paradise to the one? or what injury was the dunghill to the other? No man laid snares for the one, yet was he overthrown: the devil laid snares for the other, and yet he was crowned. Did not the devil take his property? Yes, but he did not rob him of his godliness. Did he not lay violent hands upon his sons? yes: but he did not shake his faith. Did he not tear his body to pieces? yes but he did not find his treasure. Did he not arm his wife against him? yes but he did not overthrow the soldier. Did he not hurl arrows and darts at him? yes but he received no wounds. He advanced his engines but could not shake the tower; he conducted his billows against him but did not sink the ship. Observe this law I beseech you, yea I clasp your knees, if not with the bodily hand, yet in spirit, and pour forth tears of supplication. Observe this law, I pray you, and no one can do you harm. Never call the rich man

happy; never call any man miserable save him who is living in sin: and call him happy who lives in righteousness. For it is not the nature of their circumstances, but the disposition of the men which makes both the one and the other. Never be afraid of the sword if thy conscience does not accuse thee: never be afraid in war if thy conscience is clear. Where are they who have departed? tell me. Did not all men once bow down to them? did not those who were in authority tremble greatly before them? Did they not pay court to them? But sin has come, and all things are manifested in their true lights; they who were attendants have become judges, the flatterers are turned into executioners; they who once kissed his hands, dragged him themselves from the church, and he who yesterday kissed his hand is to-day his enemy. Wherefore? Because neither did he yesterday love him with sincerity. For the opportunity came and the actors were unmasked. Didst thou not yesterday kiss his hands, and call him savior, and guardian, and benefactor? Didst thou not compose panegyrics without end? wherefore today dost thou accuse him? Why yesterday a praiser, and today an accuser? why yesterday utter panegyrics, and today reproaches? What means this change? what means this revolution?

5. But I am not like this: I was the subject of his plots, yet I became his protector. I suffered countless troubles at his hands, yet I did not retaliate. For I copy the example of my Master, who said on the cross, "Forgive them, for they know not what they do." Now I say these things that you may not be perverted by the suspicion of wicked men. Now many changes have taken place, since I had the oversight of the city, and yet no one learns self

control? But when I say no one, I do not condemn all, God forbid. For it is impossible that this rich soil when it has received seed, should not produce one ear of corn: but I am insatiable, I do not wish many to be saved but all. And if but one be left in a perishing condition, I perish also, and deem that the Shepherd should be imitated who had ninety-nine sheep, and yet hastened after the one which had gone astray. How long will money last? How long this silver and gold? how long these draughts of wine? how long the flatteries of slaves? how long these goblets wreathed with garlands? how long these satanic drinking feasts, full of diabolical activity?

Dost thou not know that the present life is a sojourn in a far country? for art thou a citizen? Nay thou art a wayfarer. Understands thou what I say? Thou art not a citizen, but thou art a wayfarer, and a traveler. Say not: I have this city and that. No one has a city. The city is above. Present life is but a journey. We are journeying on every day, while nature is running its course. Some there are who store up goods on the way: some who bury jewelry on the road. Now when you enter an inn do you beautify the inn? not so, but you eat and drink and hasten to depart. The present life is an inn: we have entered it, and we bring present life to a close: let us be eager to depart with a good hope, let us leave nothing here, that we may not lose it there. When you enter the inn, what do you say to the servant? Take care where you put away our things, that you do not leave anything behind here, that nothing may be lost, not even what is small and trifling, in order that we may carry everything back to our home. Thou art a wayfarer and traveler, and indeed more insignificant than the wayfarer. How so? I will tell you. The wayfarer knows when he is going into the inn, and when he is going out; for the egress as well as the regress is in his own power: but when I enter the inn, that is to say this present life, I know not when I shall go out: and it may be that I am providing myself with sustenance for a long time when the Master suddenly summons me saying "Thou fool, for whom shall those things be which thou hast prepared? for on this very night thy soul is being taken from thee." The time of thy departure is uncertain, the tenure of thy possessions insecure, there are innumerable precipices, and billows on every side of thee. Why dost thou rave about shadows? why desert the reality and run after shadows?

6. I say these things, and shall not cease saying them, causing continual pain, and dressing the wounds; and this not for the sake of the fallen, but of those who are still standing. For they have departed, and their career is ended, but those who are yet standing have gained a more secure position through their calamities. "What then," you say, "shall we do?" Do one thing only, hate riches, and love thy life—cast away thy goods; I do not say all of them, but cut off the superfluities. Be not covetous of other men's goods, strip not the widow, plunder not the orphan, seize not his house: I do not address myself to persons but to facts. But if any one's conscience attacks him, he himself is responsible for it, not my words. Why art thou grasping where thou brings ill-will upon thyself? Grasp where there is a crown to be gained. Strive to lay hold not of earth but of heaven. "The kingdom of Heaven belongs to violent men and men of violence take it by force." Why dost thou lay hold of the poor man who reproaches thee? Lay hold of Christ who praises thee for it. Do you see thy senselessness and madness? Do you lay hold of the poor man who has little? Christ says, "lay hold

of me; I thank thee for it, lay hold of my kingdom and take it by violence." If thou art minded to lay hold of an earthly kingdom, or rather if thou art minded to have designs upon it thou art punished; but in the case of the heavenly kingdom thou art punished if thou dost not lay hold of it. Where worldly things are concerned there is ill-will, but where spiritual there is love. Meditate daily on these things, and if two days hence thou sees another riding in a chariot, arrayed in raiment of silk, and elated with pride, be not again dismayed and troubled. Praise not a rich man, but only him who lives in righteousness. Revile not a poor man, but learn to have an upright and accurate judgment in all things.

Do not hold aloof from the Church; for nothing is stronger than the Church. The Church is thy hope, thy salvation, thy refuge. It is higher than the heaven, it is wider than the earth. It never waxes old, but is always in full vigor. Wherefore as significant of its solidity and stability Holy Scripture calls it a mountain: or of its purity a virgin, or of its magnificence a queen; or of its relationship to God a daughter; and to express its productiveness it calls her barren who has borne seven: in fact it employs countless names to represent its nobleness. For as the master of the Church has many names: being called the Father, and the way, and the life, and the light, and the arm, and the propitiation, and the foundation, and the door, and the sinless one, and the treasure, and Lord, and God, and Son, and the only begotten, and the form of God, and the image of God so is it with the Church itself: does one name suffice to present the whole truth? by no means. But for this reason there are countless names, that we may learn something concerning God, though it be but a small part. Even so the Church also is called by many names. She is called a virgin, albeit formerly she was a harlot: for this is the miracle wrought by the Bridegroom, that He took her who was a harlot and hath made her a virgin. Oh! what a new and strange event! With us marriage destroys virginity, but with God marriage hath restored it. With us she who is a virgin, when married, is a virgin no longer: with Christ she who is a harlot, when married, becomes a virgin.

7. Let the heretic who inquires curiously into the nature of heavenly generation saying "how did the Father beget the Son?" interpret this single fact, ask him how did the Church, being an harlot, become a virgin? and how did she having brought forth children remain a virgin? "For I am jealous over you," saith Paul, "with a godly jealousy, for I espoused you to one husband that I might present you as a pure virgin to Christ." What wisdom and understanding! "I am jealous over you with a godly jealousy." What means this? "I am jealous," he says: art thou jealous seeing thou art a spiritual man? I am jealous he says as God is. And hath God jealousy? yea the jealousy not of passion, but of love, and earnest zeal. I am jealous over you with the jealousy of God. Shall I tell thee how He manifests His jealousy? He saw the world corrupted by devils, and He delivered His own Son to save it. For words spoken in reference to God have not the same force as when spoken in reference to ourselves: for instance we say God is jealous, God is wroth, God repents, God hates. These words are human, but they have a meaning which becomes the nature of God. How is God jealous? "I am jealous over you with the jealousy of God." Is God wroth? "O Lord reproach me not in thine indignation." Doth God slumber? "Awake, wherefore sleeps thou, O Lord?" Doth God repent? "I repent that I

have made man." Doth God hate? "My soul hated your feasts and your new moons." Well do not consider the poverty of the expressions: but grasp their divine meaning. God is jealous, for He loves, God is wroth, not as yielding to passion, but for the purpose of chastising, and punishing. God sleeps, not as really slumbering, but as being long-suffering. Choose out the expression. Thus when thou hears that God begets the Son, think not of division but of the unity of substance. For God has taken many of these words from us as we also have borrowed others from Him, that we may receive honor thereby.

8. Do you understand what I have said? Attend carefully my beloved. There are divine names, and there are human names. God has received from me, and He Himself hath given to me. Give me thine and take mine He says. Thou hast need of mine: I have no need of thine, but thou hast of mine inasmuch as my nature is unmixed, but thou art a human being encompassed with a body, seeking also corporeal terms in order that, by borrowing expressions which are familiar to thee, thou who art thus encompassed with a body, mayest be able to think on thoughts which transcend thy understanding. What kind of names hath He received from me, and what kind hath He given to me? He Himself is God, and He hath called me God; with Him is the essential nature as an actual fact, with me only the honor of the name: "I have said ye are gods, and ye are all children of the most highest." Here are words, but in the other case there is the actual reality. He hath called me god, for by that name I have received honor. He Himself was called man, he was called Son of man, he was called the Way, the Door, the Rock. These words He borrowed from me; the others He gave from Himself to me. Wherefore was He called the Way? That

thou might understand that by Him we have access to the Father. Wherefore was He called the Rock? that thou might understand the secure and unshaken character of the faith. Wherefore was He called the Foundation? That thou might understand that He upholds all things. Wherefore was He called the Root? That thou might understand that in Him we have our power of growth. Wherefore was He called the Shepherd? Because He feeds us. Wherefore was He called a sheep? Because He was sacrificed for us and became a propitiatory offering. Wherefore was He called the Life? Because He raised us up when we were dead. Wherefore was He called the Light? Because He delivered us from darkness. Why was He called an Arm? Because He is of one substance with the Father. Why was He called the Word? Because He was begotten of the Father. For as my word is the offspring of my spirit, even so was the Son begotten of the Father. Wherefore is He called our raiment? Because I was clothed with Him when I was baptized. Why is He called a table? Because I feed upon Him when I partake of the mysteries. Why is He called a house? Because I dwell in Him. Why is He called an inmate of the house? Because we become His Temple. Wherefore is He called the Head? Because I have been made a member of His. Why is He called a Bridegroom? Because He hath taken me as His bride. Wherefore is He called undefiled? Because He took me as a virgin. Wherefore is He called Master? Because I am His bondmaid.

9. For observe the Church, how, as I was saying, she is sometimes a bride, sometimes a daughter, sometimes a virgin, sometimes a bondmaid, sometimes a queen, sometimes a barren woman, sometimes a mountain, sometimes a garden, sometimes fruitful in

children, sometimes a lily, sometimes a fountain: She is all things. Therefore having heard these things, think not I pray you that they are corporeal; but stretch thy thought further: for such things cannot be corporeal. For example: the mountain is not the maid: the maid is not the bride: the queen is not the bondmaid: yet the Church is all these things. Wherefore? because the element in which they exist is not corporeal but spiritual. For in a corporeal sphere these things are confined within narrow limits: but in a spiritual sphere they have a wide field of operation. "The queen stood on thy right hand." The queen? How did she who was downtrodden and poor become a queen? and where did she ascend? the queen herself stood on high by the side of the king. How? because the king became a servant; He was not that by nature, but He became so. Understand therefore the things which belong to the Godhead and discern those which belong to the Dispensation. Understand what He *was,* and what He *became* for thy sake, and do not confuse things which are distinct, nor make the argument of his lovingkindness an occasion for blasphemy. He was lofty, and she was lowly: lofty not by position but by nature. His essence was pure, and imperishable: His nature was incorruptible, unintelligible, invisible, incomprehensible, eternal, unchangeable, transcending the nature of angels, higher than the powers above, overpowering reason, surpassing thought, apprehended not by sight but by faith alone. Angels beheld Him and trembled, the Cherubim veiled themselves with their wings, in awe. He looked upon the earth and caused it to tremble: He threatened the sea and dried it up: he brought rivers out of the desert: He weighed the mountains in scales, and the valleys in a balance. How shall I express myself? how shall I present the truth? His greatness hath no bounds, His wisdom is beyond reckoning, His judgments are untraceable, His ways unsearchable. Such is His greatness and His power, if indeed it is safe even to use such expressions. But what am I to do? I am a human being, and I speak in human language: my tongue is of earth and I crave forgiveness from my Lord. For I do not use these expressions in a spirit of presumption, but on account of the poverty of my resources arising from my feebleness and the nature of our human tongue. Be merciful to me, O Lord, for I utter these words not in presumption but because I have no others: nevertheless I do not rest content with the meanness of my speech but soar upwards on the wings of my understanding. Such is His greatness and power. I say this, that without dwelling on the words, or on the poverty of the expressions, thou mayest also thyself learn to act in the same way. Why dost thou marvel if I do this, inasmuch as He also does the same, when He wishes to present something to our minds which transcends human powers? Since He addresses human beings He uses also human illustration, which are indeed insufficient to represent the thing spoken of, and cannot exhibit the full proportions of the matter, yet suffice for the infirmity of the hearers.

10. Make an effort, and do not grow weary of my prolonged discourse. For as when He manifests Himself, He is not manifested as He really is, nor is His bare essence manifested (for no man hath seen God in His real nature; for when He is but partially revealed the Cherubim tremble—the mountains smoke, the sea is dried up, the heaven is shaken, and if the revelation were not partial who could endure it?) as then, I say, He does not manifest Himself as He really is, but only as the beholder

is able to see Him, therefore doth He appear sometimes in the form of old age, sometimes of youth, sometimes in fire, sometimes in air, sometimes in water, sometimes in armor, not altering his essential nature, but fashioning His appearance to suit the various condition of those who are affected by it. In like manner also when anyone wishes to say anything concerning Him he employs human illustrations. For instance I say: "He went up into the mountain and He was transfigured before them, and His countenance shone as the sun, and His raiment became white as snow." He disclosed, it is said, a little of the Godhead, He manifested to them the God dwelling amongst them "and He was transfigured before them." Attend carefully to the statement. The writer says and He was transfigured before them, and His raiment shone as the light, and His countenance was as the sun. When I said "such is His greatness and power" and added "be merciful to me O Lord," (for I do not rest satisfied with the expression but am perplexed, having no other framed for the purpose) I wish you to understand, that I learned this lesson from Holy Scripture. The evangelist then wished to describe His splendor and he says, "He shone." How did He shine? tell me. Exceedingly. And how do you express this? He shone "as the sun." As the sun sayest thou? Yea. Wherefore? Because I know not any other luminary more brilliant. And He was white sayest thou as snow? wherefore as snow? Because I know not any other substance which is whiter. For that He did not really shine thus is proved by what follows: the disciples fell to the ground. If he had shone as the sun the disciples would not have fallen; for they saw the sun every day, and did not fall: but inasmuch as he shone more brilliantly than the sun or snow, they, being unable to bear the splendor, fell to the earth.

11. Tell me then, O evangelist, did He shine more brightly than the sun, and yet dost thou say, "as the sun?" Yea: wishing to make that light known to thee, I know not any other greater luminary, I have no other comparison which holds a royal place amongst luminaries. I have said these things that thou mayest not rest contentedly in the poverty of the language used: I have pointed out to thee the fall of the disciples: they fell to the earth and were stupefied and overwhelmed with slumber. "Arise" He said, and lifted them up, and yet they were oppressed. For they could not endure the excessive brightness of that shining, but heavy sleep took possession of their eyes: so far did the light which was manifested exceed the light of the sun. Yet the evangelist said, "as the sun," because that luminary is familiar to us and surpasses all the rest.

But as I was saying, He who was thus great and powerful desired a harlot. I speak of our human nature under that name. If a man indeed desire a harlot he is condemned, and doth God desire one? Yea verily. Again a man desires a harlot that he may become a fornicator: but God that He may convert the harlot into a virgin: so that the desire of the man is the destruction of her who is desired: but the desire of God is salvation to her who is desired. And why did He who is so great and powerful desire a harlot? that He might become the husband thereof. How does He act? He doth not send to her any of His servants, He sent not angel, archangel, Cherubim, or Seraphim; but He himself draws nigh Who loves her. Again when thou hears of love, deem it not sensuous. Cull out the thoughts which are contained in the words, even as an excellent bee settles on the flowers, and takes the honeycomb, but leaves the herbs God desired a harlot, and how doth He act? He does not conduct her on high; for He would not bring a harlot into Heaven, but He Himself comes down. Since she could not ascend on high, He descends to earth. He comes to the harlot and is not ashamed: He comes to her secret dwelling place. He beholds her in her drunkenness. And how doth He come? not in the bare essence of His original nature, but He becomes that which the harlot was, not in intention but in reality does He become this, in order that she may not be scared when she sees Him, that she may not rush away, and escape. He cometh to the harlot and becomes man. And how does He become this? He is conceived in the womb, he increases little by little and follows like me the course of human growth. Who is it who does this? the Deity as manifested, not the Godhead; the form of the servant not that of the Master; the flesh which belongs to me, not the essential nature which belongs to Him: He increases little by little, and has intercourse with mankind. Although He finds the harlot, human nature, full of sores, brutalized, and oppressed by devils, how does He act? He draws nigh to her. She sees Him and flees away. He calleth the wise men saying Why are ye afraid? I am not a judge, but a physician. "I came not to judge the world but to save the world." Straightway He calleth the wise men. Oh! new and strange event. The immediate first fruits of His coming are wise men. He who upholds the world lieth in a manger, and He who cares for all things is a nursling in swaddling bands. The temple is founded and the God dwelleth therein. And wise men come and straightway worship Him: the publican comes and is turned into an evangelist: the harlot comes and is turned into a maiden: the Canaanitish woman comes and partakes of his lovingkindness. This is the mark of one who loves, to forbear demanding an account of sins, and to forgive transgressions and offences. And how does He act? He takes the sinner and espouses her to himself. And what doth He give her? a signet ring. Of what nature? the Holy Spirit. Paul saith "now He who establishes us with you is God who hath also sealed us and given the earnest of the Spirit." The Spirit then He giveth her. Next, He saith "Did not I plant thee in a garden?" She saith "yea." And how didst thou fall from thence? "The devil came and cast me out of the garden." Thou was planted in the garden and he cast thee out: behold I plant thee in myself, I uphold thee. How? The devil dares not approach me. Neither do I take thee up into Heaven; but something greater than Heaven is here: I carry thee in myself who am the Lord of Heaven. The shepherd carries thee and the wolf no longer comes or rather I permit him to approach. And so the Lord carries our nature: and the devil approaches and is worsted. "I have planted thee in myself:" therefore He saith "I am the root, ye are the branches:" so He planted her in Himself. "But," she saith, "I am a sinner and unclean." "Let not this trouble thee, I am a physician. I know my vessel, I know how it was perverted. It was formerly a vessel of clay, and it was perverted. I remodel it by means of the laver of regeneration and I submit it to the action of fire." For observe: He took dust from the earth and made the man; He formed him. The devil came, and perverted him. Then the Lord came, took him again, and remolded, and recast him in baptism, and He suffered not his body to be of clay, but made it of a harder ware. He subjected the soft clay to the fire of the Holy Spirit. "He shall baptize you with the Holy Ghost and with fire:" He was baptized with water that he might be remodeled, with fire that he might be hardened. Therefore the Prophet speaking beforehand under divine guidance declared "Thou shalt dash them in pieces like vessels of the potter." He did not say like vessels of earthenware which everyone possesses for by a potter's vessels are meant those which the potter is fashioning on the wheel: now the potter's vessels are of clay, but ours are of harder ware. Speaking beforehand therefore of the remolding which is wrought by means of baptism he saith, "thou shalt dash them in pieces like vessels of a potter"—He means that He remodels and recasts them. I descend into the water of baptism, and the fashion of my nature is remolded, and the fire of the Spirit recasts it, and it is turned into a harder ware. And that my words are no empty vaunt hear what Job says, "He hath made us as clay," and Paul, "but we have this treasure in earthen vessels." But consider the strength of the earthen vessel: for it has been hardened not by fire, but by the Spirit. How was it proved to be an earthen vessel? "Five times received I forty stripes save one, thrice was I beaten with rods, once was I stoned," and yet the earthen vessel was not shattered. "A day and a night have I been in the deep." He hath been in the deep, and the earthen vessel was not dissolved: he suffered shipwreck and the treasure was not lost; the ship was submerged and yet the freight floated. "But we have this treasure" he says. What kind of treasure? a supply of the Spirit, righteousness, sanctification, redemption. Of what nature, tell me? "in the name of Jesus Christ rise up and walk." "Æneas, Jesus Christ maketh thee whole," I say unto thee thou evil spirit, go out of him.

  12. Hast thou seen a treasure more brilliant than royal treasures? For what can the pearl of a king do like that which the words of an Apostle effected? Set crowns

innumerable upon dead men, and they will not be raised: but one word went forth from an Apostle, and it brought back revoked nature, and restored it to its ancient condition. "But we have this treasure." O treasure which not only is preserved, but also preserves the house where it is stored up. Do you understand what I have said? The kings of the earth, and rulers when they have treasures, prepare large houses, having strong walls, bars, doors, guards, and bolts in order that the treasure may be preserved: but Christ did the contrary: He placed the treasure not in a stone vessel but in an earthen one. If the treasure is great wherefore is the vessel weak? But the reason why the vessel is weak is not because the treasure is great; for this is not preserved by the vessel, but itself preserves the vessel. I deposit the treasure: who is able henceforth to steal it? The devil has come, the world has come, multitudes have come, and yet they have not stolen the treasure: the vessel has been scourged, yet the treasure was not betrayed; it has been drowned in the sea, yet the treasure was not shipwrecked: it has died yet the treasure survives. He gave therefore the earnest of the Spirit. Where are they who blasphemed the Spirit's majesty? Give ye heed. "He that establishes us with you in Christ is God who also hath given the earnest of the Spirit." You all know that the earnest is a small part of the whole; let me tell you how. Someone goes to buy a house at a great price; and he says, "give me an earnest that I may have confidence: or one goes to take a wife for himself, he arranges about dowry and property, and he says, "give me an earnest." Observe: in the purchase of a slave and in all covenants there is an earnest. Since then Christ made a covenant with us (for He was about to take me as a bride) he also assigned a dowry to me not of money, but of blood. But this dowry which He assigns is the bestowal of good things "such as eye hath not seen, and ear hath not heard, neither hath entered into the heart of man." He assigned them for the dowry:—immortality, praise with the angels, release from death, freedom from sin, the inheritance of a kingdom (so great are his riches), righteousness, sanctification, deliverance from present evils, discovery of future blessings. Great was my dowry. Now attend carefully: mark what He does. He came to take the harlot, for so I call her, unclean as she was, that thou might understand the love of the bridegroom. He came; He took me: He assigns me a dowry: He saith "I give thee my wealth." How? "Hast thou lost," He saith, "paradise?" take it back. Hast thou lost thy beauty? take it back; take all these things. But yet the dowry was not given to me here.

13. Observe, this is the reason why He speaks beforehand with reference to this dowry; He warranted to me in the dowry the resurrection of the body,—immortality. For immortality does not always follow resurrection, but the two are distinct. For many have risen, and been again laid low, like Lazarus and the bodies of the saints. But in this case it is not so, but the promise is of resurrection, immortality, a place in the joyful company of angels, the meeting of the Son of Man in the clouds, and the fulfilment of the saying "so shall we ever be with the Lord," the release from death, the freedom from sin, the complete overthrow of destruction. Of what kind is that? "Eye hath not seen nor ear heard neither have entered into the heart of man the things which God hath prepared for them that love Him." Do you give me good things which I know not? He saith "yea; only be espoused to me here, love me in this world." "Wherefore dost thou

not give me the dowry here?" "It will be given when thou hast come to my Father, when thou hast entered the royal palace. Didst thou come to me! nay I came to thee. I came not that thou shouldst abide here but that I might take thee and return. Seek not the dowry here: all depends on hope, and faith. "And dost thou give me nothing in this world?" He answers. "Receive an earnest that thou mayest trust me concerning that which is to come: receive pledges and betrothal gifts." Therefore Paul saith "I have espoused you." As gifts of betrothal God has given us present blessings: they are an earnest of the future; but the full dowry abides in the other world. How so? I will tell you. Here I grow old, there I grow not old; here I die, there I die not, here I sorrow, there I sorrow not; here is poverty, and disease, and intrigue, there nothing of that kind exists: here is darkness and light, there is light alone: here is intrigue, there is liberty; here is disease, there is health; here is life which has an end, there is life which hath no end; here is sin, there is righteousness, and sin is banished; here is envy, there nothing of the kind exists. "Give me these things" one says, "Nay! wait in order that thy fellow-servants also may be saved; wait I say. He who establishes us and hath given us the earnest"—what kind of earnest? the Holy Spirit, the supply of the Spirit. Let me speak concerning the Spirit. He gave the signet ring to the Apostles, saying "take this and give it to all." Is the ring then portioned out, and yet not divided? It is so. Let me teach you the meaning of the supply of the Spirit: Peter received, and Paul also received the Holy Spirit. He went about the world, he released sinners from their sins, he restored the lame, he clothed the naked, he raised the dead, he cleansed the lepers, he bridled the devil, he strangled the demons, he held converse with God, he planted a Church, levelled temples to the earth, overturned altars, destroyed vice, established virtue, made angels of men.

14. All these things we were. But "the earnest" filled the whole world. And when I say the whole I mean all which the sun shines upon, sea, islands, mountains, valleys, and hills. Paul went hither and thither, like some winged creature, with one mouth only contending against the enemy, he the tentmaker, who handled the workman's knife and sewed skins together: and yet this his craft was no hindrance to his virtue, but the tentmaker was stronger than demons, the ineloquent man was wiser than the wise. Whence was this? He received the earnest, he bore the signet ring and carried it about. All men saw that the King had espoused our nature: the demon saw it and retreated, he saw the earnest, and trembled and withdrew: he saw but the Apostle's garments and fled. O the power of the Holy Spirit. He bestowed authority not on the soul, nor on the body, but even on raiment; nor on raiment only but even on a shadow. Peter went about and his shadow put diseases to flight, and expelled demons, and raised the dead to life. Paul went about the world, cutting away the thorns of ungodliness, sowing broadcast the seeds of godliness, like an excellent ploughman handling the ploughshare of doctrine. And to whom did he go? To Thracians, to Scythians, to Indians, to Maurians, to Sardinians, to Goths, to wild savages, and he changed them all. By what means? By means of "the earnest." How was he sufficient for these things? By the grace of the Spirit. Unskilled, ill-clothed, ill-shod he was upheld by Him "who also hath given the earnest of the Spirit." Therefore he saith "and who is sufficient for these things? But our sufficiency is of God, who hath made us

sufficient as ministers of the new Testament, not of the letter but of the Spirit." Behold what the Spirit hath wrought: He found the earth filled with demons and He has made it heaven. For meditate not on present things but review the past in your thought. Formerly there was lamentation, there were altars everywhere, everywhere the smoke and fumes of sacrifice, everywhere unclean rites and mysteries, and sacrifices, everywhere demons holding their orgies, everywhere a citadel of the devil, everywhere fornication decked with wreaths of honor; and Paul stood alone. How did he escape being overwhelmed, or torn in pieces? How could he open his mouth? He entered the Thebaid, and made captives of men, He entered the royal palace, and made a disciple of the king. He entered the hall of judgment, and the judge saith to him "almost thou persuades me to become a Christian," and the judge became a disciple. He entered the prison and took the jailor captive. He visited an island of barbarians and made a viper the instrument of his teaching. He visited the Romans and attracted the senate to his doctrine. He visited rivers, and desert places in all parts of the world. There is no land or sea which has not shared in the benefits of his labors; for God has given human nature the earnest of His signet, and when He gives it, He saith: some things I give thee now, and others I promise. Therefore the prophet saith concerning her "The queen did stand upon thy right hand in a vesture woven with gold." He does not mean a real vesture, but virtue. Therefore the Scripture elsewhere saith "How came thou in hither not having a wedding garment?" so that here he does not mean a garment, but fornication, and foul and unclean living. As then foul raiment signifies sin, so does golden raiment signify virtue. But this raiment belonged to the king. He Himself bestowed the raiment upon her: for she was naked, naked and disfigured. "The queen stood on thy right hand in a vesture woven with gold." He is speaking not of raiment but of virtue. Observe: the expression itself has great nobility of meaning. He does not say "in a vesture of gold" but "in a vesture woven with gold." Listen intelligently. A vesture of gold is one which is gold throughout: but a vesture woven with gold is one which is partly of gold, partly of silk. Why then did he say that the bride wore not a vesture of gold, but one woven with gold? Attend carefully. He means the constitution of the Church in its varied manifestations. For since we do not all belong to one condition of life, but one is a virgin, another a widow, a third lives a life of devotion—so the robe of the Church signifies the constitution of the Church.

15. Inasmuch then as our Master knew that if He carved out only one road for us, many must shrink from it, He carved out divers roads. Thou canst not enter the kingdom it may be by the way of virginity. Enter it then by the way of single marriage. Canst thou not enter it by one marriage? Perchance thou mayest by means of a second marriage. Thou canst not enter by the way of continence: enter then by the way of almsgiving: or thou canst not enter by the way of almsgiving? then try the way of fasting. If thou canst not use this way, take that—or if not that, then take this. Therefore the prophet spoke not of a garment of gold, but of one woven with gold. It is of silk, or purple, or gold. Thou canst not be a golden part? then be a silken one. I accept thee, if only thou art clothed in my raiment. Therefore also Paul saith "If any man builds upon this foundation, gold, silver, precious stones." Thou canst not be the precious stone? then be the

gold. Thou canst not be the gold? then be the silver, if only thou art resting upon the foundation. And again elsewhere, "there is one glory of the sun, and another glory of the moon, and another glory of the stars." Thou canst not be a sun? then be a moon. Thou canst not be a moon? then be a star. Thou canst not be a large star? be content to be a little one if only thou art in the Heaven. Thou canst not be a virgin? then live continently in the married state, only abiding in the Church. Thou canst not be without possessions? then give alms, only abiding in the Church, only wearing the proper raiment, only submitting to the queen. The raiment is woven with gold, it is manifold in texture. I do not bar the way against thee: for the abundance of virtues has rendered the dispensation of the king easy in operation. "Clothed in a vesture woven with gold, manifold in texture." Her vesture is manifold: unfold, if you please, the deep meaning of the expression here used, and fix your eyes upon this garment woven with gold. For here indeed some live celibate, others live in an honorable estate of matrimony being not much inferior to them: some have married once, others are widows in the flower of their age. For what purpose is a paradise? and wherefore its variety? having divers flowers, and trees, and many pearls. There are many stars, but only one sun: there are many ways of living, but only one paradise; there are many temples, but only one mother of them all. There is the body, the eye, the finger, but all these make up but one man. There is the same distinction between the small, the great, and the less. The virgin hath need of the married woman; for the virgin also is the product of marriage, that marriage may not be despised by her. The virgin is the root of marriage: thus all things have been linked together, the small with the great, and the great with the small. "The queen did stand on thy right hand clothed in a vesture wrought with gold, manifold in texture." Then follows "Hearken! O daughter." The conductor of the bride says that thou art about to go forth from thy home to the home of the bridegroom who in his essential nature far surpasses thee. I am the conductor of the bride. "Hearken O daughter." Did she immediately become the wife? Yea: for here there is nothing corporeal. For He espoused her as a wife, He loves her as a daughter, He provides for her as a handmaid, He guards her as a virgin, He fences her round like a garden, and cherishes her like a member: as a head He provides for her, as a root he causes her to grow, as a shepherd He feeds her, as a bridegroom He weds her, as a propitiation He pardons her, as a sheep He is sacrificed, as a bridegroom He preserves her in beauty, as a husband He provides for her support. Many are the meanings in order that we may enjoy a part if it be but a small part of the divine economy of grace. "Hearken O daughter" and behold and look upon things which are bridal and yet spiritual. Hearken O daughter. She was at first a daughter of demons, a daughter of the earth, unworthy of the earth and now she has become a daughter of the king. And this He wished who loved her. For he who loves does not investigate character: love does not regard uncomeliness: on this account indeed is it called love because it oftentimes hath affection for an uncomely person. Thus also did Christ. He saw one who was uncomely (for comely I could not call her) and He loved her, and He made her young, not having spot or wrinkle. Oh what a bridegroom! adorning with grace the ungracefulness of his bride! Hearken O daughter! hearken and behold! Two things He saith "Hearken" and "Behold," two which depend on thyself, one on thy eyes, the other on thy hearing. Now since her dowry depended on hearing (and although some of you have been acute enough to perceive this already, let them tarry for those who are feebler: I commend those who have anticipated the truth, and make allowances for those who only follow in their track) since the dowry then depended on hearing—(and what is meant by hearing? faith: for "faith cometh by hearing" faith as opposed to fruition, and actual experience) I said before that He divided the dowry into two, and gave some portion to the bride for an earnest, whilst He promised others in the future. What did He give her? He gave her forgiveness of sins, remission of punishment, righteousness, sanctification, redemption, the body of the Lord, the divine, spiritual Table, the resurrection of the dead. For all these things the Apostles had. Therefore He gave some parts and promised others. Of some there was experience and fruition, others depended upon hope and faith. Now listen. What did He bestow? Baptism and the Sacrifice. Of these there is experience. What did He promise? Resurrection, immortality of the body, union with angels, a place in the joyful company of archangels, and as a citizen in His kingdom, immaculate life, the good things "which eye hath not seen, nor ear heard nor have entered into the heart of man, things which God hath prepared for them that love Him."

16. Understand what is said, lest ye lose it: I am laboring to enable you to perceive it. The dowry of the bride then was divided into two portions consisting of things present and things to come; things seen and things heard, things given and things taken on trust, things experienced, and things to be enjoyed hereafter; things belonging to present life, and things to come after the

resurrection. The former things you see, the latter you hear. Observe then what He says to her that you may not suppose that she received the former things only, though they be great and ineffable, and surpassing all understanding. "Hearken O daughter and behold;" hear the latter things and behold the former that thou mayest not say "am I again to depend on hope, again on faith, again on the future?" See now: I give some things, and I promise others: the latter indeed depend on hope, but do thou receive the others as pledges, as an earnest, as a proof of the remainder. I promise thee a kingdom: and let present things be the ground of thy trust, thy trust in me. Do you promise me a kingdom? Yea. I have given thee the greater part, even the Lord of the kingdom, for "he who spared not his own son, but gave him up for us all, how shall He not with Him also freely give us all things?" Do you give me the resurrection of the body? Yea; I have given thee the greater part. What is the nature of it? Release from sins. How is that the greater part? Because sin brought forth death. I have destroyed the parent, and shall I not destroy the offspring? I have dried up the root, and shall I not destroy the produce. "Hearken O daughter and behold." What am I to behold? Dead men raised to life, lepers cleansed, the sea restrained, the paralytic braced up into vigor, paradise opened, loaves poured forth in abundance, sins remitted, the lame man leaping, the robber made a citizen of paradise, the publican turned into an evangelist, the harlot become more modest than the maid. Hear and behold. Hear of the former things and behold these. Accept from present things a proof of the others; concerning those I have given thee pledges, things which are better than they are. "What is the meaning of this thy saying?" These things are mine. "Hearken O daughter and behold." These things are my dower to thee. And what doth the bride contribute? Let us see. What I pray thee dost thou bring that thou mayest not be portionless? What can I, she answers, bring to thee from heathen altars, and the steam of sacrifices and from devils? What have I to contribute? what? sayest thou? Thy will and thy faith. "Hearken O daughter and behold." And what wilt thou have me do? "Forget thy own people." What kind of people? the devils, the idols, the sacrificial smoke, and steam, and blood. "Forget thy own people, and thy father's house." Leave thy father and come after me. I left my Father, and came to thee, and wilt thou not leave thy father? But when the word leave is used in reference to the Son do not understand by it an actual leaving. What He means is "I condescended, I accommodated myself to thee, I assumed human flesh." This is the duty of the bridegroom, and of the bride, that thou shouldest abandon thy parents, and that we should be wedded to one another. "Hearken O daughter and behold, and forget thy own people, and thy father's house." And what dost thou give me if I do forget them? "and the king shall desire thy beauty." Thou hast the Lord for thy lover. If thou hast Him for thy lover, thou hast also the things which are his. I trust ye may be able to understand what is said: for the thought is a subtle one, and I wish to stop the mouth of the Jews.

  Now exert your minds I pray: for whether one hears, or forbears to hear I shall dig and till the soil. "Hearken O daughter, and behold, forget also thy own people, and thy father's house, and the king shall desire thy beauty." By beauty in this passage the Jew understands sensible beauty; not spiritual but corporeal.

17. Attend, and let us learn what corporeal, and what spiritual beauty are. There is soul and body: they are two substances: there is a beauty of body, and there is a beauty of soul. What is beauty of body? an extended eyebrow, a merry glance, a blushing cheek, ruddy lips, a straight neck, long wavy hair, tapering fingers, upright stature, a fair blooming complexion. Does this bodily beauty come from nature, or from choice? Confessedly it comes from nature. Attend that thou mayest learn the conception of philosophers. This beauty whether of the countenance, of the eye, of the hair, of the brow, does it come from nature, or from choice? It is obvious that it comes from nature. For the ungraceful woman, even if she cultivate beauty in countless ways, cannot become graceful in body: for natural conditions are fixed, and confined by limits which they cannot pass over. Therefore the beautiful woman is always beautiful, even if she has no taste for beauty: and the ungraceful cannot make herself graceful, nor the graceful ungraceful. Wherefore? because these things come from nature. Well! thou hast seen corporeal beauty. Now let us turn inwards to the soul: let the handmaid approach the mistress! let us turn I say to the soul. Look upon that beauty, or rather listen to it: for thou canst not see it since it is invisible—Listen to that beauty. What then is beauty of soul? Temperance, mildness, almsgiving, love, brotherly kindness, tender affection, obedience to God, the fulfilment of the law, righteousness, contrition of heart. These things are the beauty of the soul. These things then are not the results of nature, but of moral disposition. And he who does not possess these things is able to receive them, and he who has them, if he becomes careless, loses them. For as in the case of the body I was saying that she who is ungraceful

cannot become graceful; so in the case of the soul I say the contrary that the graceless soul can become full of grace. For what was more graceless than the soul of Paul when he was a blasphemer and insulter: what more full of grace when he said, "I have fought the good fight, I have finished the course, I have kept the faith." What was more graceless than the soul of the robber? what more full of grace when he heard the words "Verily I say unto thee to-day shalt thou be with me in paradise?" What was more graceless than the publican when he practiced extortion? but what more full of grace when he declared his resolution. Seest thou that thou canst not alter grace of body, for it is the result not of moral disposition, but of nature. But grace of soul is supplied out of our own moral choice. Thou hast now received the definition. Of what kind are they? That the beauty of the soul proceeds from obedience to God. For if the graceless soul obeys God it puts off its ungracefulness, and becomes full of grace. "Saul! Saul!" it was said, "why persecutes thou me?" and he replied, "and who art Thou Lord?" "I am Jesus." And he obeyed, and his obedience made the graceless soul full of grace. Again, He saith to the publican "come follow me" and the publican rose up and became an apostle: and the graceless soul became full of grace. Whence? by obedience. Again He saith to the fishermen "Come ye after me and I will make you to become fishers of men:" and by their obedience their minds became full of grace. Let us see then what kind of beauty He is speaking of here. "Hearken O daughter and behold, and forget thy own people and thy father's house, and the king shall desire thy beauty." What kind of beauty will he desire? the spiritual kind. How so? because she is to "*forget*" He saith "hearken and forget." These are acts of moral choice. "Hearken!" he said: an ungraceful one hears and her ungracefulness being that of the body is not removed. To the sinful woman He has said "Hearken," and if she will obey she sees what manner of beauty is bestowed upon her. Since then the ungracefulness of the bride was not physical, but moral (for she did not obey God but transgressed) therefore he leads her to another remedy. Thou didst become ungraceful then, not by nature, but by moral choice: and thou didst become full of grace by obedience. "Hearken O daughter and behold and forget thy own people, and thy father's house, and the king shall desire thy beauty." Then that thou mayest learn that he does not mean anything visible to sense, when thou hears the word beauty, think not of eye, or nose, or mouth, or neck, but of piety, faith, love, things which are within— "for all the glory of the king's daughter is from within." Now for all these things let us offer thanks to God, the giver, for to Him alone belonged glory, honor, might, for ever and ever. Amen.

ST. CHRYSOSTOM:

A TREATISE
TO PROVE THAT NO ONE CAN HARM THE MAN WHO DOES NOT INJURE HIMSELF.

TRANSLATED BY
REV. W. R. W. STEPHENS, M.A.,

INTRODUCTION TO THE TREATISE THAT NO ONE CAN HARM THE MAN WHO DOES NOT INJURE HIMSELF.

This very beautiful treatise was composed when St. Chrysostom was in exile, probably not long before his death, and was sent with a letter to his great friend the deaconess Olympias in Constantinople.

Plato in the 10th book of his Dialogue called the "Republic" employs an argument to prove the immortality of the soul, so nearly resembling a portion of this treatise that I can scarcely doubt St. Chrysostom had it in his mind. The following is the passage in the Platonic dialogue as rendered in the excellent translation of Messrs. Davies & Vaughan. I omit a few sentences here and there.

"Have you not learned, I asked, that our soul is immortal and never dies?

He looked at me and said in amazement. No really I have not: but can you maintain this doctrine?

Yes as I am an honest man, I replied, and I think you could also. It is quite easy to do it.

Proceed by all means.

So you call one thing good and another evil?

I do.

And do we hold the same opinion as to the meaning of two terms?

What opinion do you hold?

I hold that the term evil comprises everything that destroys and corrupts, and the term good everything that preserves and benefits.

So do I.

Again, do you maintain that everything has its evil and its good? Do you say for example that the eyes are liable to the evil of ophthalmia, the entire body to disease, corn to mildew, timber to rot, copper and iron to rust or in other words that almost everything is liable to some connatural evil and malady?

I do.

And is it not the case that, whenever an object is attacked by one of these maladies it is impaired; and in the end completely broken up and destroyed by it?

Doubtless it is so?

Hence everything is destroyed by its own connatural evil and vice: otherwise if it be not destroyed by this, there is nothing else that can corrupt it. For that which is good will never destroy anything, nor yet that which is neither good nor evil.

Of course not.

If then we can find among existing things one which is liable to a particular evil which can indeed mar it, but cannot break it up or destroy it, shall we not be at once certain that a thing so constituted can never perish?

That would be a reasonable conclusion.

Well then is not the soul liable to a malady which renders it evil?

Certainly it is: all those things which we were lately discussing—injustice, intemperance, cowardice, and ignorance—produce that result."

Then having proved that although these things injure the soul they do not actually destroy it he proceeds.

"Well, it is irrational to suppose that a thing can be destroyed by the depravity of another thing, though it cannot be destroyed by its own.

True it is irrational.

Yes it is: for you must remember that we do not imagine that a body is to be destroyed by the proper depravity of its food whatever that may be, whether moldiness or rottenness or anything else. But if the depravity of the food itself produces in the body a disorder proper to the body, we shall assert that the body has been destroyed by its food remotely, but by its own proper vice or disease, immediately: and we shall always disclaim the notion that the body can be corrupted by the depravity of its food which is a different thing from the body—that is to say, the notion that the body can be corrupted by an alien evil without the introduction of its own native evil.

You are perfectly correct.

Then according to the same reasoning I continued, unless depravity of body introduces into the soul depravity of soul let us never suppose that the soul can be destroyed by an alien evil without the presence of its own peculiar disease: for that would be to suppose that one thing can be destroyed by the evil of another thing.

That is a reasonable statement.

Well then let us either refute this doctrine and point out our mistake or else, so long as it remains unrefuted, let us never assert that a fever or any other disease, or fatal violence, or even the act of cutting up the entire body into the smallest possible pieces can have any tendency to destroy the soul, until it has been demonstrated that in consequence of this treatment of the body the soul itself becomes more unjust and more unholy. For so long as a thing is exempt from its own proper evil, while an evil foreign to it appears in another subject, let us not allow it to be said that this thing whether it be a soul or anything else is in danger of being destroyed.

Well, certainly no one will prove that the souls of the dying become more unjust in consequence of death." Here follows a passage to prove that even injustice does not *destroy* the soul, after which he proceeds,

"Surely then when the soul cannot be killed and destroyed by its own depravity and its own evil, hardly will the evil which is charged with the destruction of another thing destroy a soul or anything else beyond its own appropriate object.

Hardly: at least that is the natural inference.

Hence, as it is destroyed by no evil at all, whether foreign to it or its own, it is clear that the soul must be always existing, and therefore immortal.

It must."

If anyone will compare this extract with chapters 2 to 6 in the following treatise he cannot fail to be struck by the similarity of thought and language, although in the latter case it is more apparent in the original than it can be in translation. The aim of the two writers is not indeed identical: Chrysostom's object is to prove that nothing can really injure a man except sin—depravity of soul—Plato begins by proving this, and proceeds to maintain that if even that which corrupts the soul cannot actually destroy it the soul must be imperishable. They employ the same argument, only Plato carries it a step further than Chrysostom.

A TREATISE
TO PROVE THAT NO ONE CAN HARM THE MAN
WHO DOES NOT INJURE HIMSELF.

1. I know well that to coarse-minded persons, who are greedy in the pursuit of present things, and are nailed to earth, and enslaved to physical pleasure, and have no strong hold upon spiritual ideas, this treatise will be of a strange and paradoxical kind: and they will laugh immoderately, and condemn me for uttering incredible things from the very outset of my theme. Nevertheless, I shall not on this account desist from my promise, but for this very reason shall proceed with great earnestness to the proof of what I have undertaken. For if those who take that view of my subject will please not to make a clamor and disturbance, but wait to the end of my discourse, I am sure that they will take my side, and condemn themselves, finding that they have been deceived hitherto, and will make a recantation, and apology, and crave pardon for the mistaken opinion which they held concerning these matters, and will express great gratitude to me, as patients do to physicians, when they have been relieved from the disorders which lay siege to their body. For do not tell me of the judgment which is prevailing in your mind at the present time but wait to hear the contention of my arguments and then you will be able to record an impartial verdict without being hindered by ignorance from forming a true judgment. For even judges in secular causes, if they see the first orator pouring forth a mighty torrent of words and overwhelming everything with his speech do not venture to record their decision without having patiently listened to the other speaker who is

opposed to him; and even if the remarks of the first speaker seem to be just to an unlimited extent, they reserve an unprejudiced hearing for the second. In fact the special merit of judges consists in ascertaining with all possible accuracy what each side has to allege and then bringing forward their own judgment.

Now in the place of an orator we have the common assumption of mankind which in the course of ages has taken deep root in the minds of the multitude and declaims to the following effect throughout the world. "All things" it says "have been turned upside down, the human race is full of much confusion and many are they who every day are being wronged, insulted, subjected to violence and injury, the weak by the strong, the poor by the rich: and as it is impossible to number the waves of the sea, so is it impossible to reckon the multitude of those who are the victims of intrigue, insult, and suffering; and neither the correction of law, nor the fear of being brought to trial, nor anything else can arrest this pestilence and disorder, but the evil is increasing every day, and the groans, and lamentations, and weeping of the sufferers are universal; and the judges who are appointed to reform such evils, themselves intensify the tempest, and inflame the disorder, and hence many of the more senseless and despicable kind, seized with a new kind of frenzy, accuse the providence of God, when they see the forbearing man often violently seized, racked, and oppressed, and the audacious, impetuous, low and low-born man waxing rich, and invested with authority, and becoming formidable to many, and inflicting countless troubles upon the more moderate, and this perpetrated both in town and country, and desert, on sea and land. This discourse of ours of necessity comes in by way of direct opposition to what has been alleged, maintaining a contention which is new, as I said at the beginning, and contrary to opinion, yet useful and true, and profitable to those who will give heed to it and be persuaded by it; for what I undertake is to prove (only make no commotion) that no one of those who are wronged is wronged by another, but experiences this injury at his own hands.

2. But in order to make my argument plainer, let us first of all enquire what injustice is, and of what kind of things the material of it is wont to be composed; also what human virtue is, and what it is which ruins it; and further what it is which seems to ruin it but really does not. For instance (for I must complete my argument by means of examples) each thing is subject to one evil which ruins it; iron to rust, wool to moth, flocks of sheep to wolves. The virtue of wine is injured when it ferments and turns sour: of honey when it loses its natural sweetness and is reduced to a bitter juice. Ears of corn are ruined by mildew and drought, and the fruit, and leaves, and branches of vines by the mischievous host of locusts, other trees by the caterpillar, and irrational creatures by diseases of various kinds: and not to lengthen the list by going through all possible examples, our own flesh is subject to fevers, and palsies, and a crowd of other maladies. As then each one of these things is liable to that which ruins its virtue, let us now consider what it is which injures the human race, and what it is which ruins the virtue of a human being. Most men think that there are divers things which have this effect; for I must mention the erroneous opinions on the subject, and, after confuting them, proceed to exhibit that which really does ruin our virtue: and to demonstrate clearly that no one could inflict this injury or bring this ruin upon us unless we betrayed

ourselves. The multitude then having erroneous opinions imagine that there are many different things which ruin our virtue: some say it is poverty, others bodily disease, others loss of property, others calumny, others death and they are perpetually bewailing and lamenting these things: and whilst they are commiserating the sufferers and shedding tears they excitedly exclaim to one another "What a calamity has befallen such and such a man! he has been deprived of all his fortune at a blow." Of another again one will say: "such and such a man has been attacked by severe sickness and is despaired of by the physicians in attendance." Some bewail and lament the inmates of the prison, some those who have been expelled from their country and transported to the land of exile, others those who have been deprived of their freedom, others those who have been seized and made captives by enemies, others those who have been drowned, or burnt, or buried by the fall of a house, but no one mourns those who are living in wickedness: on the contrary, which is worse than all, they often congratulate them, a practice which is the cause of all manner of evils. Come then (only, as I exhorted you at the outset, do not make a commotion), let me prove that none of the things which have been mentioned injure the man who lives soberly, nor can ruin his virtue. For tell me if a man has lost his all either at the hands of calumniators or of robbers, or has been stripped of his goods by knavish servants, what harm has the loss done to the virtue of the man?

But if it seems well let me rather indicate in the first place what is the virtue of a man, beginning by dealing with the subject in the case of existences of another kind so as to make it more intelligible and plain to the majority of readers.

3. What then is the virtue of a horse? is it to have a bridle studded with gold and girths to match, and a band of silken threads to fasten the housing, and clothes wrought in divers colors and gold tissue, and head gear studded with jewels, and locks of hair plaited with gold cord? or is it to be swift and strong in its legs, and even in its paces, and to have hoofs suitable to a well bred horse, and courage fitted for long journeys and warfare, and to be able to behave with calmness in the battle field, and if a rout takes place to save its rider? Is it not manifest that these are the things which constitute the virtue of the horse, not the others? Again, what should you say was the virtue of asses and mules? is it not the power of carrying burdens with contentment, and accomplishing journeys with ease, and having hoofs like rock? Shall we say that their outside trappings contribute anything to their own proper virtue? By no means. And what kind of vine shall we admire? one which abounds in leaves and branches, or one which is laden with fruit? or what kind of virtue do we predicate of an olive? is it to have large boughs, and great luxuriance of leaves, or to exhibit an abundance of its proper fruit dispersed over all parts of the tree? Well, let us act in the same way in the case of human beings also: let us determine what is the virtue of man, and let us regard that alone as an injury, which is destructive to it. What then is the virtue of man? not riches that thou shouldest fear poverty: nor health of body that thou shouldest dread sickness, nor the opinion of the public, that thou shouldest view an evil reputation with alarm, nor life simply for its own sake, that death should be terrible to thee: nor liberty that thou shouldest avoid servitude: but carefulness in holding true doctrine, and rectitude in life. Of these things not even the devil himself will be

able to rob a man, if he who possesses them guards them with the needful carefulness: and that most malicious and ferocious demon is aware of this. For this cause also he robbed Job of his substance, not to make him poor, but that he might force him into uttering some blasphemous speech; and he tortured his body, not to subject him to infirmity, but to upset the virtue of his soul. But nevertheless when he had set all his devices in motion, and turned him from a rich man into a poor one (that calamity which seems to us the most terrible of all), and had made him childless who was once surrounded by many children, and had scarified his whole body more cruelly than the executioners do in the public tribunals (for their nails do not lacerate the sides of those who fall into their hands so severely as the gnawing of the worms lacerated his body), and when he had fastened a bad reputation upon him (for Job's friends who were present with him said "thou hast not received the chastisement which thy sins deserve," and directed many words of accusation against him), and after he had not merely expelled him from city and home and transferred him to another city, but had actually made the dunghill serve as his home and city; after all this, he not only did him no damage but rendered him more glorious by the designs which he formed against him. And he not only failed to rob him of any of his possessions although he had robbed him of so many things, but he even increased the wealth of his virtue. For after these things he enjoyed greater confidence inasmuch as he had contended in a more severe contest. Now if he who underwent such sufferings, and this not at the hand of man, but at the hand of the devil who is more wicked than all men, sustained no injury, which of those persons who say such and such a man injured and damaged me will have any defense to make in future? For if the devil who is full of such great malice, after having set all his instruments in motion, and discharged all his weapons, and poured out all the evils incident to man, in a superlative degree upon the family and the person of that righteous man nevertheless did him no injury, but as I was saying rather profited him: how shall certain be able to accuse such and such a man alleging that they have suffered injury at their hands, not at their own?

4. What then? someone will say, did he not inflict injury on Adam, and upset him, and cast him out of paradise? No: he did it not, but the cause was the listlessness of him who was injured, and his want of temperance and vigilance. For he who applied such powerful and manifold devices and yet was not able to subdue Job, how could he by inferior means have mastered Adam, had not Adam betrayed himself through his own listlessness? What then? Has not he been injured who has been exposed to slander, and suffered confiscation of his property, having been deprived of all his goods, and is thrown out of his patrimony, and struggles with extreme poverty? No! he has not been injured, but has even profited, if he be sober. For, tell me, what harm did this do the apostles? Were they not continually struggling with hunger, and thirst and nakedness? And this was the very reason why they were so illustrious, and distinguished, and won for themselves much help from God. Again what harm was done to Lazarus by his disease, and sores, and poverty and dearth of protectors? Were they not the reasons why garlands of victory were more abundantly woven for him? Or what harm was done to Joseph by his getting evil reported of,

both in his own land, and in the land of strangers for he was supposed to be both an adulterer and fornicator: or what harm did servitude do him or expatriation? Is it not especially on account of these things that we regard him with admiration and astonishment? And why do I speak of removal into a foreign land, poverty, and evil report, and bondage? For what harm did death itself inflict on Abel, although it was a violent and untimely death, and perpetrated by a brother's hand? Is not this the reason why his praise is sounded throughout the whole world? Seest thou how the discourse has demonstrated even more than it promised? For not only has it disclosed the fact that no one is injured by anybody, but also that they who take heed to themselves derive the greater gain (from such assaults). What is the purpose then it will be said of penalties and punishments? What is the purpose of hell? What is the purpose of such great threatening, if no one is either injured or injures? What is it thou sayest? Why dost thou confuse the argument? For I did not say that no one injures, but that no one is injured. And how is it possible, you will say, for no one to be injured when many are committing injury? In the way which I indicated just now. For Joseph's brethren did indeed injure him, yet he himself was not injured: and Cain laid snares for Abel, yet he himself was not ensnared. This is the reason why there are penalties and punishments. For God does not abolish penalties on account of the virtue of those who suffer; but he ordains punishments on account of the malice of those who do wickedly. For although they who are evil entreated become more illustrious in consequence of the designs formed against them, this is not due to the intention of those who plan the designs, but to the courage of those who are the victims of them. Wherefore for the latter the rewards of philosophy are made ready and prepared, for the former the penalties of wickedness. Hast thou been deprived of thy money? Read the word "Naked came I out of my mother's womb, and naked shall I return thither." And add to this the apostolic saying "for we brought nothing into this world; it is certain we can carry nothing out." Art thou evil reported of, and have some men loaded thee with countless abuse? Remember that passage where it is said "Woe unto you when all men shall speak well of you" and "rejoice ye and leap for joy when they shall cast upon you an evil name." Hast thou been transported into the land of exile? Consider that thou hast not here a fatherland, but that if thou wilt be wise thou art bidden to regard the whole world as a strange country. Or hast thou been given over to a sore disease? quote the apostolic saying "the more our outward man decayed, so much the more is the inward man renewed day by day." Has anyone suffered a violent death? consider the case of John, his head cut off in prison, carried in a charger, and made the reward of a harlot's dancing. Consider the recompense which is derived from these things: for all these sufferings when they are unjustly inflicted by any one on another, expiate sins, and work righteousness. So great is the advantage of them in the case of those who bear them bravely.

5. When then neither loss of money, nor slander, nor railing, nor banishment, nor diseases, nor tortures, nor that which seems more formidable than all, namely death, harms those who suffer them, but rather adds to their profit, whence can you prove to me that any one is injured when he is not injured at all from any of these things? For I will endeavor to prove the reverse, showing that they who are most injured and insulted, and suffer the most

incurable evils are the persons who do these things. For what could be more miserable than the condition of Cain, who dealt with his brother in this fashion? what more pitiable than that of Phillip's wife who beheaded John? or the brethren of Joseph who sold him away, and transported him into the land of exile? or the devil who tortured Job with such great calamities? For not only on account of his other iniquities, but at the same time also for this assault he will pay no trifling penalty. Do you see how here the argument has proved even more than was proposed, shewing that those who are insulted not only sustain no harm from these assaults, but that the whole mischief recoils on the head of those who contrive them? For since neither wealth nor freedom, nor life in our native land nor the other things which I have mentioned, but only right actions of the soul, constitute the virtue of man, naturally when the harm is directed against these things, human virtue itself is no wise harmed. What then? Suppose someone does harm the moral condition of the soul? Even then if a man suffers damage, the damage does not come from another but proceeds from within, and from the man himself. "How so," do you say? When anyone having been beaten by another, or deprived of his goods, or having endured some other grievous insult, utters a blasphemous speech, he certainly sustains a damage thereby, and a very great one, nevertheless it does not proceed from him who has inflicted the insult, but from his own littleness of soul. For what I said before I will now repeat, no man if he be infinitely wicked could attack any one more wickedly or more bitterly than that revengeful demon who is implacably hostile to us, the devil: but yet this cruel demon had not power to upset or overthrow him who lived before the law, and before the time of grace, although he discharged so many and such bitter weapons against him from all quarters. Such is the force of nobility of soul. And what shall I say of Paul? Did he not suffer so many distresses that even to make a list of them is no easy matter? He was put in prison, loaded with chains, dragged hither and hither, scourged by the Jews, stoned, lacerated on the back not only by thongs, but also by rods, he was immersed in the sea, oftentimes beset by robbers, involved in strife with his own countrymen, continually assailed both by foes and by acquaintance, subjected to countless intrigues, struggling with hunger and nakedness, undergoing other frequent and lasting mischances and afflictions: and why need I mention the greater part of them? he was dying every day: but yet, although subjected to so many and such grievous sufferings, he not only uttered no blasphemous word, but rejoiced over these things and gloried in them: and one time he says "I rejoice in my sufferings," and then again "not only this but we also glory in afflictions." If then he rejoiced and gloried when suffering such great troubles what excuse will you have, and what defense will you make if you blaspheme when you do not undergo the smallest fraction of them.

6. But I am injured in other ways, one will say, and even if I do not blaspheme, yet when I am robbed of my money, I am disabled from giving alms. This is a mere pretext and pretense. For if you grieve on this account know certainly that poverty is no bar to almsgiving. For even if you are infinitely poor you are not poorer than the woman who possessed only a handful of meal, and the one who had only two mites, each of whom having spent all her substance upon those who were in need was an object of surpassing admiration: and such

great poverty was no hindrance to such great lovingkindness, but the alms bestowed from the two mites was so abundant and generous as to eclipse all who had riches, and in wealth of intention and superabundance of zeal to surpass those who cast in much coin. Wherefore even in this matter thou art not injured but rather benefited, receiving by means of a small contribution rewards more glorious than they who put down large sums. But since, if I were to say these things for ever, sensuous characters which delight to grovel in worldly things, and revel in present things would not readily endure parting from the fading flowers (for such are the pleasant things of this life) or letting go its shadows: but the better sort of men indeed cling to both the one and the other, while the more pitiable and abject cling more strongly to the former than to the latter, come let us strip off the pleasant and showy masks which hide the base and ugly countenance of these things, and let us expose the foul deformity of the harlot. For such is the character of a life of this kind which is devoted to luxury, and wealth and power: it is foul and ugly and full of much abomination, disagreeable and burdensome, and charged with bitterness. For this indeed is the special feature in this life which deprives those who are captivated by it of every excuse, that although it is the aim of their longings and endeavors, yet is it filled with much annoyance and bitterness, and teems with innumerable evils, dangers, bloodshed, precipices, crags, murders, fears and trembling, envy and ill-will, and intrigue, perpetual anxiety and care, and derives no profit, and produces no fruit from these great evils save punishment and revenge, and incessant torment. But although this is its character it seems to be to most men an object of ambition, and eager contention, which is a sign of the folly of those who are captivated by it, not of the blessedness of the thing itself. Little children indeed are eager and excited about toys and cannot take notice of the things which become full grown men. There is an excuse for them on account of their immaturity: but these others are debarred from the right of defense, because, although of full age they are childish in disposition, and more foolish than children in their manner of life.

  Now tell me why is wealth an object of ambition? For it is necessary to start from this point, because to the majority of those who are afflicted with this grievous malady it seems to be more precious than health and life, and public reputation, and good opinion, and country, and household, and friends, and kindred and everything else. Moreover the flame has ascended to the very clouds: and this fierce heat has taken possession of land and sea. Nor is there anyone to quench this fire: but all people are engaged in stirring it up, both those who have been already caught by it, and those who have not yet been caught, in order that they may be captured. And you may see every one, husband and wife, household slave, and freeman, rich and poor, each according to his ability carrying loads which supply much fuel to this fire by day and night: loads not of wood or faggots (for the fire is not of that kind), but loads of souls and bodies, of unrighteousness and iniquity. For such is the material of which a fire of this kind is wont to be kindled. For those who have riches place no limit anywhere to this monstrous passion, even if they compass the whole world: and the poor press on to get in advance of them, and a kind of incurable craze, and unrestrainable frenzy and irremediable disease possesses the souls of all. And this affection has conquered every other kind and thrust it away expelling it from the soul: neither friends nor kindred are taken into account: and why do I speak of friends and kindred? not even wife and children are regarded, and what can be dearer to man than these? but all things are dashed to the ground and trampled underfoot, when this savage and inhuman mistress has laid hold of the souls of all who are taken captive by her. For as an inhuman mistress, and harsh tyrant, and savage barbarian, and public and expensive prostitute she debases and exhausts and punishes with innumerable dangers and torments those who have chosen to be in bondage to her; and yet although she is terrible and harsh, and fierce and cruel, and has the face of a barbarian, or rather of a wild beast, fiercer than a wolf or a lion, she seems to those who have been taken captive by her gentle and loveable, and sweeter than honey. And although she forges swords and weapons against them every day, and digs pitfalls and leads them to precipices and crags and weaves endless snares of punishment for them, yet is she supposed to make these things objects of ambition to those who have been made captive, and those who are desiring to be captured. And just as a sow delights and revels in wallowing in the ditch and mire, and beetles delight in perpetually crawling over dung; even so they who are captivated by the love of money are more miserable than these creatures. For the abomination is greater in this case, and the mire more offensive: for they who are addicted to this passion imagine that much pleasure is derived from it: which does not arise from the nature of the thing, but of the understanding which is afflicted with such an irrational taste. And this taste is worse in their case than in that of brutes: for as with the mire and the dung the cause of pleasure is not in them, but in the irrational nature of the creatures who plunge into it; even so count it to be in the case of human beings.

7. And how might we cure those who are thus disposed? It would be possible if they would open their ears to us, and unfold their heart, and receive our words. For it is impossible to turn and divert the irrational animals from their unclean habit; for they are destitute of reason: but this the gentlest of all tribes, honored by reason and speech, I mean human nature, might, if it chose, readily and easily be released from the mire and the stench, and the dung hill and its abomination. For wherefore, O man, do riches seem to thee worthy such diligent pursuit? Is it on account of the pleasure which no doubt is derived from the table? or on account of the honor and the escort of those who pay court to thee, because of thy wealth? is it because thou art able to defend thyself against those who annoy thee, and to be an object of fear to all? For yon cannot name any other reasons, save pleasure and flattery, and fear, and the power of taking revenge; for wealth is not generally wont to make any one wiser, or more self-controlled, or more gentle, or more intelligent, or kind, or benevolent, or superior to anger, or gluttony or pleasure: it does not train any one to be moderate, or teach him how to be humble, nor introduce and implant any other piece of virtue in the soul. Neither could you say for which of these things it deserves to be so diligently sought and desired. For not only is it ignorant how to plant and cultivate any good thing, but even if it finds a store of them it mars and stunts and blights them; and some of them it even uproots, and introduces their opposites, unmeasured licentiousness, unseasonable wrath, unrighteous anger, pride, arrogance,

foolishness. But let me not speak of these; for they who have been seized by this malady will not endure to hear about virtue and vice, being entirely abandoned to pleasure and therefore enslaved to it. Come then let us forego for the time being the consideration of these points, and let us bring forward the others which remain, and see whether wealth has any pleasure, or any honor: for in my eyes the case is quite the reverse. And first of all, if you please, let us investigate the meals of rich and poor, and ask the guests which they are who enjoy the purest and most genuine pleasure; is it they who recline for a full day on couches, and join breakfast and dinner together, and distend their stomach, and blunt their senses, and sink the vessel by an overladen cargo of food, and waterlog the ship, and drench it as in some shipwreck of the body, and devise fetters, and manacles, and gags, and bind their whole body with the band of drunkenness and surfeit more grievous than an iron chain, and enjoy no sound pure sleep undisturbed by frightful dreams, and are more miserable than madmen and introduce a kind of self-imposed demon into the soul and display themselves as a laughing stock to the gaze of their servants, or rather to the kinder sort amongst them as a tragical spectacle eliciting tears, and cannot recognize any of those who are present, and are incapable of speaking or hearing but have to be carried away from their couches to their bed;—or is it they who are sober and vigilant, and limit their eating by their need, and sail with a favorable breeze, and find hunger and thirst the best relish in their food and drink? For nothing is so conducive to enjoyment and health as to be hungry and thirsty when one attacks the viands, and to identify satiety with the simple necessity of food, never overstepping the limits of this, nor imposing a load upon the body too great for its strength.

8. But if you disbelieve my statement study the physical condition, and the soul of each class. Are not the bodies vigorous of those who live thus moderately (for do not tell me of that which rarely happens, although some may be weak from some other circumstance, but form your judgment from those instances which are of constant occurrence), I say are they not vigorous, and their senses clear, fulfilling their proper function with much ease? whereas the bodies of the others are flaccid and softer than wax, and beset with a crowd of maladies? For gout soon fastens upon them, and untimely palsy, and premature old age, and headache, and flatulence, and feebleness of digestion, and loss of appetite, and they require constant attendance of physicians, and perpetual dosing, and daily care. Are these things pleasurable? tell me. Who of those that know what pleasure really is would say so? For pleasure is produced when desire leads the way, and fruition follows: now if there is fruition, but desire is nowhere to be found, the conditions of pleasure fail and vanish. On this account also invalids, although the most charming food is set before them, partake of it with a feeling of disgust and sense of oppression: because there is no desire which gives a keen relish to the enjoyment of it. For it is not the nature of the food, or of the drink, but the appetite of the eaters which is wont to produce the desire and is capable of causing pleasure. Therefore also a certain wise man who had an accurate knowledge of all that concerned pleasure, and understood how to moralize about these things said "the full soul mocked at honeycombs:" showing that the conditions of pleasure consist not in the nature of the meal, but in the

disposition of the eaters. Therefore also the prophet recounting the wonders in Egypt and in the desert mentioned this in connection with the others "He satisfied them with honey out of the rock." And yet nowhere does it appear that honey actually sprang forth for them out of the rock: what then is the meaning of the expression? Because the people being exhausted by much toil and long travelling, and distressed by great thirst rushed to the cool spring, their craving for drink serving as a relish, the writer wishing to describe the pleasures which they received from those fountains called the water honey, not meaning that the element was converted into honey, but that the pleasure received from the water rivalled the sweetness of honey, inasmuch as those who partook of it rushed to it in their eagerness to drink.

Since then these things are so and no one can deny it, however stupid he may be: is it not perfectly plain that pure, undiluted, and lively pleasure is to be found at the tables of the poor? whereas at the tables of the rich there is discomfort, and disgust and defilement? as that wise man has said "even sweet things seem to be a vexation."

9. But riches someone will say procure honor for those who possess them, and enable them to take vengeance on their enemies with ease. And is this a reason, pray, why riches seem to you desirable and worth contending for;—that they nourish the most dangerous passion in our nature, leading on anger into action, swelling the empty bubbles of ambition, and stimulating and urging men to arrogance? Why these are just the very reasons why we ought resolutely to turn our backs upon riches, because they introduce certain fierce and dangerous wild beasts into our heart depriving us of the real honor which we might receive from all, and

introducing to deluded men another which is the opposite of this, only painted over with its colors, and persuading them to fancy that it is the same, when by nature it is not so, but only seems to be so to the eye. For as the beauty of courtesans, made up as it is of dyes and pigments, is destitute of real beauty, yet makes a foul and ugly face appear fair and beautiful to those who are deluded by it when it is not so in reality: even so also riches force flattery to look like honor. For I beg you not to consider the praises which are openly bestowed through fear and fawning: for these are only tints and pigments; but unfold the conscience of each of those who flatter you in this fashion, and inside it you will see countless accusers declaring against you, and loathing and detesting you more than your bitterest adversaries and foes. And if ever a change of circumstances should occur which would remove and expose this mask which fear has manufactured, just as the sun when it emits a hotter ray than usual discloses the real countenances of those women whom I mentioned, then you will see clearly that all through the former time you were held in the greatest contempt by those who paid court to you, and you fancied you were enjoying honor from those who thoroughly hated you, and in their heart poured infinite abuse upon you, and longed to see you involved in extreme calamities. For there is nothing like virtue to produce honor,—honor neither forced nor feigned, nor hidden under a mask of deceit, but real and genuine, and able to stand the test of hard times.

10. But do you wish to take vengeance on those who have annoyed you? This, as I was saying just now, is the very reason why wealth ought especially to be avoided. For it prepares thee to thrust the sword against

thyself, and renders thee liable to a heavier account in the future day of reckoning, and makes thy punishment intolerable. For revenge is so great an evil that it actually revokes the mercy of God and cancels the forgiveness of countless sins which has been already bestowed. For he who received remission of the debt of ten thousand talents, and after having obtained so great a boon by merely asking for it then made a demand of one hundred pence from his fellow servant, a demand, that is, for satisfaction for his transgression against himself, in his severity towards his fellow servant recorded his own condemnation; and for this reason and no other he was delivered to the tormentors, and racked, and required to pay back the ten thousand talents; and he was not allowed the benefit of any excuse or defense, but suffered the most extreme penalty, having been commanded to deposit the whole debt which the lovingkindness of God had formerly remitted. Is this then the reason, pray, why wealth is so earnestly pursued by thee, because it so easily conducts thee into sin of this kind? Nay verily, this is why you ought to abhor it as a foe and an adversary teeming with countless murders. But poverty, someone will say, disposes men to be discontented and often also to utter profane words, and condescend to mean actions. It is not poverty which does this, but littleness of soul: for Lazarus also was poor, aye! Very poor: and besides poverty he suffered from infirmity, a bitterer trial than any form of poverty, and one which makes poverty more severely felt; and in addition to infirmity there was a total absence of protectors, and difficulty in finding any to supply his wants, which increased the bitterness of poverty and infirmity. For each of these things is painful in itself, but when there are none to minister to the sufferer's wants, the suffering becomes greater, the flame more painful, the distress more bitter, the tempest fiercer, the billows stronger, the furnace hotter. And if one examines the case thoroughly there was yet a fourth trial besides these—the unconcern and luxury of the rich man who dwelt hard by. And if you would find a fifth thing, serving as fuel to the flame, you will see quite clearly that he was beset by it. For not only was that rich man living luxuriously, but twice, and thrice, or rather indeed several times in the day he saw the poor man: for he had been laid at his gate, being a grievous spectacle of pitiable distress, and the bare sight of him was sufficient to soften even a heart of stone: and yet even this did not induce that unmerciful man to assist this case of poverty: but he had his luxurious table spread, and goblets wreathed with flowers, and pure wine plentifully poured forth, and grand armies of cooks, and parasites, and flatterers from early dawn, and troops of singers, cupbearers, and jesters; and he spent all his time in devising every species of dissipation, and drunkenness, and surfeiting, and in reveling in dress and feasting and many other things. But although he saw that poor man every day distressed by grievous hunger and the bitterest infirmity, and the oppression of his many sores, and by destitution, and the ills which result from these things, he never even gave him a thought: yet the parasites and the flatterers were pampered even beyond their need; but the poor man, and he so very poor, and encompassed with so many miseries, was not even vouchsafed the crumbs which fell from that table, although he greatly desired them: and yet none of these things injured him, he did not give vent to a bitter word, he did not utter a profane speech; but like a piece of gold which shines all the more brilliantly when it is purified by excessive heat, even so he, although oppressed by these sufferings, was superior to all of them, and to the agitation which in many cases is produced by them. For if generally speaking poor men, when they see rich men, are consumed with envy and racked by malicious ill-will, and deem life not worth living, and this even when they are well supplied with necessary food, and have persons to minister to their wants; what would the condition of this poor man have been had he not been very wise and noble hearted, seeing that he was poor beyond all other poor men, and not only poor, but also infirm, and without any one to protect or cheer him, and lay in the midst of the city as if in a remote desert, and wasted away with bitter hunger, and saw all good things being poured upon the rich man as out of a fountain, and had not the benefit of any human consolation, but lay exposed as a perpetual meal for the tongues of the dogs, for he was so enfeebled and broken down in body that he could not scare them away? Do you perceive that he who does not injure himself suffers no evil? for I will again take up the same argument.

11. For what harm was done to this hero by his bodily infirmity? or by the absence of protectors? or by the coming of the dogs? or the evil proximity of the rich man? or by the great luxury, haughtiness and arrogance of the latter? Did it enervate him for the contest on behalf of virtue? Did it ruin his fortitude? Nowhere was he harmed at all, but that multitude of sufferings, and the cruelty of the rich man, rather increased his strength, and became the pledge for him of infinite crowns of victory, a means of adding to his rewards, an augmentation of his recompense, and a promise of an increased requital. For he was crowned not merely on account of his poverty, or

of his hunger or of his sores, or of the dogs licking them: but because, having such a neighbor as the rich man, and being seen by him every day, and perpetually overlooked he endured this trial bravely and with much fortitude, a trial which added no small flame but in fact a very strong one to the fire of poverty, and infirmity and loneliness.

And, tell me, what was the case of the blessed Paul? for there is nothing to prevent my making mention of him again. Did he not experience innumerable storms of trial? And in what respect was he injured by them? Was he not crowned with victory all the more in consequence,—because he suffered hunger, because he was consumed with cold and nakedness, because he was often tortured with the scourge, because he was stoned, because he was cast into the sea? But then someone says he was Paul, and called by Christ. Yet Judas also was one of the twelve, and he too was called of Christ; but neither his being of the twelve nor his call profited him, because he had not a mind disposed to virtue. But Paul although struggling with hunger, and at a loss to procure necessary food, and daily undergoing such great sufferings, pursued with great zeal the road which leads to heaven: whereas Judas although he had been called before him, and enjoyed the same advantages as he did, and was initiated in the highest form of Christian life, and partook of the holy table and that most awful of sacred feasts, and received such grace as to be able to raise the dead, and cleanse the lepers, and cast out devils, and often heard discourses concerning poverty, and spent so long a time in the company of Christ Himself, and was entrusted with the money of the poor, so that his passion might be soothed thereby (for he was a thief) even then did not become any better, although he had been favored with such great condescension. For since Christ knew that he was covetous, and destined to perish on account of his love of money he not only did not demand punishment of him for this at that time, but with a view to softening down his passion he was entrusted with the money of the poor, that having some means of appeasing his greed he might be saved from falling into that appalling gulf of sin, checking the greater evil beforehand by a lesser one.

12. Thus in no case will anyone be able to injure a man who does not choose to injure himself: but if a man is not willing to be temperate, and to aid himself from his own resources no one will ever be able to profit him. Therefore also that wonderful history of the Holy Scriptures, as in some lofty, large, and broad picture, has portrayed the lives of the men of old time, extending the narrative from Adam to the coming of Christ: and it exhibits to you both those who are upset, and those who are crowned with victory in the contest, in order that it may instruct you by means of all examples that no one will be able to injure one who is not injured by himself, even if all the world were to kindle a fierce war against him. For it is not stress of circumstances, nor variation of seasons, nor insults of men in power, nor intrigues besetting thee like snow storms, nor a crowd of calamities, nor a promiscuous collection of all the ills to which mankind is subject, which can disturb even slightly the man who is brave, and temperate, and watchful; just as on the contrary the indolent and supine man who is his own betrayer cannot be made better, even with the aid of innumerable ministrations. This at least was made manifest to us by the parable of the two men, of whom the one built his house upon the rock, the other upon the sand: not that we are to think of sand and rock, or of a building

of stone, and a roof, or of rivers, and rain, and wild winds, beating against the buildings, but we are to extract virtue and vice as the meaning of these things, and to perceive from them that no one injures a man who does not injure himself. Therefore neither the rain although driven furiously along, nor the streams dashing against it with much vehemence, nor the wild winds beating against it with a mighty rush, shook the one house in any degree: but it remained undisturbed, unmoved: that thou mightiest understand that no trial can agitate the man who does not betray himself. But the house of the other man was easily swept away, not on account of the force of the trials (for in that case the other would have experienced the same fate), but on account of his own folly; for it did not fall because the wind blew upon it, but because it was built upon the sand, that is to say upon indolence and iniquity. For before that tempest beat upon it, it was weak and ready to fall. For buildings of that kind, even if no one puts any pressure on them, fall to pieces of themselves, the foundation sinking and giving way in every direction. And just as cobwebs part asunder, although no strain is put upon them, but adamant remains unshaken even when it is struck: even so also they who do not injure themselves become stronger, even if they receive innumerable blows; but they who betray themselves, even if there is no one to harass them, fall of themselves, and collapse and perish. For even thus did Judas perish, not only having been unassailed by any trial of this kind, but having actually enjoyed the benefit of much assistance.

13. Would you like me to illustrate this argument in the case of whole nations? What great forethought was bestowed upon the Jewish nation! was not the whole visible creation arranged with a view to their service? was

not a new and strange method of life introduced amongst them? For they had not to send down to a market, and so they had the benefit of things which are sold for money without paying any price for them: neither did they cleave furrows nor drag a plough, nor harrow the ground, nor cast in seed, nor had they need of rain and wind, and annual seasons, nor sunshine, nor phases of the moon, nor climate, nor anything of that kind; they prepared no threshing floor, they threshed no grain, they used no winnowing fan for separating the grain from the chaff, they turned no mill-stone, they built no oven, they brought neither wood nor fire into the house, they needed no baker's art, they handled no spade, they sharpened no sickle, they required no other art, I mean of weaving or building or supplying shoes: but the word of God was everything to them. And they had a table prepared off hand, free of all toil and labor. For such was the nature of the manna; it was new and fresh, nowhere costing them any trouble, nor straining them by labor. And their clothes, shoes, and even their physical frame forgot their natural infirmity: for the former did not wear out in the course of so long a time nor did their feet swell although they made such long marches. Of physicians, and medicine, and all other concern about that kind of art, there was no mention at all amongst them; so completely banished was infirmity of every kind: for it is said "He brought them out with silver and gold; and there was not one feeble person among their tribes." But like men who had quitted this world, and were transplanted to another and a better one, even so did they eat and drink, neither did the sun's ray when it waxed hot smite their heads; for the cloud parted them from the fiery beam, hovering all round them, and serving like a portable shelter for the whole body of the people. Neither at night did they need a torch to disperse the darkness, but they had the pillar of fire, a source of unspeakable light, supplying two wants, one by its shining, the other by directing the course of their journey; for it was not only luminous, but also conducted that countless host along the wilderness with more certainty than any human guide. And they journeyed not only upon land but also upon sea as if it had been dry land; and they made an audacious experiment upon the laws of nature by treading upon that angry sea, marching through it as if it had been the hard and resisting surface of a rock; and indeed when they placed their feet upon it the element became like solid earth, and gently sloping plains and fields; but when it received their enemies it wrought after the nature of sea; and to the Israelites indeed it served as a chariot, but to their enemies it became a grave; conveying the former across with ease, but drowning the latter with great violence. And the disorderly flood of water displayed the good order and subordination which marks reasonable and highly intelligent men, fulfilling the part at one time of a guardian, at another of an executioner, and exhibiting these opposites together on one day. What shall one say of the rocks which gave forth streams of water? what of the clouds of birds which covered the whole face of the earth by the number of their carcasses? what of the wonders in Egypt? what of the marvels in the wilderness? what of the triumphs and bloodless victories? For they subdued those who opposed them like men keeping holiday rather than making war. And they vanquished their own masters without the use of arms; and overcame those who fought with them after they left Egypt by means of singing and music; and what they did was a festival rather than a campaign, a religious ceremony rather than a battle. For all these wonders took place not merely for the purpose of supplying their need, but also that the people might preserve more accurately the doctrine which Moses inculcated of the knowledge of God; and voices proclaiming the presence of their Master were uttered on all sides of them. For the sea loudly declared this, by becoming a road for them to march upon, and then turning into sea again: and the waters of the Nile uttered this voice when they were converted into the nature of blood; and the frogs, and the great army of locusts, and the caterpillar and blight declared the same thing to all the people; and the wonders in the desert, the manna, the pillar of fire, the cloud, the quails, and all the other incidents served them as a book, and writing which could never be effaced, echoing daily in their memory and resounding in their mind. Nevertheless after such great and remarkable providence, after all those unspeakable benefits, after such mighty miracles, after care indescribable, after continual teaching, after instruction by means of speech, and admonition by means of deeds, after glorious victories, after extraordinary triumphs, after abundant supply of food, after the plentiful production of water, after the ineffable glory with which they were invested in the eyes of the human race, being ungrateful and senseless they worshipped a calf, and paid reverence to the head of a bull, even when the memorials of God's benefits in Egypt were fresh in their minds, and they were still in actual enjoyment of many more.

14. But the Ninevites, although a barbarous and foreign people who had never participated in any of these benefits, small or great, neither words, nor wonders, nor works, when they saw a man who had been saved from

shipwreck, who had never associated with them before, but appeared then for the first time, enter their city and say "yet three days and Nineveh shall be overthrown," were so converted and reformed by the mere sound of these words, and putting away their former wickedness, advanced in the direction of virtue by the path of repentance, that they caused the sentence of God to be revoked, and arrested the threatened disturbance of their city, and averted the heaven-sent wrath, and were delivered from every kind of evil. "For," we read, "God saw that every man turned from his evil way and was converted to the Lord." How turned? I ask. Although their wickedness was great, their iniquity unspeakable, their moral sores difficult to heal, which was plainly shown by the prophet when he said "their wickedness ascended even unto the heaven:" indicating by the distance of the place the magnitude of their wickedness; nevertheless such great iniquity which was piled up to such a height as to reach even to the heaven, all this in the course of three days in a brief moment of time through the effect of a few words which they heard from the mouth of one man and he an unknown shipwrecked stranger they so thoroughly abolished, removed out of sight, and put away, as to have the happiness of hearing the declaration "God saw that everyone turned from his evil way, and He repented of the evil which God said He would do them." Seest thou that he who is temperate and watchful not only suffers no injury at the hands of man but even turns back Heaven-sent wrath? whereas he who betrays himself and harms himself by his own doing, even if he receives countess benefits, reaps no great advantage. So, at least, the Jews were not profited by those great miracles, nor on the other hand were the Ninevites harmed by having no share in them; but inasmuch as they were inwardly well-disposed, having laid hold of a slight opportunity they became better, barbarians and foreigners though they were, ignorant of all divine revelation, and dwelling at a distance from Palestine.

15. Again, I ask, was the virtue of the "three children" corrupted by the troubles which beset them? Whilst they were still young, mere youths, of immature age, did they not undergo that grievous affliction of captivity? had they not to make a long journey from home, and when they had arrived in the foreign country were they not cut off from fatherland and home and temple, and altar and sacrifices, and offerings, and drink offerings, and even the singing of psalms? For not only were they debarred from their home, but as a consequence from many forms of worship also. Were they not given up into the hands of barbarians, wolves rather than men? and, most painful calamity of all, when they had been banished into so distant and barbarous a country, and were suffering such a grievous captivity were they not without teacher, without prophets, without ruler? "for," it is written, "there is no ruler, nor prophet, nor governor, nor place for offering before Thee and finding mercy." Yea moreover they were cast into the royal palace, as upon some cliff and crag, and a sea full of rocks and reefs, being compelled to sail over that angry sea without a pilot or signal man, or crew, or sails; and they were cooped up in the royal court as in a prison. For inasmuch as they knew spiritual wisdom, and were superior to worldly things, and despised all human pride and made the wings of their soul soar upwards, they counted their sojourn there as an aggravation of their trouble. For had they been outside the court, and dwelling in a private house they

would have enjoyed more independence: but having been cast into that prison (for they deemed the splendor of the palace no better than a prison, no safer than a place of rocks and crags) they were straightway subjected to cruel embarrassment. For the king commanded them to be partakers of his own table, a luxurious, unclean and profane table, a thing which was forbidden them, and seemed more terrible than death; and they were lonely men hemmed in like lambs amongst so many wolves. And they were constrained to choose between being consumed by famine or rather led off to execution, and tasting of forbidden meats. What then did these youths do, forlorn as they were, captives, strangers, slaves of those who commanded these things. They did not consider that this strait or the absolute power of him who possessed the state sufficed to justify their compliance; but they employed every device and expedient to enable them to avoid the sin, although they were abandoned on every side. For they could not influence men by money: how should they, being captives? nor by friendship and social intercourse? how should they being strangers? nor could they get the better of them by any exertion of power: how was it possible being slaves? nor master them by force of numbers: how could they being only three? Therefore they approached the eunuch who possessed the necessary authority and persuaded him by their arguments. For when they saw him fearful and trembling, and in an agony of alarm concerning his own safety, and the dread of death which agitated his soul was intolerable: "for I fear" said he "my lord the king, lest he should see your countenances sadder than the children which are of your sort and so shall ye endanger my head to the king,"908 having released him from this fear they persuaded him to grant them the favor. And inasmuch as they brought to the work all the strength which they had, God also henceforth contributed his strength to it. For it was not God's doing only that they achieved those things for the sake of which they were to receive a reward, but the beginning and starting point was from their own purpose, and having manifested that to be noble and brave, they won for themselves the help of God, and so accomplished their aim.

16. Dost thou then perceive that if a man does not injure himself, no one else will be able to harm him? Behold at least youthfulness, and captivity and destitution, and removal into a foreign land, and loneliness, and dearth of protectors, and a stern command, and great fear of death assailing the mind of the eunuch, and poverty, and feebleness of numbers, and dwelling in the midst of barbarians, and having enemies for masters, and surrender into the hands of the king himself, and separation from all their kindred, and removal from priests and prophets, and from all others who cared for them, and the cessation of drink offerings and sacrifices, and loss of the temple and psalmody, and yet none of these things harmed them; but they had more renown then than when they enjoyed these things in their native land. And after they had accomplished this task first and had wreathed their brows with the glorious garland of victory, and had kept the law even in a foreign land, and trampled underfoot the tyrant's command, and overcome fear of the avenger, and yet received no harm from any quarter, as if they had been quietly living at home and enjoying the benefit of all those things which I mentioned, after they had thus fearlessly accomplished their work they were again summoned to other contests. And again they were

the same men; and they were subjected to a more severe trial than the former one, and a furnace was kindled, and they were confronted by the barbarian army in company with the king: and the whole Persian force was set in motion and everything was devised which tended to put deceit or constraint upon them: divers kinds of music, and various forms of punishment, and threats, and what they saw on every side of them was alarming, and the words which they heard were more alarming than what they saw; nevertheless inasmuch as they did not betray themselves, but made the most of their own strength, they never sustained any kind of damage: but even won for themselves more glorious crowns of victory than before. For Nabuchadonosor bound them and cast them into the furnace, yet he burnt them not, but rather benefited them, and rendered them more illustrious. And although they were deprived of temple (for I will repeat my former remarks) and altar, and fatherland, and priests and prophets, although they were in a foreign and barbarous country, in the very midst of the furnace, surrounded by all that mighty host, the king himself who wrought this looking on, they set up a glorious trophy, and won a notable victory, having sung that admirable and extraordinary hymn which from that day to this has been sung throughout the world and will continue to be sung to future generations.

  Thus then when a man does not injure himself, he cannot possibly be hurt by another: for I will not cease harping constantly upon this saying. For if captivity, and bondage, and loneliness and loss of country and all kindred and death, and burning, and a great army and a savage tyrant could not do any damage to the innate virtue of the three children captives, bondmen, strangers though they were in a foreign land, but the enemy's assault became to them rather the occasion of greater confidence: what shall be able to harm the temperate man? There is nothing, even should he have the whole world in arms against him. But, someone may say, in their case God stood beside them, and plucked them out of the flame. Certainly He did; and if thou wilt play thy part to the best of thy power, the help which God supplies will assuredly follow.

17. Nevertheless the reason why I admire those youths, and pronounce them blessed, and enviable, is not because they tramped on the flame, and vanquished the force of the fire: but because they were bound, and cast into the furnace, and delivered to the fire for the sake of true doctrine. For this it was which constituted the completeness of their triumph, and the wreath of victory was placed on their brows as soon as they were cast into the furnace and before the issue of events it began to be weaved for them from the moment that they uttered those words which they spoke with much boldness and freedom of speech to the king when they were brought into his presence. "We have no need to answer thee concerning this thing: for our God in Heaven whom we serve is able to rescue us out of the burning fiery furnace: and He will deliver us out of thy hands, O King. But if not, be it known unto thee, O King, that we will not serve thy Gods nor worship the golden image which thou hast set up." After the utterance of these words I proclaimed them conquerors; after these words having grasped the prize of victory, they hastened on to the glorious crown of martyrdom, following up the confession which they made through their words with the confession made through their deeds. But if when they had been cast into it, the fire

had respect for their bodies, and undid their bonds, and suffered them to go down into it without fear, and forgot its natural force, so that the furnace of fire became as a fountain of cool water, this marvel was the effect of God's grace and of the divine wonder-working power. Yet the heroes themselves even before these things took place, as soon as they set foot in the flames had erected their trophy, and won their victory, and put on their crown, and had been proclaimed conquerors both in Heaven and on earth, and so far as they were concerned nothing was wanting for their renown. What then wouldst thou have to say to these things? Hast thou been driven into exile, and expelled from thy country? Behold so also were they. Hast thou suffered captivity, and become the servant of barbarian masters. Well! this also thou wilt find befell these men. But thou hast no one present there to regulate thy state nor to advise or instruct thee? Well! of attention of this kind these men were destitute. Or thou hast been bound, burned, put to death? for thou canst not tell me of anything more painful than these things. Yet lo! these men having gone through them all, were made more glorious by each one of them, yea more exceedingly illustrious, and increased the store of their treasures in Heaven. And the Jews indeed who had both temple, and altar, and ark and cherubim, and mercy-seat, and veil, and an infinite multitude of priests, and daily services, and morning and evening sacrifices, and continually heard the voices of the prophets, both living and departed, sounding in their ears, and carried about with them the recollection of the wonders which were done in Egypt, and in the wilderness, and all the rest, and turned the story of these things over in their hands, and had them inscribed upon their door posts and enjoyed the benefit at that time of much supernatural power and every other kind of help were yet no wise profited, but rather damaged, having set up idols in the temple itself, and having sacrificed their sons and daughters under trees, and in almost every part of the country in Palestine having offered those unlawful and accursed sacrifices, and perpetrated countless other deeds yet more monstrous. But these men although in the midst of a barbarous and hostile land, having their occupation in a tyrant's house, deprived of all that care of which I have been speaking, led away to execution, and subjected to burning, not only suffered no harm there from small or great, but became the more illustrious. Knowing then these things, and collecting instances of the like kind from the inspired divine Scriptures (for it is possible to find many such examples in the case of various other persons) we deem that neither a difficulty arising from seasons or events, nor compulsion and force, nor the arbitrary authority of potentates furnish a sufficient excuse for us when we transgress. I will now conclude my discourse by repeating what I said at the beginning, that if any one be harmed and injured he certainly suffers this at his own hands, not at the hands of others even if there be countless multitudes injuring and insulting him: so that if he does not suffer this at his own hands, not all the creatures who inhabit the whole earth and sea if they combined to attack him would be able to hurt one who is vigilant and sober in the Lord. Let us then, I beseech you, be sober and vigilant at all times, and let us endure all painful things bravely that we may obtain those everlasting and pure blessings in Christ Jesus our Lord, to whom be glory and power, now and ever throughout all ages. Amen.

Find this and other great works of the Early Church Fathers at lighthousechristianpublishing.com.

St. John Chrysostom

Our Father who art in heaven, hallowed be thy name.
Thy kingdom come, Thy will be done, on earth as it is in heaven.
Give us this day our daily bread and forgive us our trespasses as we forgive those who trespass against us.
And lead us not into temptation, but deliver us from evil, for Thine is the kingdom, the power and the glory. Forever and ever.

Amen

Hail Mary full of grace, the Lord is with thee. Blessed art thou amongst women and blessed is the fruit of thy womb Jesus. Holy Mary mother of God, pray for us sinners, now and the hour of our death.

www.ingramcontent.com/pod-product-compliance
Lightning Source LLC
Chambersburg PA
CBHW052131070526
44585CB00017B/1786